POLITICS AND BUREAUCRACY
IN THE EUROPEAN COMMUNITY

A PORTRAIT OF THE COMMISSION OF THE E.E.C.

POLITICS AND BUREAUCRACY IN THE EUROPEAN COMMUNITY

A PORTRAIT OF THE COMMISSION OF THE E.E.C.

BY

DAVID COOMBES

PEP
Political and Economic Planning
12 Upper Belgrave Street

London
GEORGE ALLEN AND UNWIN LTD
RUSKIN HOUSE   MUSEUM STREET

FIRST PUBLISHED IN 1970

DR

382.9142

30. MAY 1970

PRINTED IN GREAT BRITAIN
in 10 *on* 12*pt Times*
BY UNWIN BROTHERS LIMITED
WOKING AND LONDON

PREFACE

This book is the product of a study undertaken for PEP by David Coombes, of the Department of Politics at the University of Reading. The original research necessitated intensive interviewing of officials in Brussels and would not have been possible without a good deal of generosity and forebearance on their part. In particular, the author is indebted to those members of the Official Spokesman's Group at the Commission, who to his great surprise, never flinched from his tiresome requests for assistance in arranging interviews and advising on suitable contacts. The author was also greatly assisted in organizing his research by John Lambert, who contributed much advice and guidance on matters of fact. In addition, a number of other scholars of European unity in Britain and abroad have talked to the author, and have commented upon numerous drafts of the final work. Naturally, however, none of them can be held responsible for the views expressed or errors committed which are those of the author himself.

The study was financed from a grant from the Ford Foundation.

FOREWORD

The 'abdication' of General de Gaulle in May 1969 and the course of the electoral campaign to find a new President for the French fifth Republic led to renewed optimism regarding the prospects of European unity and of British entry to the existing European Communities. The issue of European integration (and Britain's part in it) had already been the subject of considerable high-level discussion and diplomatic activity in the year or two preceding these dramatic events in France. However, the prospects of the postwar movement for political unity in Europe had rarely seemed so bleak as they did in the period before the General's departure. In particular, the European Economic Community—the movement's major achievement so far—seemed to have reached the lowest point in its whole existence and was only just emerging from eighteen months of near deadlock arising from the British application for membership. This crisis concerned issues far wider than enlarging the Community's membership and involved a number of other basic questions regarding the Community's future political development. To many observers the real obstacle was the General himself and his departure from the political scene has therefore been seen as a strangely unexpected, but nevertheless heaven-sent, opportunity for taking up again where the European Movement left off in the early 1960s.

On the other hand, the critical self-examination which occupied the European Movement in the few years before de Gaulle's resignation may well turn out to be more important and more influential on the future course of events than the pragmatic, optimistic reactions which have followed it. Indeed, the present book was written mainly during that more pessimistic period and seeks to assess the contribution of the institutions of the EEC to European political unity from a fairly rigorous viewpoint. However, the analysis presented here goes deeper than the level of contemporary national politics. Its findings regarding the problems of political unification and how these might be solved have not been significantly affected by recent political events—even those as important as the resignation of General de Gaulle. Indeed, since there is now more ground for hope of early British entry to the Communities and of new steps towards political union, the book is now all the more timely. For its main finding

is that the existing institutions of the Community are inadequate
for achieving political unity and that some radical changes are now
required. The task of applying the book's findings to the contemporary situation belongs to policy-makers and activists engaged in
the present. The book thus hopes to be able to warn the latter not to
overlook some fundamental questions regarding the nature of
political unification and of political activity in general and not to
be preoccupied by the events and the atmosphere of the time in
which they act.

The book seeks to go beyond both the more journalistic and
personal accounts of the European Communities published in recent
years and the more general, purely descriptive and summary text-
books and tries to reach conclusions based on a programme of
intensive empirical research. In this respect it fills a significant gap
in the literature of European unity. While a few studies of different
political aspects of the EEC based on original research were published
after the first four or five years of the Community's existence[1] these
suffered from being written at a time of what has since proved to be
exceptional euphoria within the Communities. Now, with ten years'
experience to draw upon, there is a much wider range of moods to
take into account. Moreover, it was still too early in 1962 to have
a clear idea as to how the Community would make the transition
from the stage of removing barriers to trade to that of setting up
and administering common social and economic policies.

The present book was inspired by a conviction that there was
great need for a comprehensive study of the role of the key institution of the Community, the Commission, in order to ascertain what
kind of organization it really is. As the work progressed it became
increasingly apparent that such a study had to take in a number of
more general aspects of the Community and that it led in fact to
valuable conclusions about the whole Community experience, as
well as to useful comparisons of different methods of undertaking
political unification. The author was led to an interest in the role of
the EEC Commission through a concern with the general relationship
between politics and administration, particularly with reference to

[1] A valuable review of the current state of research and publication on the
problem of European unification can be found in Roy Pryce, 'Political Science
and Integration in Europe', *Government and Opposition*, London, Vol. 2, No. 3,
April–July 1967, pp. 457–61.

bodies like the Commission, which seem to fit completely into neither side of this distinction. Before joining PEP to undertake research on the Commission he had treated this problem in the context of national systems and at the level of general theory. For reasons which will become obvious as the book proceeds, the Community proved to be an excellent vehicle for testing out ideas in this field. Conversely, however, study of the unification process seemed to benefit from the application of concepts and theories derived from the study of national politics and public administration, and it appeared that a number of the problems which troubled those interested in the Communities could be elucidated considerably by this approach. At the same time, there has been a conscious attempt in writing this book not to submit to the current trend in political science to write according to some experimental methodology such as structure-function analysis, cybernetics, games theory or whatever. No original methodological system is propounded; nor can the book claim to justify or exemplify any previously tried technique or system. Thus jargon and methodological digression have been kept to the barest minimum possible for a study which still tries to be original and to communicate on a fairly broad level of generality. The aim was to continue in PEP's tradition of applying academic disciplines to current problems of policy-making in such a way as to prove informative and useful to both scholars and practitioners.

The book begins with a brief introduction to the European Movement from which the European Communities emerged in an attempt to distinguish some of the main political forces and currents of thought involved. At the same time an attempt is made to elucidate some of the most important concepts involved in the study of political unification in the postwar European context. There follows in Part II a straightforward descriptive account of the nature of the European Economic Community, of its different legal, institutional and human elements, and of its objectives, which leads to an introduction to the body with which the book is chiefly concerned, the Commission of the EEC. This account is based largely on existing secondary sources. The heart of the book is contained in Part III, which consists chiefly of an analysis of the role of the Commission in the political process of the EEC as it has evolved in practice. The concept of bureaucracy is introduced (in Chapter Five) from the study of comparative politics and public administration, in order to show its relevance to

11

the institutional problems of the European Communities and to raise a number of new questions. The next five chapters are each based on first-hand observation of the Commission's organization at work, partly through a study of personnel administration in the Commission,[1] partly through two case studies of decision and partly through a review of some general problems of decision-making within the organization. In Chapter 11 the consequences of this empirical research are discussed in the light of the present and future tasks of the Commission. The concluding part of the book tries to relate these findings to the future prospects of the European Communities and of European unity in general and also to the general study of comparative politics.

[1] This research was originally reported in D. Coombes, *Towards a European Civil Service*, London, PEP/Chatham House, April 1967.

CONTENTS

PART ONE

INTRODUCTION

CHAPTER 1

EUROPEAN UNITY

This book is concerned with one particular attempt at political unification—the European Communities resulting from the Treaties of Paris and Rome; and it concentrates within that context on one particular Community—the European Economic Community (EEC). We are mainly concerned with examining the extent to which this Community has succeeded in achieving a degree of political unity and how far it is likely to succeed in future. Quite recently there was a wide consensus that the EEC represented a major advance towards European political unity, and that its experience had helped to validate, or at least to strengthen, certain general theories regarding the unification of nation states. This book will aim, therefore, not only to test the viability of the Community as a growing political union, but also to throw more light on the particular approaches to unification with which it has been associated. In this introductory chapter we shall attempt first to describe briefly the intellectual and political milieu out of which the European Communities emerged and then to elucidate some of the theoretical problems which arise in a discussion of political unification.

European unity, seen as a process of establishing common political institutions and not simply as co-operation or consultation between existing nation states, is an end valued both by numbers of people in positions of public eminence and responsibility and also, as far as one can tell, by many playing a less participant role in public affairs. The arguments in its favour—whether from an economic, military, cultural or straightforwardly political view—are already well known and have been widely discussed in Britain and on the continent for a number of years now. We shall not attempt to rehearse these arguments here. Nor shall we apologise for the book's concentration on this interpretation of the future of Europe, rather than on conceptions which seek above all to preserve or enhance the role of nation states. However, the author does not represent—either formally or even in terms of purely intellectual commitment—any of the various bodies which have campaigned for European unity; the book is not in any way a manifesto or *apologia* and it has no consciously proselytizing function. As it happens, the author began work on this subject with an objective (not to say cynical) frame of mind with regard to the aims of the European Movement. It is only honest to admit that frequent trips to and from Brussels and intensive work on the subject have done something to affect this attitude and have fanned a spark of enthusiasm which he did not really know was there. This was just as well, as it provided the energy with which to complete a work which seemed to grow remorselessly as time went on. However, the enterprise was not conceived out of conscious conviction (so its conclusions may seem all the more surprising), but rather out of a professional interest in the role of political institutions, not only in the international context but within the national framework as well.

This book is, however, largely about the role of conviction in politics and its subject is a near perfect example of an attempt to actuate movement towards a political ideal in a world primarily devoted to the pursuit of material welfare. The ideal is the uniting of the nation states of Europe into a common political framework. This objective emerged from the second world war as something valued by western European politicians and statesmen of all but the most extreme political tendencies.[1] As peacetime conditions returned, however, it became more and more obvious that there were serious differences among these men. They differed both in their conception of how the ultimate goal should be approached and in their commitment towards it relative to other ends. At one level many leading statesmen of the late 1940s and early 1950s were willing to pay lip-service to the idea of a politically united Europe, but, when faced with practical proposals towards that end, they flinched from the necessary surrender of national sovereignty and retreated to a position

---

[1] This is not to neglect the existence of Federalist movements before and during the war. See Henri Brugmans, *L'Idée Européenne, 1918–1965*, Cahiers de Bruges, N–S 12, Bruges, De Tempel, 1966, Chapters 1–3.

favouring a more traditional form of inter-governmental co-operation. This seems to have been the attitude of most British leaders of both parties and it was the spirit which was dominant in the formation of the Council of Europe in 1949. This organization, while providing an invaluable forum for the activity of the various European movements, never represented an advance towards common institutions with real power.[1] At another level, leaders of European industry, trade unionists, commercial and financial interests anxiously sought the recovery of European trade and industry and found that this demanded a wider perspective than the purely national one. This same view was held by the Government of the United States on whose support in the Marshall Plan the recovery of continental Europe largely depended in the early years. The Marshall Plan resulted in the establishment of the Organization for European Economic Co-operation (OEEC).[2] This never became more than a purely technical and advisory institution and, while the spirit behind the economic resurgence of the years after the Marshall Plan was later to prove a major element in rendering the idea of 'supranational' European institutions concrete, it was always an essentially pragmatic affair.

The real vision of political union was nurtured and sustained at another level altogether, that of voluntary clubs, societies and movements, including groups representing the main political parties and interest groups. This vision and the association of men of various countries around it was largely inherited from the wartime resistance movement. The most strongly committed of these associations came together in December 1946 to form the European Union of Federalists, which held its first congress at Montreux in August 1947. The Union campaigned for the establishment of a federal system of government, a truly 'United States of Europe'. Within it, however, there was a serious division between two different approaches. One of these was associated mainly with the Italian *Movimento Federalista Europeo*, led by Altiero Spinelli, which believed that immediate steps should be taken towards a full political union established by means of a European Constituent Assembly. Later, repeatedly disappointed in the ability of the national governments to support

---

[1] See J. Lambert, M. Palmer, *et al.*, *European Unity*, London, Allen & Unwin for PEP, 1968, pp. 111–66.

[2] See *ibid.*, pp. 75–110, 422 ff.

17

movement towards a federal Europe, this part of the Federalist Movement adopted a very radical, almost revolutionary, position, calling for direct mobilization of popular opinion in favour of federalist objectives, if necessary without the support of the national governments and parliaments.[1] The other part of the Union of Federalists consisted largely of elements which were far more conservative and 'gradualist' in approach than Spinelli and his followers. These elements were represented in the beginning mainly by the French organization, *La Fédération*, which considered that a Constituent Assembly would be altogether premature in 1947 and which favoured an approach based on integration by sectors and on first seeking the support of key political groups in the countries of western Europe. In this gradualist approach were the roots of the functional integration which was eventually to find expression in the foundation of the European Communities.[2]

THE COMMUNITY METHOD

The various parts of the Union of Federalists, along with the numerous other groups and associations which had sprung up to support European unity, but which were mainly divided on political or social lines, were known collectively as the 'European Movement'. From 1947 the ideas which dominated this movement belonged essentially to those who favoured a 'gradualist' approach, avoiding any direct challenge to the existing structures of government, and seeking to proceed only with the support of the political leaders of the countries of Western Europe. These 'functionalist' ideas were soon to find concrete expression in the formation of the Coal and Steel Community.

This early success of the functionalist approach owed much to the support of certain individual statesmen, mainly members of Christian Democratic parties in their own countries, and all with personal reasons for inclining towards European unity. The most noted of these were Schuman, from France, Adenauer, from Western Ger-

[1] Brugmans, *op. cit.*, pp. 99–102, 175–80; Altiero Spinelli, *The Eurocrats, Conflict and Crisis in the EEC*, translated by C. Grove Haines, Baltimore, Johns Hopkins Press, 1966, pp. 10–26.

[2] *ibid.*, pp. 99–102. The European Union of Federalists later (1956) split up into a number of separate associations, mainly because these more 'gradualist' elements could not accept the 'radial' views mentioned above.

many, and de Gasperi, from Italy. The European Movement benefited greatly from the fact that these three men all held positions of great authority within their own countries in the early 1950s. However, the intellectual leader of the European Movement during this time (and ever since) was Jean Monnet, a Frenchman of varied background and experience, but who had made himself famous with *cognoscenti* both in his own country and in international circles by his skill at organizing imaginative and daring undertakings. He was very much in the tradition of the French Civil Service in that, although most of his life had been spent either in commercial affairs or in a public official capacity, he had never valued anonymity or impersonality as professional virtues, but had rather shown considerable personal conviction in most of the enterprises he had been associated with. There was enough of an administrator about him, however, to be greatly attracted by the gradualist, or functionalist, approach to European unity and from the late 1940s onwards this cause was to dominate his life to such an extent that it has been identified ever since as the Monnet approach.

Monnet's influence in the creation of each of the three European Communities was enormous, and it was he who helped to draft the declaration of the French Foreign Minister, Schuman, which eventually led to the establishment of the Coal and Steel Community in 1951. 'The Schuman Plan' was a model of pragmatism, both in its approach to unification, and in the way it arose from a seemingly insoluble political problem. The Plan was seen initially as a solution to problems arising from control of German heavy industry by the International Authority for the Ruhr. It was used by Monnet and Schuman as an opportunity to propose collective action by the states of western Europe in the direction of real economic, and eventually political, union. The Plan announced that 'The French Government proposes to place Franco-German production of coal and steel under a common High Authority, within the framework of an organization open to the participation of the other countries of Europe.' It also stated, however, that the objectives of this proposal were to foster world peace (by making future war between France and Germany impossible), and to 'lay the real foundations' for economic unification of the member countries.[1]

[1] Text of the statement made by M. R. Schuman, French Foreign Minister, on May 9, 1950.

19

Here was the essence of what has since become known as 'The Community Method': namely, progress towards political unity by integrating one sector at a time, as this could be made acceptable to the statesmen of the countries concerned. A political objective was made explicit, but the initial approach was not to attempt to establish an overtly political union. The first steps were taken in the economic sector, and in certain clearly defined parts of that sector. A central organization was established in these fields for making the necessary collective decisions, but this would not at first challenge the existing structures of government in the member states. Progress towards political unification would be essentially gradual and would depend on the success of the new central institutions in proving their value in the spheres to which they were at first confined. However, the central institutions were expected to prove their effectiveness and their indispensability and thus to foster an extension of the scope of integration into new fields and even to whole new sectors.[1]

As for the institutional arrangements themselves, these were to contain a substantial measure of 'supranationality' providing for an element which would be independent of the member states and able to make decisions on its own. The main idea was to get away from the traditional form of international co-operation in which member governments simply negotiated with each other and to provide real means of collective action. This 'supranational' element in the case of the Coal and Steel Community was the High Authority which, though appointed by the member governments, was given substantial formal powers of decision of its own and the right to raise its own financial resources. An essential part of the scheme, however, was that the High Authority should be directly responsible to a European Assembly, consisting of members elected by the national parliaments. At the same time it was required on most matters to consult a Council of Ministers representing the member governments. It is widely acknowledged that Monnet saw the adoption of these institutional provisions as a major step towards a 'United States of Europe', and expected that in time the Assembly would be directly elected by citizens of the member countries.[2] The type of

[1] R. Pryce, *The Political Future of the European Community*, London, John Marshbank Ltd., 1962, pp. 26 ff.; D. Sidjanski, *Dimensions Européennes de la Science Politique*, Paris, Librairie de Droit et de Jurisprudence, 1963, pp. 157–73.
[2] Brugmans, *op. cit.*, p. 135.

institutional structure contained in the Coal and Steel Community represented another major element in the gradualist approach to political unity. Monnet's own faith in the power of institutions to affect the behaviour of men and in the importance of such a process for achieving political ends is witnessed by his famous quotation from the Swiss philosopher, Amiel:

'L'expérience de chaque homme se recommence. Seules les institutions deviennent plus sages, elles accumulent l'expérience collective et, de cette expérience et de cette sagesse, les hommes soumis aux mêmes règles verront non pas leur nature se changer, mais leur comportement graduellement se transformer.'[1] Monnet himself became the first President of the High Authority and its headquarters in Luxembourg became a magnet for numbers of committed Europeans and the centre of their energies and hopes: 'No one who lived in his entourage during the initial period in the decrepit building in the Place de Metz, will ever forget those years of fervour and of inspiring work in the service of the High Authority.'[2]

To the more radical elements among the Federalists, of course, the Coal and Steel Community was a disappointment, but even so it went too far in the direction of 'supranationality' for many of the governments of Europe at that time and so the 'Europe of the Six' was born, consisting of France, Germany and Italy, and the three Benelux countries, Belgium, Luxembourg and the Netherlands. In a few years, however, another opportunity was to arise for proposing more radical steps towards a federal Europe (and also for widening the membership of the potential union). This too, however, came as a response to a particular international problem and was again largely the initiative of leading national statesmen. The problem this time arose from the United States proposal for a German national army to form part of the Atlantic Alliance, a proposal which itself arose from the difficulties inherent in the allied military occupation of Western Germany. Again the only acceptable solution seemed to be a European initiative and the French Government responded by proposing a European Defence Community containing

---

[1] Jean Monnet, *Les Etats-Unis d'Europe ont commencé*, Paris, Robert Laffont, 1955, p. 44.
[2] Brugmans, *op. cit.*, p. 172. For an account of the early history of the Coal and Steel Community, see R. Mayne, *The Community of Europe*, London, 1962, pp. 85–99.

21

a supranational military organization. A European Army would be made responsible to a European Minister of Defence in turn responsible to a European Assembly. The proposal was initially accepted by the French National Assembly and international negotiations began. It soon became evident that integration in such a key sector of government as national defence would necessitate some form of concrete political union, and under pressure from the European Movement, an *ad hoc* European Assembly was set up (with virtually the same membership as the Assembly of the Coal and Steel Community) to consider draft constitutional proposals for a European Political Community.

The more extreme Federalists now proposed the establishment of a Political Community with extensive powers, involving an immediate and substantial cession of sovereignty by the national governments. The more moderate view in the European Movement was in favour of providing common institutions which were independent of national influence but which did not make any new demands for sacrifice of national sovereignty.[1] It was finally proposed to establish a European Executive Council, directly responsible to two chambers, one of which was to be directly elected and the other appointed by the national parliaments.[2] The final draft constitution went much nearer the more radical Federalist position than anything before, but it concealed numerous compromises on questions of principle.[3] The draft treaty for a Defence Community (which contained only vague references to the future establishment of democratic institutions) had already been ratified in four of the six countries (the other countries of Europe having again recoiled from 'supranationalism'), but support for it in France was becoming weaker and weaker. Finally, on August 30, 1954, the draft treaty was rejected by the French National Assembly, and with it died also the hopes of a Political Community.

The main reasons for the unpopularity of the idea of a Defence Community in France, it has been suggested, were reluctance to give up control over the French army, growing political difficulties in France's foreign relations, particularly with regard to her dependen-

---

[1] Brugmans, *op. cit.*, 161–3.
[2] See Miriam Camps, *Britain and the European Communities, 1955–63*, Oxford University Press, 1964, pp. 15–16; Mayne, *op. cit.*, pp. 102–3.
[3] Spinelli, *op. cit.*, pp. 19, 20

cies overseas, and a change of government unfavourable to European unity. Basically, however, the proposal for a Defence Community faced too many enemies on all sides, most of whom were not necessarily anti-European; it was opposed by idealistic, pacifist elements, by those who opposed or feared the American alliance, and by those who were still suspicious of German power. Moreover, from many points of view the early exclusion of Britain from the negotiations had weakened the case for a European Army.[1]

The downfall of the proposals for a Defence Community had the effect of strengthening the case for a 'gradualist' approach. In the period that followed it the expectations of the European Movement became far more sober. Attention reverted to the economic sector and Monnet himself was known to favour attempting a limited step towards sectoral integration in the sphere of atomic energy. Following the August 30th vote in the National Assembly he resigned as President of the High Authority and thus acquired greater freedom in which to organize a campaign for some new initiative in this direction. He did this as President of a 'Committee of Action for the United States of Europe', which became the new spearhead of the European Movement. This organization was essentially 'functionalist' in outlook and in character and consisted of representatives of the main interest groups and political parties in the countries of the Six.[2] Partly resulting from pressure by this Committee, but following an initiative by ministers of the three Benelux countries, a conference of the Six was called at Messina and took place in June 1955. The Treaties of Rome, establishing the European Economic Community and Euratom, were negotiated on the basis of the reports from this conference. The two new Communities came into being at the beginning of 1958.

The two new Communities were seen as forming a logical extension of the movement started by the establishment of the Coal and Steel Community in that they had the same membership and were based on the same fundamental principles. There were a number of differences of practice: the new Treaty establishing the EEC envisaged integration of the whole economic sector and not simply part of it; most of the major decisions were not taken by the Treaty but were fixed for later dates; and the Executives of the new Communities,

---

[1] Camps, *op. cit.*, p. 16; Mayne, *op. cit.*, pp. 103–5.
[2] See Mayne, *op. cit.*, pp. 109–110.

(the Commissions), had fewer powers of decision than the High Authority, while the representatives of the member governments in the Council of Ministers had a greatly expanded role. However, these institutional arrangements simply reflected what had been actual practice in the Coal and Steel Community, for the High Authority had always tended to seek the agreement of the member governments before taking major decisions. Moreover, the three Communities would have two institutions in common: the Assembly (later called the European Parliament) and the Court of Justice.

It is now possible to draw together some of the main themes in the approach to political unity represented by 'The Community Method'. First of all, although the Communities resulted mainly from the action of members of the European Movement, who saw as their aim a 'United States of Europe', they did not represent any formal commitment to a particular type of political union. The building of a political union was left to the future, a future which was essentially uncharted. This was considered to be a highly commendable way of avoiding destructive arguments of principle and ideology. Two fundamental principles were clear, however: namely, that there was no intention to destroy the sovereignty of the nation states completely, but rather to develop some type of central organization as the need arose; and that whatever new structures emerged would have to be based on democratic principles.[1] As we shall see, these issues do really need careful elaboration, for it is vital to have some idea of how much national sovereignty has to be ceded before a political union can be said to exist, and also to know what particular type of central institutions are required. Certainly, however, the Communities represented a political undertaking, not only because of the political motivation of the governments and political groups who supported them, but also because the Treaties expressed a commitment to take more and more political decisions in common as time went on.[2]

Secondly, there is an important stress in this approach to unification on integrating specific fields and sectors. Certainly this approach was to lead to numerous problems, not the least of which is the existence of three separate Communities, whose functions sometimes overlap in the same field and whose policies are not always co-ordinated.

[1] Pryce, *op. cit.*, pp. 23–5.
[2] *ibid.*, pp. 13–23.

24

However, the value of this approach was said to be its realism, designed as it was to carry the support of key social and economic interests for further integration. Writing in 1962 one author was able to conclude that, in spite of the kinds of problem we have mentioned, '. . . by advancing step by step the six countries have been gradually drawn closer together, and not merely at the level of governments but also—and increasingly—by the activity of private economic interests. The interpenetration of the hitherto separate economies has proceeded apace, and the establishment of a multiplicity of new trading and industrial links has given substance to the formal provisions of the three treaties.'[1] We shall not question here the effects of the sectoral approach in bringing governments and social and economic interests closer together, but it is important to question just how constructive this 'interpenetration' is in terms of political unification. It is far from clear, for example, how important it is relative to the establishment of strong central institutions.

Finally, however, 'the Community Method' relies to a great extent on the existence of central institutions (in particular the three Community Executives) which are independent of the national governments in some vital respects, and which according to the treaties will take over more and more formal powers of decision from the member governments. In no case are these institutions directly responsible to the people of the Six countries, or even to an assembly which represents the people directly, but this was not thought to prevent them from mobilizing support for further integration. The authority of these institutions was expected to lead gradually to a significant 'restructuring' of the behaviour of political parties and groups. Not only were the members of the Community Executives independent of the member governments (except in so far as they were appointed by them), but in some matters they exercised direct authority over people living in the six countries.

'In contrast with international organizations, which generally give rise only to little, if any, change in attitudes or structures within member states, the Communities are distinguished by the breadth of the process of integration which they have set in motion both inside member countries and across their frontiers. The Communities' powers are important and are of an immediate significance. Citizens of the member countries are aware that these powers impose on

[1] Pryce, *op. cit.*, p. 30.

them obligations and direct measures which can be followed up by sanctions. In fact, instead of the state acting as a screen and filtering the influence of the Communities, the latter bears directly upon individuals, pressure groups, political parties, and so on. It arouses their interest, and obliges them to defend themselves by reacting to European power and intervening at its source.'[1]

Thus 'The Community Method' is a process of unification by which 'supranational' institutions, acting initially within limited sectors, are expected to have wide-ranging effects on political behaviour and by this means to provide an impetus for growing political union. The pace of that growth and the nature of the final union are left mainly to the member states themselves to determine, but it is expected that the latter can be influenced in these respects by favourable experience of integration in the initial period. This is an undertaking which falls some way short of the objectives of many European Federalists. Many would argue, in fact, that key issues such as the pace and scope of integration and the nature of the final union are too important to leave undetermined or at the mercy of national governments. As we shall see, a key factor here is the role of the 'supranational' institutions provided in the Community Treaties. These questions are all related, however, to a wider problem of deciding what federalism and political union really entail in terms of institutional development and extending the scope of unification. That is, indeed, the main subject of the present book. In the next section we shall examine some of the immediate difficulties which arise in trying to theorize about political unification.

FEDERALISM AND POLITICAL UNION

Those who regard the European Communities as a major opportunity for progress towards a federal system of government in Europe probably do not have a very precise conception of what a federal system should be like. However, the use of the term by political activists is clearly meant to evoke comparisons with known cases of political union and to imply certain distinct criteria of unification. As we have seen, some of those closely involved in the European Movement have called themselves 'Federalists', as if this term

---

[1] Sidjanski, *op. cit.*, pp. 157–8.

distinguished them and their objectives in some significant ways.[1] Moreover, a number of academic scholars have attempted to define the term 'federal government' and to distinguish it from other types. The expression has been widely used in practice to describe various political systems and so it has become increasingly necessary to clarify its meaning.

We are not concerned here to enter into the academic debate about federalism—how it can be distinguished from other types, on what conditions it depends, in what circumstances it is suitable, and so on—but rather to draw on existing knowledge as a basis for our own study. In particular, we are not interested here in one of the main aspects of the debate on federalism, namely, the relative advantages of federal and unitary systems of government. To discuss this in the context of a possible union of the states of western Europe is clearly of only academic interest while the main problem is whether or not such a union is possible at all. Our concern with the subject of federalism, therefore, centres on how and why different states unite under a common government and on the extent to which different stages of the unifying process can be usefully distinguished from one another.

The chief means of defining the term 'federal government' is to compare a large number of existing cases and determine what features they have in common. The main problem, however, is to decide which kind of feature is most important; different scholars have stressed different kinds, namely, the legal or constitutional characteristics of federal government, the underlying economic and social conditions, or the political circumstances in which federal governments have emerged. We shall try to draw to some extent on each of these three approaches. In addition, however, a distinction can be drawn between those scholars who have tried to define federal government descriptively, in terms of a static set of institutions and relationships, and those who treat federalism as a process by means of which more and more decisions come to be taken in common. The latter approach has the distinct advantage that it allows for greater flexibility, which is very desirable in view of the great variety of conditions to which the term 'federal' has been applied, and also in view of the lack of precision of those (for example, in the European Movement) who have claimed to be 'Federalists'.

[1] See pp. 17–18 above.

27

On the other hand, much of the popular debate about European unification has relied on analogy with existing cases of federal government (such as that of the United States of America and Switzerland), so that it will probably be valuable to take note of both the static and dynamic accounts of federalism.

The best known account of federal government as a particular constitutional system is that of Sir Kenneth Wheare, who (writing in 1946) limited the application of the term to four existing systems of government: the USA, Switzerland, the Dominion of Canada, and the Commonwealth of Australia.[1] According to this definition, the fundamental principle of federalism is that there should be separate central and regional governments which are 'co-ordinate', in the sense that each government is limited to its own sphere and within that sphere is independent of the other. One qualification to this, however, is that there might be a second legislative chamber at the centre which is appointed by the regional government.[2] Other characteristics are listed by Wheare as being more or less essential to the maintenance of a federal system and some of these are of interest for our main theme. For example, there must be some means of settling constitutional disputes regarding the division of authority between central and regional governments by an impartial body, such as a supreme court or constitutional council. Another important constitutional requirement is that the amendment of the federal constitution should be shared between the central and regional governments. As we shall see below, the provisions of the Treaty of Rome go some way towards meeting these and other formal, constitutional prerequisites of federalism.[3] On the other hand, it is noticeable that one of the key features of the Community institutions —their direct authority over citizens in the member States—is regarded by Wheare as not being a prerequisite of federal government and as being a different matter from exercising 'separate and co-ordinate' authority.[4] Significantly enough, however, Wheare stresses the importance of such elements as a strong central executive authority, supported by a coherent and stable party system founded

[1] K. C. Wheare, *Federal Government*, 3rd edn., London, Oxford University Press, 1953.
[2] *ibid.*, pp. 1–15.
[3] See pp. 43–4, below.
[4] Wheare, *op. cit.*, pp. 14–15.

on a federal basis[1], and he remarks that existing federal governments, in addition to being separately elected and being accountable mainly to central institutions, normally find it essential to control their own financial resources and to have the power to tax.[2] It is also normal in existing federations for the central governments to have more or less complete control over the conduct of foreign relations, at least in so far as the constituent states may not make separate treaties of their own with other powers.[3] Unfortunately, Wheare is not able to come to any definite conclusions as to which sectors of government a federal system must include if it is to remain a federation and not break down into independent units, although in each of the four federations he considers the powers of the central government cover in practice foreign affairs, defence, and civil order, as well as trade, economics, and social policy.

This characterisation of federal government is useful for it gives us an idea of some possible standards and objectives for a 'federal Europe'. Indeed, as is now well known, the European Communities already have some of these 'federal' characteristics. What, however, are the chances that the present Communities will develop into a federal system with a strong central government like that of the United States of America? On what conditions must such a development depend? Wheare lists six factors which seemed to have been present to a greater or lesser degree at the time of the formation of each of the four federations he examined:

(1) 'A sense of military insecurity and of the consequent need for common defence',

(2) 'a desire to be independent of foreign powers and a realization that only through union could independence be secured',

(3) 'a hope of economic advantage from union',

(4) 'some political association of the communities concerned prior to their federal union',

(5) 'geographical neighbourhood', and

(6) 'similarity of political institutions'.[4]

It is clear that in the case of the countries of western Europe (and in particular the six members of the Communities) the last four of

[1] Wheare, *op. cit.*, pp. 86-7.
[2] *ibid.*, pp. 97ff.
[3] *ibid.*, pp. 175–96.
[4] *ibid.*, pp. 36–7.

these factors were to some degree present at the time of the first steps towards political unity in 1950 and 1951 and are present now. The need for common defence has been satisfied primarily up to now for the countries of western Europe by means of the North Atlantic alliance, and in any event the sense of military insecurity arising from the Cold War cannot be said to have affected all these countries (or all members of the Six) to the same degree or in the same way. Furthermore, the independence of the states of western Europe has not been directly threatened, nor has federal union presented itself to the statesmen of Europe as in any sense *prerequisite* for preserving that independence. On the other hand, some Europeans have attempted to take advantage of growing discomfort in western Europe about the increasing role of American investment in European industry and increasing American influence in all spheres.[1] Moreover, the need for Europe to act as a 'Third Force' in world affairs in order to counterbalance the power of the United States and the Soviet Union has been stressed throughout as a motive of European unification.

However, the presence of factors such as those just listed does not of itself determine that states will move in the direction of a federal union. Nor does it necessarily imply that the formation of a federal union would be the most desirable or effective response. It is mainly in an attempt to deal with the second of these two issues—the conditions suited to federalism—that a number of American scholars have compared various attempts at union in great detail in order to test the social and economic conditions upon which successful integration depends. Here a much more general view of political union is adopted than Wheare's rather strict definition of federal government in terms of an identifiable type of constitution. Yet there is still no conclusive evidence that differences in cultural matters, such as language, race, religion, nationality, or even social institutions need prevent integration in other sectors such as economics, defence, or even the sharing of common political institutions (although a certain amount of cultural integration may become necessary if union is to advance beyond a certain stage).[2] Even Wheare

---

[1] Note, in particular, the reactions to Servan-Schreiber's book *Le Défi Americain*. See pp. 301–7 below.

[2] A. Etzioni, *Political Unification: A Comparative Study of Leaders and Forces*, New York, Holt, Rinehart and Winstone, 1965, pp. 16–27, 34–7.

found that such cultural differences were compatible with the working of a federal constitution.[1] However, while it did not succeed in finding a definite set of conditions on which federalism could be said to depend, this approach contributed greatly to directing attention away from the consideration of purely formal and static governmental structures and towards the examination of integration as a process. Indeed, the use of the term 'federalism' to describe the process of unification has tended to give way in popularity to vaguer and more general expressions such as 'integration' and 'political unification'; the end product has been treated less as a fixed type of governmental structure and more as a sociological phenomenon, a 'political community' or a 'union'.[2]

No doubt, the optimism of scholars regarding the prospects of growing unity among the countries of western Europe following the establishment of the Communities owed a lot to the popularity of this approach. In effect, the pragmatic, gradualist approach of Monnet and his followers found theoretical justification in the work of many American students of international integration. In particular, the 'sectoral' approach represented by the setting up of the Coal and Steel Community (and later of the other two Communities), was interpreted as a major advance towards political unification by what was known as the 'spillover' theory. According to this theory the process of integration could be expected to pass from one sector of society to another in a more or less automatic fashion. As social functions in one sector were generalised and held in common, this would create the need for integration in other, related sectors and so there would develop a natural impetus towards integration of all social functions. Thus the establishment of a common market in coal and steel seemed to have led to the adoption of common investment policies and common working conditions in this sector and then eventually to demands for a full common market in industrial goods and common economic policies.[3] The establishment of a common market in industrial goods along with the adoption of common economic policies was similarly expected to result in new

[1] Wheare, *op. cit.*, pp. 37–40.
[2] See, in particular, K. W. Deutsch, *et al.*, *Political Community and the North Atlantic Area*, Princeton, 1957; Elmer Plischke (ed.), *Systems of Integrating the International Community*, Princeton, 1964; Ernst B. Haas, *The Uniting of Europe*, London, Oxford University Press, 1958; Etzioni, *op. cit.*
[3] Haas, *op. cit.*, pp. 103–110, 271 ff.

demands on economic policy-making by governments and thus to take the process of integration beyond the industrial sector altogether to affect political parties and other groups. Vital sectors of government such as defence and foreign policy would ultimately be drawn in.[1]

Furthermore, integration in one sector necessarily led to the establishment of a common centre for decision-making, (embodied in the case of the Coal and Steel Community in a 'supranational bureaucracy', the High Authority). This in itself could be expected to provide a natural impetus towards further integration, for such a bureaucracy would seek to increase its own functions and to resist attempts to reduce them. Together with the 'spillover' effect, this would tend to give the process of unification a motive power of its own.[2] The key to political unification was seen by these theorists as the establishment of a common centre of decision-making in a major economic sector. This was seen to have ramifications beyond the sector immediately concerned, in particular by 'restructuring' the activity of national political parties and interest groups on to a Community basis in response to the expanding role of the central authorities. Much of the study of European unification has, therefore, been directed at measuring the effectiveness of the present Communities in eliciting such a response. It has been readily assumed that the Communities should be studied as if they formed an embryonic political system, the main subject for empirical analysis being the political behaviour of key groups within the system: political parties, interest groups, national ministers and officials, and so on.[3] This is in spite of the fact that the present institutional arrangements do not constitute a federal system according to any formal, constitutional description, and in spite of the fact that the main power of decision in most sectors still rests with the national governments.

The main concern of this approach is with examining the conditions which facilitate a process of integration. This means that a number of problems are overlooked or underestimated. First, there is no satisfactory definition of what a 'political union' is as opposed

[1] Sidjanski, op. cit., pp. 157–77; Etzioni, op. cit., pp. 51–5.
[2] Etzioni, op. cit., pp. 53–4.
[3] See, for example, the plan of research prescribed by Sidjanski, op. cit., pp. 75–86, 177–83; and see Pryce, op. cit., pp. 52–93; Leon Lindberg, The Political Dynamics of European Economic Integration, London, Oxford University Press, 1964.

to an 'economic union' or even to a 'common market'. It is surely far too glib simply to assume that integration in industrial and economic affairs could be the same thing qualitatively as political integration.[1] This is affected by a second gap in the existing theory, namely, the failure to determine what are the key sectors in which the process of integration is to be set in motion. Are all sectors of the same value in this respect? Will the process run smoothly through all social functions, or will some prove more difficult to integrate than others? Finally, what guarantee is there that a 'supranational bureaucracy' will expand its role and not be prevented from doing so by a lack of resources, whether financial, political or otherwise?

One crucial element which is overlooked in much of the theory of integration is the role of political leadership, in particular the attitude of the national governments concerned in the process of unification. It is ironic, perhaps, that even Wheare cautioned that the presence of the various political, economic and social conditions he listed would not of itself produce a desire to unite: 'a great deal will depend, for example, on leadership or statesmanship at the right time'.[2]

A more recent writer, the American, Etzioni, attempts to take some account of the role of political leaderships, or *élites* as he calls them, in his inquiry into the conditions which underlie successful efforts to initiate a process of unification.[3] Etzioni's approach is to ask the question, 'Who is unifying and by what kinds of power?' in relation to four recent attempts at unification: the United Arab Republic, the Federation of the West Indies, the Nordic Union, and the European Economic Community. The relatively short time-span over which he is able to consider these attempts at union (writing in 1964) combined with his insistence on testing propositions of a rather extreme generality make it impossible for Etzioni to reach any very definite conclusions which might be applied in a concrete

[1] Ernst B. Haas defines 'political integration' as: 'the process whereby political actors in several distinct national settings are persuaded to shift their loyalties, expectations and political activities toward a new center, whose institutions possess or demand jurisdiction over the pre-existing national states', *op. cit.*, p. 16; Etzioni defines a 'union' as an international system 'whose level of integration and scope is higher than that of a typical international organization and lower than that of an established political community', *op. cit.*, p. 12n.

[2] Wheare, *op. cit.*, pp. 39–40.

[3] Etzioni, *op. cit.*

case such as the one with which we are concerned. However, some of the propositions he is able to formulate do serve to provide a useful emphasis for our own work.

First of all, there is the stress placed on the role of *élites*, which might be 'a person (for example, General de Gaulle), a group of persons (for example, the British aristocracy), or a state (for example, the United States for the Western World)'[1] According to this definition an *élite* exercises political leadership, rather than leadership in economic, cultural or other matters, and is defined as 'a unit that devotes a comparatively high proportion of its assets to guiding a process and leading other units to support it'. Etzioni's treatment of the role of *élites* in political unification is concerned partly with the role of an 'external *élite*', that is, an outsider influencing a process of unification (the USA in the case of the European Economic Community, and partly with that of 'member-*élites*', meaning chiefly the national governments directly involved in the process. The influence of an outsider in the direction of unification is greatest, according to Etzioni, when it can be 'internalized' so that the union becomes 'independent'. However, unification will be made more difficult in so far as the functions and powers internalized are taken over by national governments rather than by the union itself and if the power of the 'external *élite*' is internalized in some sectors but not in others (such as the economic but not the military). As for the relations between national governments within the union, three alternatives seem to emerge as being most likely: first, if there is only one national government acting as a political leadership for the whole union, then the union will be decisive but there will be alienation and a lack of commitment to the union among the other members; secondly, if there is an 'egalitarian union' in which there is no identifiable 'member-*élite*', then the union will be indecisive but commitment will be relatively high; finally, where there are two or more leading national governments, it will be essential for the success of the union for these to act in coalition rather than in conflict.[2] Unfortunately, Etzioni does not extend his account to analyse what factors determine the behaviour of 'member *élites*', (which are really nothing more than national governments as far as his empirical analysis is concerned). Nor does he consider the effect of

1 Etzioni, *op. cit.*, pp. 45–7.
2 *ibid.*, pp. 294–300.

34

different kinds of '*élite*' (which would involve some fairly complex analysis of the nature of power and authority). His main conclusion on the question of political leadership seems to be that 'the most effective unions are expected to be ruled by system-*élites* rather than by member-*élites*', meaning by 'system-*élite*' a unit which belongs to the union as a whole (such as the federal government of the USA) and is not simply a member of it (such as an individual state).

'A system-*élite* combines the decisiveness found in member-*élites* with the ability to generate commitment found in egalitarian unions; the decisiveness is gained from the existence of one superior centre of decision-making, while commitments are generated because the system-*élite* is representing all the members of the union as well as the union as a collectivity.'[1] There is little guidance, however, as to how such a central political leadership might emerge, nor as to the possible bases of its power. In what sense, moreover, does it 'represent' all the members of the union—are these members the national governments, and, if so, what is their formal relationship with the central authority so that it 'represents' them? Etzioni clearly regards the Commission of the EEC as forming a kind of 'system-*élite*' but feels that the Community is not as effective a union as it might be if this 'system-*élite*' were stronger.[2]

He does provide, however, an interesting analysis of the different kinds of power required to maintain the process of integration, typifying three kinds: 'utilitarian' power, generated by the use of economic possessions, technical and administrative capabilities, manpower, and so on; 'coercive' power, resulting when physical force is used; and 'indentitive' power, depending on an ability to convince others that a particular course of action is consistent with, or an expression of, certain shared values. Leaving aside for the sake of our own study the question of 'coercive' power, we can regard 'utilitarian' power as referring in the case of the European Communities to the power arising from the promise of economic benefits from the union and 'identitive' power as referring to power based on acceptance of the 'European idea'. Etzioni concludes from his brief review of the experience of the EEC up to 1963 that in terms of 'utilitarian' power the member States have gained more or less

[1] Etzioni, *op. cit.*, pp. 269–7.
[2] *ibid.*, p. 299.

35

equally (producing in the 'utilitarian' sector an egalitarian union), and that the initiation and growth of the EEC were largely supported by 'utilitarian' power. This development was 'enhanced by the presence of, and pre-existing identitive commitments to, the idea of European unification, which the EEC has drawn upon and been able to expand'.[1] However, he remarks that 'in political matters', General de Gaulle, or at least the French regime, seems to have acted as a single 'member-*élite*'. 'Moreover, whether the "European" idea has really penetrated enough to provide the identitive power needed to support a European integration broad in scope, leading towards a political community, remains to be seen.'[2]

His review of four attempts at unification leads Etzioni to the fairly obvious conclusion that 'the more utilitarian and identitive power supporting a particular unification effort, the farther it advances, and vice versa.' (This is not true of coercive power.)[3] However, he offers little enlightenment on two questions of major importance: first, how must these different kinds of power be combined to produce an effective political union? And secondly, how is effective 'identitive' power built up? In the first place, this leads us back to the question as to what is an effective political union. Etzioni defines a 'union' very flexibly as an international system 'whose level of integration and scope is higher than that of a typical international organization and lower than that of an established political community'.[4] A 'political community' must be able to maintain itself by its own processes and without having to rely on other systems or its own members. It must have effective control over the use of means of violence, must be able to affect significantly the allocation of resources and rewards throughout the community, and must be the dominant focus of 'political identification for the large majority of politically aware citizens'. (In other words it must have access to the exercise of coercive, utilitarian and identitive power.)[5] This does not tell us at what point a growing union must exercise 'identitive' power before it can continue to grow in the 'utilitarian' sector. Etzioni implies that such a point must be reached by his remarks that the level of 'utilitarian' integration in

1 Etzioni, *op. cit.*, pp. 37–40, and p. 305.
2 *ibid.*, p. 307.
3 *ibid.*, p. 306.
4 *ibid.*, p. 12n.
5 *ibid.*, pp. 6–8.

the EEC may be approaching a point 'at which some political unification will probably be required'.[1]

As for the nature of 'identitive' power, it is far from clear whether this can be exercised on the basis of the shared values of individuals or national governments. Etzioni seems to mean the former, for he says that to be effective, an ideology favouring unification 'must be accepted by the majority of the politically active citizens'.[2] However, little attention is paid throughout the study to the role of groups within the member States belonging to a union. When he writes of the need for 'intermediate responsiveness' on the part of the leaders of the union, that is, enough responsiveness to avoid excessive conflict but not so much as to prevent an independent line or course of action being taken, he does not specify to which groups the leadership should be responding. In his account he refers most often to the national governments. There is no discussion of the relationship between the power of political leaders and the support of groups and individuals through different means of legitimation. However, this would seem to be a key issue in deciding the effectiveness of a central political leadership.

One approach to filling these twin gaps in the theory of unification is to reintroduce the notion of federalism as a particular stage in the unifying process and to discover by a wide comparative study the conditions which made the reaching of this stage of development possible in some actual cases. 'Federalism' might simply be defined as the existence of two levels of government, each of which has at least one area of action in which it is autonomous and in which its autonomy is 'guaranteed'.[3] Thus another American scholar, W. H. Riker, concludes from an empirical study of a large number of different situations where union has been attempted (mainly in developing countries) that federalism of this type always resulted from a political bargain between the political leaders of the states concerned.[4] This leads him to state two conditions as being necessary for the striking of such a federal 'bargain':

(1) The existence of politicians who wish to expand their area of influence without the use of force, 'either to meet an external military

[1] Etzioni, op. cit., p. 305.
[2] ibid., p. 307.
[3] See W. H. Riker, Federalism: Origin, Operation, Significance, Boston and Toronto, 1964, p. 11.
[4] ibid., p. 12.

37

or diplomatic threat or to prepare for military or diplomatic aggression'.

(2) A willingness on the part of these politicians to give up some independence for the sake of the union, either because they desire protection from a military or diplomatic threat or because they desire to participate in the potential aggression of the union.[1] It is particularly interesting that Riker should reach such limiting conclusions regarding the possibilities of federation from a review mainly of countries with only a very short experience of independent nationhood and partly of countries which had much to gain in 'utilitarian' terms from unification.[2]

Some of these questions and their implications lead far beyond our present study. Indeed, they raise the whole issue of the nature of political authority and invite some treatment of the role of nationalism as a political ideology. Nevertheless, our own study, which is limited to one particular case of attempted political union— the European Communities—can contribute to an advance in knowledge of political unification in some vital respects. Thus one focus of our study will be the assumption made by some Europeans that integration in the economic or 'utilitarian' sector is preferable to a frontal attack in the political sector. The viability of a union based primarily on the 'spillover' resulting from the formation of a common market in industrial products needs to be tested. One question is how far economic or 'utilitarian' union can itself be sustained without some advance in political union. This begs the question as to whether political union can be distinguished qualitatively from other kinds of union, but recent work on the theory of federalism and political unification would seem to imply that it certainly can. The same line of inquiry will lead us to an even more far-reaching question which is whether in the long run 'The Community Method' represents an effective means towards political union at all in view of the vital role of political leadership in protecting national sovereignty and interests.

If the assumptions about the importance of political leadership are correct, then we can view the 'supranational' institutions estab-

1 Riker, *op. cit.*
2 See also the excellent article, modifying Riker's analysis in certain respects, by A. H. Birch, Approaches to the Study of Federalism, *Political Studies*, Vol. XIV, No. 1, February 1966, pp. 15–33.

lished as part of 'The Community Method' as facing a major challenge to their own competence, aptitude and legitimation. At present these are clearly not the normal institutions of a federal government, nor were they intended to be. However, they were given some formal attributes enigmatically similar to those of a federal government, and were expected to substitute in some way for real federal institutions. Just as the establishment of a federal system was rejected as a viable course of action by the European Movement and the 'gradualist', 'functionalist' approach of 'The Community Method' adopted instead, so the Community institutions reflect a pragmatic, but ingenious, attempt to avoid a head-on conflict regarding national sovereignty. In so far as such a conflict would be inevitable before institutions with real legitimacy could be established (based, for example, on direct representation of electorates or elected assemblies and possessing real executive powers), can it be postponed indefinitely? Or can a 'supranational bureaucracy' exercise political leadership of the kind which might well be essential, not just for extending the scope and level of integration tow ards a federal Europe, but even for sustaining a union based primarily on economic integration? In answering this question we shall be led into the whole subject of the role of bureaucracy in the modern political system. The substance of the empirical research reported in this book is really a case study of 'de-politization' or 'technocracy', designed to see whether there are natural limitations to bureaucratic leadership. First, however, we need to look more closely at 'The Community Method' itself at work, in order to obtain a clear picture of what kind of union is being created.

PART TWO

THE EUROPEAN ECONOMIC COMMUNITY

CHAPTER 2

THE PARTS OF THE COMMUNITY

The three European Communities are normally regarded as forming one common enterprise, designed to culminate in a political union of the countries of western Europe. Some writers distinguish the two later Communities—the European Economic Community and Euratom (set up in 1958)—from the first—the Coal and Steel Community (set up in 1952)—as representing a change in approach to European unification. In particular, it is felt that the fate of the projected Defence and Political Communities, which ran aground in 1954, was chastening, so that the initiatives which led to the Treaty of Rome were far more cautious than earlier approaches. This is illustrated by the fact that in the case of the EEC and Euratom, as we shall see later in this chapter, the main powers of decision are shared between the independent Commission and the Council of Ministers representing the governments of the member States. The formal powers of the Coal and Steel Community were entrusted largely to a single, independent High Authority.[1] Nevertheless, although the mood of the European Movement might have changed when the Treaty of Rome was conceived and negotiated, the two new Communities were regarded essentially as a continuation of the process set under way by the foundation of the Coal and Steel Community. The same six countries were involved, the same guiding spirits were present, and the same basic principles of the 'gradualist' or 'functionalist' approach were applied.

Indeed, although the approach to 'supranationality' in the Treaty

---

[1] R. Mayne, *The Community of Europe*, London, Gollancz, 1962, pp. 92–100.

of Rome may seem to a constitutional lawyer to be much more tentative than in the Treaty of Paris[1] the scope of integration which is envisaged in the Treaty of Rome is of a different order altogether, directly involving as it does the whole economic sector and including important elements of social policy. Mainly for this reason the EEC has become the central part of the Communities and represents the core of their promised expansion into non-economic sectors. Most students of the Communities concentrate on the EEC, treating the other two Communities as ancillary to it.

Moreover, the member States signed a Treaty on April 8, 1965, designed to merge the three Communities in two stages—first, by creating a single Council of Ministers and a single Commission by July 1, 1967, (the European Parliament, the Economic and Social Committee and the Court of Justice already being common institutions), and second, by negotiating another treaty by 1970 to amalgamate the Communities themselves.[2] Thus, although until that date the EEC is a separate legal entity, the existence of three separate Communities is intended to be only a temporary feature.

We shall also adopt another common practice among students of the Communities which is to treat the EEC as an evolving political system. Thus, the Community has a 'constitution'—the Treaty of Rome; it has a set of political institutions (all of which are now shared with the other Communities); and it has a number of voluntary political groups and associations (most of which again belong to all three Communities). Just how far these various parts have developed characteristics normally associated with a political system is a question which this chapter will seek to clarify.[3] In the next chapter we shall examine the objectives of the EEC, as these are laid down in the Treaty of Rome and as they have been stated since the Treaty by official representatives of the Communities in the Com-

[1] See, for example, F. Dehousse, *L'avenir institutionnel des Communautés Européennes*, Nancy, Centre Européen Universitaire, 1967, pp. 25–7.

[2] Treaty establishing a single Council and a single Commission of the European Communities, 1965.

[3] It is not our intention here to contribute to the current academic debate concerning the application of the concept of 'system' in social science to relations between states. Even if one accepts the assumptions upon which this debate is based, it is clear that findings which are relevant in empirical research will not be available for a long time, if at all. It is our conviction that valuable research and discussion can still take place meanwhile in a more conventional conceptual framework.

B*   41

mission and in the Council of Ministers, and shall ask how far these objectives do envisage an eventual political union of Europe.

THE TREATY OF ROME

The Treaty of Rome can be considered as the constitution of the Community: in addition to setting out the objectives of the Community, it lays down the essential organization and structure of its institutions and determines the relations between them. It vests these institutions with the power to make Community laws and provides means by which these laws may be enforced.

Two particular features of the Treaty are worth emphasizing at this point. First, while some of the aims of the Community are stated quite precisely along with a timetable for their achievement, other objectives are expressed only vaguely and are left very much to the initiative of the Community institutions and of the member States. Secondly, the Treaty is the result of hard-won compromise between pragmatic national interests and the various supporters of the European Movement.[1] As a direct result of these two facts, the Treaty (not unlike most written constitutions) is only a limiting framework for actual practice.

In addition to the provisions of the Treaty itself, Community law consists of the official legislative acts of the Community institutions. According to the Treaty these are of three possible kinds: Regulations, which are binding upon member governments and upon individuals within each member State; Directives, which bind each member government so designated to achieve certain ends by whatever means it may choose; and Decisions which bind whichever individuals or governments they specifically designate. In addition, the Community institutions may issue Recommendations and Opinions which have no binding force. Regulations have to be published in the official gazette of the Community, the *Journal Officiel*. The task of ensuring that this system of law is observed is shared between the Community institutions and the national authorities.

While the Treaty owes something to ideas of European federalists, it does not provide for a federal system of government. On the other hand, the institutional arrangements provided differ from those of an ordinary international organization. First of all, there is no withdrawal

[1] See pp. 18–24 above.

clause in the Treaty. Secondly, the Treaty imposes certain deadlines by which agreement on steps towards further integration must be reached. Thirdly, the Community itself is given power to make laws and to sign treaties with third countries without the need for ratification by member States' parliaments. Finally, the subjects of Community law are not simply member States, as in most international organizations, but also private individuals and corporations.[1] Furthermore, as we are about to see, the institutional arrangements which have been provided can be interpreted in some ways as representing a federal government in embryo.

THE COMMUNITY INSTITUTIONS

The Treaty provides for a Parliament, a Commission and a Council of Ministers, and a Court of Justice. This might be interpreted as implying a separation of powers—legislative, executive, judicial—along the lines conventionally associated with a federal government (that of the USA, for example).

The Treaty provides that the Parliament shall eventually be elected by direct universal suffrage in each of the member States.[2] The Commission is responsible to the Parliament in the sense that the latter could, if a two-third majority of its members wished, pass a motion of censure on the Commission forcing its members to resign [3] The Parliament discusses the Commission's annual report and may put oral and written questions to the Commission, whose members may appear before it.[4] The Council can also appear before the Parliament but it is in no way responsible to it. To many 'committed Europeans' this implies that the Commission is the real federal executive in embryo, which should become completely responsible to the Parliament as soon as the latter is directly elected, while the Council should be reduced to an advisory role or to acting as a kind of Senate representing the interests of member States.[5] Indeed, in the earlier Coal and Steel Community, executive authority was vested in a single body, the High Authority.

[1] See also pp. 25–6 above.
[2] Treaty establishing the European Economic Community, 1957, Article 138.5.
[3] ibid., Article 144.
[4] ibid., Article 140.
[5] See, for example, R. Pryce, *The Political Future of the European Community*, London, John Marshbank Ltd, 1962, pp. 60–74.

43

In the two later Communities the main decision-making body is the Council of Ministers, consisting of ministers representing the member States, the Commission acting as an independent spokesman of the common interest with an important right of initiative. The new arrangement largely formalizes the existing practice as it had evolved in the Coal and Steel Community, where the 'Special Council of Ministers' (originally a purely advisory body) had become much more important than was really intended. Moreover, the failure of the proposals for a Defence Community and a Political Community had lowered the sights of the leading figures in the European Movement. At the same time, of course, the member States could be expected to be particularly reluctant to give authority to an independent, 'supranational' executive in the case of full economic union.[1] The fact is that the way executive authority is divided between Commission and Council represents a departure from the normal conception of federal government. This has led most students of the Community institutions to treat these arrangements as *sui generis*, being typical neither of a federal system of government nor of an ordinary international organization, but containing elements of both.[2]

The members of the Commission are appointed unanimously by the governments of the member States for a renewable term of four years; (the offices of President and Vice-President are subject to renewal every two years). The Treaty provides that the members of the Commission should be chosen for their 'general competence' and they take an oath of independence from their national governments.[3] The Commission takes part in the sessions of the Council and plays a full and active part in its deliberations. It has the right to put forward such proposals as it thinks fit on any matter covered by the Treaty.[4] Except in a few rare cases, decisions of the Council of Ministers must be taken on the basis of a proposal of the Commission, and the Council can amend a Commission proposal only by a unanimous vote.[5] This procedure sets up a sort of dialogue

[1] See R. Mayne, *The Institutions of the European Community*, London, PEP/Chatham House, 1968, pp. 12–15.
[2] M. Camps, *What Kind of Europe?*, Oxford University Press, 1965, pp. 124–31; S. Holt, *The Common Market*, London, Nelson, 1967, pp. 30–8.
[3] Treaty establishing the EEC, Article 157.
[4] *ibid.*, Article 155.
[5] *ibid.*, Article 149.

between Commission and Council, out of which Community legislation results: the Commission seeking to promote the Community interest and the Council seeking to protect the interests of the member States.

Gradually, according to the Rome Treaty, the Council can take more and more decisions by a majority vote thus eliminating the possibility of a national veto. In fact, majority voting is the general rule laid down by the Treaty.[1] However, the present French regime is opposed to majority voting and has tried to prevent its introduction. This led to a major constitutional crisis in the Community between 1965 and 1966, the settlement of which included an agreement by all member States that majority voting would not be used where a vital national interest was at stake.[2] The practice of unanimous voting in the Council of the Ministers clearly makes more difficult the Commission's task of bringing about compromise between the representatives of the member States while ensuring that the solution reached is in the best interests of the Community.

The dialogue between the two executive bodies is the source of all major decisions taken in the name of the Community. The roles of the Parliament and to a lesser extent the Court of Justice are no more than supplementary. The Parliament is composed of 142 members nominated by the parliaments of the member States. Some parliaments nominate members in proportion to party strengths in one or both houses, some by a majority vote in both houses, but no members are directly elected to the European Parliament by people living in the six countries. The European Parliament cannot be regarded as truly representative of the peoples of the Community. One outstanding illustration of this is that, although the French and Italian Communist Parties have consistently polled about 25 per cent of the total vote in their respective countries in recent general elections, they have not so far been represented at all in the European Parliament.[3] Moreover, it can be safely assumed that the majority of members of the Parliament have been selected largely because of their willingness to serve and because of an existing

[1] For details of the voting procedures in the Council of Ministers, see J. Lambert, M. Palmer, *et al.*, *European Unity*, London, George Allen & Unwin for PEP, 1968, pp. 174–5. See also pp. 277–83.

[2] See also pp. 277–83 below.

[3] M. Forsyth, *The Parliament of the European Communities*, PEP Planning, Vol. XXX, No. 478, March 9, 1964, pp. 19–25.

interest in or loyalty towards the European Movement. Although there is a small group in the Parliament which opposes the basic principles of European unity, the general nature of its membership, along with the limitations on its powers, disqualifies it as a possible source of Opposition to the Community's executive branch.

The Parliament holds only six or seven plenary sessions a year each lasting about five days, but its main work is performed through specialized standing committees which meet quite frequently throughout the year. These committees draft reports on which Parliamentary debates are based and also carry out the more general task of keeping the Parliament abreast of the Community's activities. Members of the Commission and their staff often attend committee meetings and explain their actions and policies.[1] The Parliament's role is accurately described in the Treaty as 'advisory and supervisory'. It has to be consulted on policy proposals of the Commission and may take votes and make recommendations on its own initiative. However, its right to censure the Commission has never been used and is of only limited usefulness as a means of control in that the Parliament cannot appoint a new Commission if the existing one is forced to resign.[2] In so far as the Commission fulfils its intended role as representative of the common interest, the real check upon it, and the real source of opposition, is the Council of Ministers, which in all the most important cases decides whether or not measures become Community law. The Parliament has no effective means of preventing measures passing into law or of otherwise controlling the Council, which is not accountable to it. This is another major difference between the formal institutional arrangements of the Community and those of a typical federal system of government.[3]

Alongside the Parliament, but with a rather different standing, is another consultative body called the Economic and Social Committee consisting of 121 members appointed by the Council of Ministers by unanimous vote as 'representatives of the various categories of economic and social life'.[4] One third of its members are chosen to represent employers' organizations, one third the trade unions,

1 Forsyth, *op. cit.*, pp. 52–5.
2 *ibid.*, pp. 47–52.
3 See pp. 29–30 above.
4 Treaty establishing the EEC, Article 193.

and the remainder to defend 'the general interest'. In certain cases the Council has to obtain the Committee's opinion on proposals from the Commission and in other cases such consultation is optional but is, in practice, frequent. Its opinions are not binding but some important economic and social groups are represented on the Committee. There are about six plenary sessions a year and eight specialized sections of the Committee meet more frequently to prepare drafts for the full Committee to debate.[1]

The essential duty of the Court of Justice is to act as a court of appeal against breaches of the Treaty and of Community legislation. In practice, however, it has proved incompetent to deal with constitutional clashes involving member States. It consists of seven judges and two advocates general, all appointed for six-year renewable terms by agreement between the member governments. Cases of breach of the Treaty or of Community law can be brought before the Court by the Commission, the member States, or firms in the Community. (In addition, individual suits may be filed by personnel of the Community institutions.) The Court's ruling is binding on all parties and is not subject to appeal. It may award damages and impose sanctions for the non-execution of its decisions.[2]

In addition to these major Community institutions, there are also other bodies, some purely consultative, but others with some executive responsibilities. Some of these miscellaneous bodies were set up by the Treaty; others have come into being as the Community has developed. In the first category are the European Investment Bank and the European Social Fund.[3] There is also a Monetary Committee, consisting of government and central bank officials which 'keeps under review the monetary and financial situation of the member States and of the Community', reports regularly to the Council and to the Commission on this subject, and formulates opinions at the latter's request or on its own initiative.[4] In the course of the development of the Community, a number of committees have been set up in a variety of fields, consisting partly of national officials and partly of representatives of the Commission, designed either to assist the Commission in drawing up proposals for the Council

---

[1] J. Lambert, M. Palmer, *et al.*, *op. cit.*, pp. 185–7.
[2] *ibid.*, pp. 187–9.
[3] Treaty establishing the EEC, Articles 129–30, and 123–8, respectively.
[4] *ibid.*, Articles 105.2.

47

of Ministers or to lighten the burden of the Council of Ministers in discussing proposals already formulated. This growth of committees of a mixed nature as additions to the executive branch of the Community system has, as we shall see later, proved to be an institutional development of great importance.[1]

MEMBER GOVERNMENTS

The ministers and officials of the member governments have a vital role to perform in the Community system. Dr Erhard is quoted as saying that nearly a third of the civil servants in the relevant departments in the Federal Republic are occupied solely with papers to do with the Community, produced in Bonn and in Brussels.[2] The member governments are involved in the following ways.

First, the Treaty provides for a few acts to be performed by the member governments 'acting together' or 'by unanimous agreement', such as appointing the members of the Commission and of the Court of Justice. Secondly, the member governments take responsibility in many cases for implementing policy decided by the Community institutions, for example, when Directives are addressed to a member government requiring it to take the necessary measures to achieve some stated end. Thirdly, and of much greater importance, the ministers of the member governments sit on the Council of Ministers which is the main decision-making body of the Community. The member governments also maintain special staffs in Brussels in the manner of delegations to the Community known as Permanent Representatives. These national envoys sit together in the Committee of Permanent Representatives which is itself divided into specialized committees and working groups. The establishment of such a committee was provided for in the Treaty, its duties and powers being determined by the Council of Ministers.[3] Its aim is to try to reach agreement before meetings of the Council so as to limit negotiations between ministers to points which cannot be agreed at the level of officials.

Fifthly, there are other consultative specialized committees, set up either by the Treaty or by the Council of Ministers in the course of

---

[1] See pp. 86–100 and 242–7 below.
[2] Quoted in M. Camps, *op. cit.*, p. 93.
[3] Treaty establishing the EEC, Article 151.

time, like the Monetary Committee already mentioned. National officials, whether permanently attached to the committee concerned or to the country's Permanent Representative or specially sent from the capital, sit on these committees along with officials of the Commission and sometimes other national experts. Thus, there are committees concerned with agricultural policy (the Special Agriculture Committee), with trade negotiations with third countries (the 'Article 111 Committee'), and with economic policy (the Medium- and Short-Term Economic Policy Committees).[1] Of particular interest because of the way they are sometimes referred to as a model of future organization in other fields are the *management committees* set up under the common agricultural policy. These committees, which have been established for each main group of commodities, consist of representatives of the member States along with a representative of the Commission who acts as chairman but has no vote. Most of the more important matters on which the Commission is empowered to rule must be discussed in the *management committee* concerned, which gives an opinion either unanimously or by a qualified majority. The procedure according to which the Commission's decision is then ratified is incredibly complicated, as is typical of most of the procedures by which Community decisions are taken. The main point is that, if the Commission's decision disagrees with the *management committee's* opinion, then the matter is referred to the Council of Ministers, which has one month in which to amend the decision by a qualified majority vote. If no such majority can be obtained within the time-limit, the Commission's decision is applied.[2]

Finally, the officials of member governments are frequently consulted by the Commission when it is drawing up its proposals before submitting them to the Committee of Permanent Representatives and the Council. Several hundred meetings are held annually with this end in view and a variety of national government departments are involved.

In spite of their extensive and elaborate involvement in the decision-making process of the Community, none of the national representatives to which we have referred is accountable to the European

[1] See J. Lambert, M. Palmer *et al.*, *op. cit.*, pp. 223–6.
[2] For a fuller account, see R. Mayne, *Institutions of the European Community*, *op. cit.*, p. 38.

49

Parliament. Although the member governments constitute a crucial part of the Community they continue to be responsible for the role they play only to their own national Parliaments or to the electors in their own countries.

POLITICAL ORGANIZATIONS

These fall into three types: political parties, interest groups and promotional groups. If we take as our definition of political party, an organization based on common interest or ideology which aims to gain representation on bodies exercising political authority, then the political parties of the Community are basically the separate national parties. The reason for this is clearly that appointment to institutions wielding political authority in the Community is still in the hands of the member governments and not in those of any Community institution. But another important reason for the lack of Community-wide political parties is that the Community is still concerned with only a limited range of issues and its institutions exercise only a limited amount of power.

However, in the European Parliament national affiliations have been less important than party allegiances and the members of the Parliament sit according to party, not national, groupings during plenary sessions. The different party groups (Socialist, Christian Democrat, Liberal and Gaullist) play a vital part in the organization and conduct of sessions. However, the extent to which they act cohesively varies somewhat and there is no doubt that their members still consider themselves primarily as members of their national party and only secondarily as members of a European party group. To many committed Europeans, on the other hand, the emergence of European political parties, at least in this skeleton form, is extremely encouraging.[1]

Interest groups, such as trade unions, associations of employers and traders, professional associations, and so on, have gone very much further than political parties in organizing themselves into European units. The reasons for this are fairly obvious in that the Community institutions have acquired some important powers in fields such as tariff protection, agriculture, and competition between

[1] See M. Forsyth, *op. cit.*, pp. 25–36, and S. Henig (ed.), *European Political Parties*, London, George Allen & Unwin for PEP, 1969.

enterprises, which affect the members of these organizations very closely indeed. The limitations are similar, however, in that, in so far as representatives of the member governments continue to be responsible before their own national institutions for the main decisions, the attention of interest groups must still be directed primarily at their own national authorities. However, there are some special reasons why interest groups find it essential to have some means of effective Community-wide representation. As one student of Community interest groups has written:

'An interest group can still hope to have its views taken into account and defended in the Council by its national government. But even if it succeeds in persuading a minister to do this, the final stages of the bargaining process that precedes any Council decision are usually so complex that it is unlikely that the final outcome will be very satisfactory from its point of view. It is inevitable that compromises have to be reached, and national support for particular interests either withdrawn or modified.'[1] As a result, it is essential for groups to focus their activity, to some extent at least, on the Commission as representative of the common interest. Furthermore, it may well be too late by the time a proposal of the Commission gets to the Council of Ministers for a group to exert effective pressure.

Indeed, the Commission adopted very early on a general policy of refusing to deal with national interest groups, and encouraged the formation of Community-wide associations. There are now as many as three or four hundred of these, ranging from associations representing wide sectors of economic or social interest, such as the *Union des Industries de la Communauté Européenne* (UNICE), to the many specialized trade and professional associations. These Community 'federations' have proved extremely important as agents for helping to harmonize standards and terminology within their respective sectors. They also manage to exert some influence on the Community decision-making process in technical matters. However, as in the case of parties, the degree of cohesiveness of these European groups varies, and the power of the groups is limited in that they have no real sanctions to apply to institutions at a Community level.[2]

Promotional groups are societies, clubs and associations, not

[1] R. Pryce, Interest Groups in the EEC, *European Community*, European Community Information Service, May 1968, p. 13.
[2] *ibid.*, pp. 12–13.

necessarily based on common social or economic interest, but concerned primarily with promoting some commonly held principle or cause. The only examples of such organizations at a Community level are groups of enthusiasts for European unity who tend to support the initiative which led to the founding of the Community, and seek to draw attention to the need for taking up that initiative in the interests of further integration. Many of these existed before the Community came into existence, such as the various Federalist associations.[1] Perhaps the most effective pressure group to have arisen after the Treaty of Rome is Jean Monnet's Action Committee for the United States of Europe, of which the national Christian Democratic, Socialist and Liberal parties are members along with the main trade unions of the six countries. Monnet himself has always been regarded as 'the father' of the European Communities and his Committee is now widely seen as a powerful source of inspiration for committed Europeans of different countries, even outside the Community itself.

The symbolic importance of the Community for the various branches of the European Movement is shown by the great attention paid to it by all the various European and Federalist groups in different parts of Europe. The Press and Information Service of the Commission has actively encouraged the dissemination of information to such centres and has occasionally sponsored their activities. Such groups are often important sources of personnel for the Community institutions, and provide much intellectual and ideological stimulation for those actively concerned with running the Community. Some of the European groups are based on educational centres, some of which, like the College of Europe at Bruges, are especially concerned with the advancement of learning in the field of European unity. The former students of this College, from a variety of European countries, maintain an active association and publish their own journal on European affairs. However, with the exception of Jean Monnet's Committee, a lot of these movements are confined to intellectuals and committed activists, and their activities only rarely and indirectly impinge on the lives of the vast mass of the people living in the six countries. In no case could any of the promo-

[1] See pp. 17–23 above. For a fuller account of political groups in the Community, see A. Spinelli, *The Eurocrats*, New York, Johns Hopkins Press, 1967 pp. 112–203.

THE PARTS OF THE COMMUNITY

tional groups organized on a Community basis be described as mass movements or as groups widely representative of public opinion.

The fact is, therefore, that interest groups are the only bodies with large memberships that have effectively organized themselves at a Community level, while, even in their case, the maintenance of European federations is only a secondary consideration compared with national activity. This emphasizes the fact that the Community is still strictly a business of narrow economic interest. It is scarcely accurate yet to speak of it as a political system. Political activity in the six countries is still overwhelmingly concentrated at the national level. This is a source of disappointment for many of the original supporters of the Community, who believed that the establishment of Community institutions with growing power in economic fields would promote new European political movements and create a kind of European constituency in which the electors would come to vote for European candidates and issues.[1]

[1] See, in particular, D. Sidjanski, *Dimensions Européennes de la Science Politique*, Paris, Librairie Général de Droit et de Jurisprudence, 1962, pp. 45–102, 177–83.

CHAPTER 3

THE OBJECTIVES OF THE COMMUNITY

The immediate objectives of the Community as expressed in the Treaty of Rome are the creation of a customs union by the removal of all restrictions to trade between the six countries and the creation of an economic union by the establishment of common policies. A number of authors have suggested that these two objectives are essentially related in that the removal of barriers to trade itself creates a demand for concerted action on economic policies. However, the two objectives are regarded as quite separate by some who aim at a common market which does not attempt to go as far as economic union. It has been suggested that for this reason it is desirable to distinguish between two kinds of integration: 'negative' and 'positive'. 'Negative integration' refers to that part of economic integration which consists of the removal of discrimination, while 'positive integration' refers to the formulation and application of co-ordinated common policies designed to fulfil broad economic and welfare objectives.[1] As we shall see, the provisions of the Treaty of Rome contain elements of both types of integration, although it falls short of complete negative integration, and provides for positive integration only in somewhat vague terms. The distinction is important, for, as we shall see in a later chapter, many economists believe that a viable economic union cannot be achieved by negative integration alone.[2]

There was also a strong feeling among the founders of the Community that economic union would be only a first step towards other kinds of integration between the countries of Europe. Although not particularly articulate in this respect, the Treaty of Rome is clearly about much more than the removal of restrictions to trade and the evolution of common economic policies, and is intended to

[1] John Pinder, Positive Integration and Negative Integration, *The World Today*, March 1963, Vol. 24, No. 3, pp. 88–110.
[2] See pp. 301–7, below.

lead eventually to a political union. This arises mainly from the dynamic nature of the Community. Not only does its constitution (the Treaty of Rome) contain a number of inarticulate premisses which invite interpretation and development, but the whole idea of having common economic policies implies transferring a substantial power of discretion to new centres of decision-making at a Community level.[1] Moreover, economic policies are never particularly precise or articulate even at the national level, and are notorious for the leeway they give to the authorities which have to apply them. Any attempt to re-define them in a new context, as seems to be intended in the case of the Community, provides an important reason for concerning the Community in politics.

The roles of the various parts of the Community differ with respect to each of these levels of integration. As far as negative integration is concerned (or the creation of a common market), the relevant authorities are given fairly well-defined tasks, namely ensuring that restrictions and other distortions to trade are removed according to the timetable agreed and that escape clauses are properly administered. However, in the case of positive integration (or the adoption of common economic policies), the arrangements provided by the Treaty allow for greater elasticity in the reaching of decisions. As for the timetable according to which common policies have to be adopted, this has not proved as flexible in practice as it might have been, mainly on account of political factors. Thus the French Government insisted that the establishment of a common agricultural policy should precede progress beyond a certain stage towards a custom union. On the other hand, the Treaty is quite often silent as to the actual content of common policies and this is something which has to be settled by a general process of bargaining between the Commission and the member States. Finally, the Treaty refers only in vague and general terms to the ultimate prospect of a political union[2] and this is something which is left almost entirely to the initiative of Community institutions and member States.

---

[1] R. Pryce, *The Political Future of the European Communities*, London, John Marshbank Ltd, 1962, pp. 17–23.

[2] In the Preamble to the Treaty of Rome, the member States express their determination 'to establish the foundations of an ever-closer union between the peoples of Europe'. Article 2 of the Treaty states 'closer relations between the States' as a general objective of the Community.

AN INDUSTRIAL CUSTOMS UNION

The Treaty of Rome laid down that free trade in industrial goods within the Community should be achieved step by step in the course of a Transitional Period timed to end at December 31, 1969. In fact, the removal of trade barriers has proved the easiest of the objectives to achieve and was completed on July 1, 1968, eighteen months earlier than planned. At the same time the Community adopted a common external tariff to all imports from the rest of the world (the level of this having been fixed in 1960). In 1960 and 1963 the Council of Ministers was able to 'accelerate' the cuts provided in the timetable set by the Treaty and in the same way to ensure that almost all quantitative restrictions were removed by December 31, 1961.[1]

The achievement of a full common market involves more than the removal of barriers to trade, so the Treaty provides that by the end of the Transitional Period there shall be free movement of workers within the Community and freedom to establish businesses and to supply services and also requires the progressive abolition of restrictions on movement of capital 'to the extent necessary for the proper functioning of the common market'.[2] To all intents and purposes the free movement of labour has already been achieved in the course of the Transitional Period. However, before the right of establishment can be assured and the supply of services properly freed, measures have to be taken to harmonise legislation and other standards in the member States regarding qualifications, company law and so on; work in this direction has been more difficult, and has progressed slowly throughout the Transitional Period.

REGULATION OF COMPETITION

One basic principle of the Treaty is that the activities of the Community shall include 'the establishment of a system ensuring that

---

[1] Details regarding the timetable of tariff cuts since the first reduction of 10 per cent in January 1959 can be found in J. Lambert, M. Palmer *et al.*, *European Unity*, London, George Allen and Unwin for PEP, 1968, pp. 195.

[2] Restrictions on current capital payments were removed as required by the end of the first stage.

competition shall not be distorted in the common market'.[1] The most important machinery for enforcing this principle is contained in Articles 85 to 94 of the Treaty of Rome. These prohibit any associations, agreements or practices by states, enterprises or other organizations which might affect trade across frontiers and have as their object or result the distortion of competition. The provisions define what kinds of agreement are to be banned and explain the grounds on which some might be exempted. A Regulation to implement these provisions came into effect in March 1962 and required that all agreements between firms should be registered with the Commission, which is empowered to determine exemptions from the general prohibition. It has since been the duty of the Commission to develop a case law on restrictive trade practices in the Community.[2]

Abuse of a 'dominant position' by one or more firms is also prohibited by the Treaty but no action has yet been taken under this article. The Commission has extensive powers to ensure the abolition of a number of state aids which are designed to favour certain firms or sectors of production and which in so doing adversely affect trade between member countries. There are however a number of exceptions which the Commission can take into account. The Commission has already acted in a large number of cases, authorizing some forms of aid and having others amended or abolished.[3]

AN AGRICULTURAL COMMON MARKET

Two facts, in particular, have made the pursuit of this objective possibly the most dramatic feature of the Community so far. On the one hand, the criteria for achieving free trade in agriculture were vastly more complicated than those for industrial goods.

[1] Articles 100–102 of the Treaty of Rome lay down the terms under which action might be taken by Community institutions to ensure the alignment of national legislation which might otherwise result in disparities in trade between member countries. According to Article 226 special safeguard measures may be taken to protect certain uncompetitive basic industries, for example, Italian sulphur, but an effort has been made by the Community institutions with the co-operation of the member governments concerned to make such special measures unnecessary.

[2] See D. Swann and D. L. McLachlan, *Competition Policy in The European Community*, London, Oxford University Press, 1968, pp. 54–9.

[3] J. Lambert, M. Palmer et al., *op. cit.*, pp. 199–201.

In each member country there existed a managed and protected market for agriculture and there were significant differences in prices and in structure between them. At the same time the inclusion of agriculture was essential to provide a balance of interests between member states. Thus it is clear that in this area negative integration could not be contemplated before substantial agreement on some measures of positive integration had already been reached. On the other hand, the Treaty laid down the principles and objectives of the common agricultural policy in very general terms, leaving it entirely up to the Commission to take the initiative in preparing the ground for a policy after holding a conference of representatives from the member States (this conference was held at Stresa in July 1958). A common agricultural market, centrally financed from a common fund, had been largely established by July 1, 1968, at the same time as free trade was achieved for all major agricultural products. This point has been reached gradually since 1962 in a series of stages dealing with one product or group of products at a time.

The general objectives of the common agricultural policy were set out in the Treaty as:

(a) to increase agricultural productivity by developing technical progress and by ensuring the rational development of agricultural production and the optimum utilization of the factors of production, particularly labour;

(b) to ensure thereby a fair standard of living for the agricultural population, particularly by increasing the individual earnings of persons engaged in agriculture;

(c) to stabilize markets;

(d) to guarantee regular supplies;

(e) to ensure reasonable prices in supplies to consumers.

It was agreed that there should be a common organization of markets at a Community level and three alternative systems were laid down by the Treaty.[1] From these the member States chose on the Commission's initiative to adopt the system requiring a separate common market organization for each main product. The basis of the organization in each sector is the fixing of an annual common price supported mainly with the help of common import levies and subsidies to

[1] Treaty establishing the EEC, Articles 39–40.

producers. At the same time, a common Fund (FEOGA) provides support for structural improvements of agriculture and of predominantly agricultural areas within the Community. It also pays out refunds to exporters and helps to maintain price levels in the various agricultural markets.[1]

The Commission has recently made a major effort to shift the emphasis of the policy away from the fixing of price levels by laying more stress on the general reform of agriculture. Measures recently proposed include reducing the present acreage of farmland within the Community and increasing the average size of farm holdings.[2] This is a major attempt to advance towards positive integration in the agricultural sector, but the Commission's proposals have met with strong resistance from some governments who do not believe it is the Community's business to get involved in such far-reaching questions. The Commission's proposals have yet to be approved by the member States.

The most difficult aspect of the common agricultural policy so far has been the question of finance. In 1962 it was agreed that the receipts from import levies should go directly to the Community when the common policy was finally adopted, thus giving the Community an independent source of revenue (such as was enjoyed by the High Authority of the Coal and Steel Community). However, this agreement has since led to severe conflict within the Community with the result that the introduction of self-financing has had to be postponed. Up to now the Community Fund for agriculture (FEOGA) has had to be financed from member States' contributions, paid partly from the import levies which go to the member States for the time being. The main cause of this deadlock has been failure to agree on the institutional arrangements which should accompany the Community's acquisition of its own financial resources. Because of this, the agricultural common market has not turned out to be nearly so positive a form of integration as was initially hoped and, ostensibly at least, it has not so far taken the members of the Community any farther towards political unity.

[1] For a full account of how the policy works in practice, see T. K. Warley, *Agriculture: The Cost of Joining the Common Market*, London, PEP/Chatham House, April 1967.

[2] *European Community*, London, European Communities Information Service, January 1969, pp. 4–5.

COMMON SOCIAL AND ECONOMIC POLICIES

The Treaty requires that common policies should be put into effect in a number of other fields in addition to competition and agriculture. Transport, in particular, is an essential element in economic union, given its importance to trade and given also its similarity to agriculture in being nearly everywhere subject to managed market conditions. The Treaty stipulates quite categorically that a common transport policy should be achieved by 1970.[1] But progress in this sector has proved extremely difficult and most of what has been achieved so far consists of the removal by means of Community regulations of certain discriminations between nationalities, although some progress has also been made towards establishing common rules for competition in inland transport. The bulk of measures taken towards this end were agreed in two stages, first, in June 1965 and, second, in June 1968. So far the policy consists of the fixing of common upper and lower limits for rates charged in road and rail transport, the introduction of Community quotas for the granting of road transport licences, and the harmonisation of various national safety regulations and rules governing working conditions. Government subsidies to certain kinds of transport undertaking have been prohibited.[2] However, these developments have not taken place against the background of any overall policy for the transport sector. While studies have been in progress for several years on national expenditure on transport infrastructure, there is little or nothing in the way of common agreement on the future size and shape of the Community transport system. The representatives of the road transport industry in the Six criticized the 1968 measures as being far too piecemeal in that they 'could not be considered as constituting a real common transport policy'.[3]

Progress towards a common transport policy received something of a blow in 1967 when the German Government produced a national transport plan, (aimed mainly at diverting road traffic on to the railways within the Federal Republic), which threatened to increase the differences between the national policies of the Six and included some measures which would be inconsistent with the Treaty of Rome.

[1] Treaty establishing the EEC, Articles 74–5.
[2] J. Lambert, M. Palmer *et al.*, *op. cit.*, pp. 217–20.
[3] *European Community*, September 1968, European Communities Information Service, pp. 10–12.

The Commission has applied pressure on the German Government to modify this plan.[1]

Although the Treaty makes no reference to a common social policy, it involves the Community in a number of important functions in this respect. One aim of the Treaty is to 'promote improvement in the living and working conditions of labour so as to allow them to be harmonized in an upward direction'. This is to be achieved, however, largely by co-ordinating national activity rather than by agreeing to specific Community policies. Nevertheless, the Community institutions are responsible for ensuring the free movement of workers and complete equality of status for all Community workers was achieved in July 1968. There is also the European Social Fund administered by the Commission and designed to reimburse part of member governments' costs for schemes of vocational retraining and resettlement in order to ensure the re-employment of workers who have to change their jobs as a result of the Common Market. The Fund is financed out of member States' contributions. In 1965 the Commission recommended that its role should be extended but nothing has come of this as yet.

Another aspect of the Community which is mainly left to the governments of member States 'acting together' is economic policy in the more general sense, meaning policy for dealing with fluctuations in the business cycle and in the national balance of payments, monetary policy, and long-term economic planning. According to Article 103 of the Treaty:

'Member States shall consider their short-term economic policy as a matter of common interest. They shall consult with each other and with the Commission on measures to be taken in response to current circumstances.' The member States are also enjoined to co-ordinate their economic policies and to ensure that their respective central banks and administrative services collaborate with one another. The Monetary Committee is provided to keep the monetary and financial situation of the Community under review and to report to the other Community institutions. A similar committee has been set up to assist in co-ordinating member States' budgetary policies. Article 108 of the Treaty provides for 'mutual assistance' to be given to any member State in balance-of-payments difficulties. The Com-

[1] *European Community*, September 1968, European Communities Information Service, pp. 10–12.

mission is empowered to recommend appropriate measures to any member government when the latter finds itself in difficulties which are 'likely to prejudice the functioning of the common market', power which was used in May and June 1964 when Italy faced a serious balance-of-payments crisis. There has also been an attempt to co-ordinate economic policy-making over the longer term and to this end a Medium-term Economic Policy Committee was set up in 1965. Five-year programmes were presented by the Committee and were approved by the Commission in 1966 and in 1968 respectively. The aim of these programmes is to provide a basis for recommendations on the kinds of economic and social policies member States should pursue and also for securing consistency between the various policies being worked out at a Community level. This approach to common long-term economic policy, however, is very much more moderate and less elaborate than the proposals originally worked out by the Commission in 1962 and 1963.[1]

The development of some kind of economic union is implied but not explained in the Treaty of Rome and progress depends largely on the initiative and will-power of the Community institutions and national governments. According to the 'spill-over' theory movement towards common economic and social policies should follow more or less automatically from the achievement of a common market.[2] Moreover, it is argued by many economists that the full benefits of free trade cannot be achieved unless the opening of barriers to trade is accompanied by co-ordinated efforts to achieve balanced economic and social development in all parts of the area concerned.[3] Again, it is repeatedly stressed that the pricing arrangements adopted in the common agricultural policy will make closer monetary co-operation essential, if not inevitable.[4] Presumably, in an ideal world, the Community would be already moving close to the adoption of a common currency with a common central bank. Movement in this sort of direction, however, is proving qualitatively quite different from the removal of discrimination and the establishment of a common market. This is a field where political differences as to the proper role of public authorities in economic management may become

[1] G. Denton, *Planning in the EEC*, London, PEP/Chatham House, 1967.
[2] See pp. 31–3, above.
[3] See J. Pinder, *op. cit.*
[4] See, for example, M. Camps, *What Kind of Europe?*, London, Oxford University Press, 1965, pp. 59–62.

crucial and may prevent agreement on further measures of integration. For a long time progress towards the adoption of common economic policies, including co-ordination of long-term strategy, was held up by the existence of a strongly neo-liberal government in Germany committed to free trade rather than economic planning. Moreover, it is extremely difficult to provide for effective common policies in a treaty between a number of different States, and some authors criticize the Treaty of Rome for being particularly 'vague and permissive' where the integration of economic policies is concerned.[1]

In spite of this, the Commission took from the start a very positive attitude. For example, it placed the emphasis in its *Action Programme for the Second Term* 'on a positive goal, public responsibility in economic affairs' and aimed 'gradually to forge national economic policies into a common short-term and long-term policy designed to secure the fastest expansion possible, economic stability, and a smoothing out of cyclical swings and national or regional disequilibria'.[2] However, there has been evidence of an ideological division within the Community, not only as there was at the outset between 'free traders' and 'planners', but also increasingly between those who believe that economic policy must be left to the member States themselves to determine and those who consider that the full benefits of integration can be gained only by developing Community policies and by making provision for Community action.[3]

There remain six specific areas where common policies are regarded by at least some actors in the Community as being necessary or desirable objectives. These are, respectively, taxation, regional and commercial policies, energy, industry and technology. In only one of these fields, however, has anything like real progress been made. This is in the harmonization of taxation, and in particular the harmonization of practices associated with business turnover taxes, (provided for in Article 99 of the Treaty). Agreement in this respect was achieved in 1967 and will involve the adoption throughout the Community of a modified version of the French system of value added taxation (TVA). Otherwise the Commission has got no further

---

[1] Pinder, *op. cit.*
[2] *Memorandum of the Commission on the Action Programme for the Second Stage*, 1962, European Economic Community, Brussels.
[3] See G. Denton, *op. cit.*

than the stage of initiating discussions on such problems as distortions to trade resulting from different levels of indirect taxation or from different relative levels of indirect and direct taxation.[1] Indeed, there is so far no element of positive integration in Community policy on taxation and what has been aimed and achieved so far is essentially in the form of removing distortions to trade.

In the case of regional policy, where the Treaty expresses only a declaration of intent, progress has been very slow indeed. The major difficulties here have been, respectively, the lack of regional policies within certain member States, and the reluctance of others (such as France) to allow regional policy to become a matter of Community concern. In 1965 the Community did, however, set out the general lines of a Community regional policy, designed to bring living standards in less-favoured parts of the Community up towards the levels of the more prosperous areas and to give help to those declining areas of the Community which had suffered as a result of the increased freedom of trade. Yet most of the instruments for promoting regional development are the responsibility of the member governments; for example, the European Investment Bank, while it has to take account of the Commission's recommendations in allocating its funds, is controlled by a board consisting of the national finance ministers.[2]

There are three particular areas where the development of Community policies has become of increasing interest and importance in spite of receiving no specific treatment in the Treaty of Rome. The first of these is energy policy. Until the merger of the three Community executives in July 1967 responsibility for different sources of energy was divided between the three different executive bodies of the different Communities. Nevertheless, a Protocol of Agreement had been signed in April 1964 laying down the objectives of a common policy. This had been considered necessary because of the vital importance of energy as a proportion of industrial costs. The merger has now increased hopes of concerted efforts in the implementation of a common policy in this field.

The establishment of a single market among the six countries, together with the challenge of American competition from outside,

---

[1] For a full account, see D. Dosser and S. Han, *Taxes in the EEC and Britain: The Problem of Harmonization*, London, PEP/Chatham House, 1968.
[2] J. Lambert, M. Palmer *et al.*, *op. cit.*, pp. 227–8.

presents industries of the Community with the need to develop new structures which are more suited to the changed conditions. It is thought by many that this challenge can be taken up satisfactorily only if a series of Community measures in the field of industrial policy are taken and in recent years increasing attention has been paid to this within the Community. The sort of measures envisaged include the formation of a Community-wide capital market capable of making funds available where and when they are needed, the harmonization of national company law (so as to permit the establishment of 'European companies'), and the development of a Community patent law as well as of a common policy on science and technology.[1]

Financial policy, economic programming, regional development, policies for industry, energy, and science and technology are all now regularly spoken of as important objectives of the Community, in spite of vagueness or silence on the part of the Treaty of Rome itself. However, these are all fields where progress is only just beginning and where there are important underlying differences of approach between the different parts of the Community. These differences arise not just over the role of Community institutions, but also over the desirability or practicability of framing policies at all. Above all, to achieve common economic and social policies on this dimension necessitates a broad measure of political consensus among those concerned and a level of institutional and political integration which does not seem to exist in the Community at the present time.

In contrast, the Treaty was quite specific in the case of a common commercial policy, providing for the adoption of such a policy for external trade by the end of the Transitional Period.[2] Here too, however, the *political* challenge is proving to be too great. Each Community country agreed to offer the members the opportunity of consultation as from July 1, 1961, before concluding any new trade agreement with non-member countries and not to sign any bilateral trade agreements extending beyond the Transitional Period. In April 1964 the Commission submitted a series of proposals to the Council for moves towards a common commercial policy, but little progress has been made with these.

---

[1] *Tenth General Report on the Activities of the Communities*, 1968, Commission of the European Communities, sec. 24–31.

[2] Treaty establishing the EEC, Articles 111–12.

It is important to note, however, that in many ways common action in commercial policy has been achieved *de facto* in that the Commission has already negotiated on behalf of the Community in a number of important (and conclusive) trade negotiations with third countries, for example, in the framework of GATT. On the other hand, agreement on general policies on external trade (particularly with 'problem' countries such as those in eastern Europe) still seems a forlorn hope, and many in the Community doubt its real practicability.

This is the area of policy where the requirements of an economic union overlap most clearly with questions of foreign policy, which remain the prerogative of the national governments, and the lack of progress towards a political union has not helped in creating a willingness to work towards a genuine common policy in trade matters.[1]

AN OUTWARD-LOOKING COMMUNITY

That the Community should play a major constructive role in world economic affairs was undoubtedly an aim of the founders of the Treaty. However, the Treaty itself offers very little guidance on this point[2] and in fact very many of the actions which have been taken at a Community level have been reactions to the initiatives of third countries. It is in this area above all others that the lack of political unity, in particular the absence of any common foreign policy, has proved most inhibiting to joint action by the six countries. Four objectives of the Community in the field of external relations are particularly important: the maintenance of an Association with the former overseas dependencies of certain member States, the maintenance of Association Agreements with other third countries, the consideration of new applications for membership, and the conduct of trade negotiations with third countries and with other international organizations.

The Association with former dependent territories was established

---

[1] J. Lambert, M. Palmer *et al.*, *op. cit.*, p. 238.
[2] The Preamble to the Treaty of Rome states as general objectives of the Community, 'the gradual suppression of restrictions to international trade', and to 'consolidate . . . the safeguards of peace and liberty', and calls on the other peoples of Europe who share their ideal to join in the enterprise.

for a period of five years by Part IV of the Treaty of Rome and involved freeing trade between the Six and their associates at the same tempo as within the Community. Following the Association, the Community has granted direct aid in the form of investment and joint institutions have been set up. By 1960 the Belgian Congo and most of the French colonies in Africa had attained independence and the Association with these countries was re-negotiated on an equal footing by the member States and the Commission during 1961 and 1962. The resulting Yaoundé Convention was signed in June 1964 and renewed the Association for another five years more or less along the lines of the original Association. The institutions of the Association consist of a Council of Ministers, a Secretariat established in Brussels with a joint African and European staff, a Parliamentary Conference and a Court of Arbitration. After three years of negotiations a special Association Treaty with Nigeria was signed in July 1966 to last for three years. The Community has also concluded trade agreements with Israel and Iran, and a trade and technical assistance agreement with the Lebanon.[1]

According to the Treaty, association with the Community is open to all countries. The form of association is left to the Community institutions and the member States to decide. However, serious difficulty has been encountered in negotiating association agreements with certain Mediterranean countries. So far separate agreements have been signed with Greece and Turkey, each Association having its own set of institutions. The agreement with Greece provides for the establishment of a customs union with the Community and the harmonization of economic policies, as well as the award of a four-year development grant by the Community through the European Investment Bank. However, the Community refused a Greek request to be allowed to take part in the arrangements provided by the common agricultural policy. At the time of the agreement (1961) the Greek government expressed its complete readiness to accept the political implications of eventual full membership of the Community, but recent political events in Greece have led to a considerable hardening of the Community's attitude within the Association.[2]

Negotiations for the association of Algeria, Morocco and Tunisia opened in 1965. The Italian Government has objected to the growing

[1] J. Lambert, M. Palmer et al., op. cit., pp. 237–9.
[2] ibid., p. 244–5.

67

extension of terms of association to Mediterranean countries which are her competitors in certain agricultural products and has suggested that association should be confined to those countries which are potential full members. Italy has also resisted the full membership of Austria, and, since Austria's state of neutrality as bound by the State Treaty of 1955 makes her membership something of a special problem, association with that country has been proposed as a substitute. Negotiations have been under way since 1965. An application for association was received from Spain in 1962 and renewed in 1964 and negotiations for a trade agreement were opened in 1967. However, some member countries are opposed to the establishment of any institutional links with this country on account of the nature of its present regime.[1] Clearly, therefore, there seem to be certain natural limits to the policy of association imposed, on the one hand, by individual trading policies of member States, and, on the other, by differences between the political systems of member States and those of would-be associates. As yet, however, although no articulate common policy exists, there has been no major clash between members of the Community on the criteria for extending association to third countries.

The same cannot be said for the admission of new members to Community. On two occasions the very existence of the Community has been threatened by disagreement between France and her partners on the desirability of admitting Britain (along with other smaller European countries) to full membership. Article 237 of the Treaty states that 'any European state may apply to become a member of the Community', and rules that the decision to admit a new member shall be taken by the Council of Ministers by unanimous vote after obtaining the opinion of the Commission. The first approach for membership came from Britain and was made in August 1961. Applications followed from Denmark, Norway and Ireland. The British request for negotiation was formally accepted by the Council and in the course of the next eighteen months of negotiation Britain accepted the provisions of the Treaty relating to economic union and the texts approved up to that time by the Council, as well as the basic principles of the common agricultural policy. On January 14, 1963, however, President de Gaulle gave his famous press conference expressing the view that Britain was not yet ready

1 J. Lambert, M. Palmer et al., op. cit., pp. 247–8.

for membership of the Community and negotiations were broken off (with all the four applicant countries) shortly afterwards.[1] In 1967 a second British application was made and the Commission issued a favourable opinion on the idea of reopening negotiations. For a second time, however, General de Gaulle applied his veto in November 1967. The British application remains on the table, but no negotiations have been undertaken, although prospects are now brighter following the resignation of General de Gaulle.

In spite of the absence of a common commercial policy, as we have already seen, the Community has succeeded in negotiating as one unit in trade negotiations within the framework of GATT. Its most striking success in this respect was its part in the Kennedy Round of tariff and trade negotiatons between 1963 and 1967. The Commission conducted these negotiations under directives from the Council.[2]

DEVELOPMENT TOWARDS A POLITICAL UNION

The main step taken so far towards developing the institutional framework established by the Treaties has been the merger of the three Executives (the Commissions of the EEC and Euratom and the High Authority of the Coal and Steel Community), into a single Commission of the European Communities, and the establishment of a single Council of Ministers. A Treaty to this effect was signed by the member governments on April 8, 1965, and came into effect after some delay on July 1, 1967. Many members of the European Movement may have wished that this merger would increase the formal powers of the Commission in the Economic and Atomic Energy Communities to match the role of the High Authority in the Coal and Steel Community.[1] For the time being, however, the new single Commission and Council will continue to implement the three separate Community treaties, and the only real advantage for unification will be that the new joint institutions will be better able to

---

[1] For a full account of the negotiations, see M. Camps, *Britain and the European Communities, 1958–63,* London, Oxford University Press, 1964, pp. 367–413, 455–506.

[2] This example is considered in detail as a special case study at pp. 166–216, below.

[3] See pp. 43–6, above.

take an overall view of certain issues, such as energy policy, responsibility for which was previously divided up between the different separate Executives.[1] The new single Commission will, however, be responsible for drawing up plans for a merger of the three Communities. This objective has been approached with some caution for fear that the French Government will oppose any attempt to strengthen the Community institutions at the expense of the national governments.

The fact that the merger of the executives is the only major institutional development which can be pointed to is rather a depressing fact for the European Movement. Indeed most of the leading actors in the Communities had aimed, in one sense or another, at some kind of political union, including an extension of the present Treaties to cover foreign affairs and defence. The Commission itself has from the very beginning been conscious of the wider political implications of what was intended in the Treaty of Rome.[2] However, two different kinds of development have been envisaged and they should be considered separately. First, there is development of the institutions within the existing framework set up by the Treaties, concentrating on the means by which the Community obtains its financial resources, on the role of the Parliament and of the Commission, and on the voting procedures in the Council of Ministers. Secondly, there is a desire to extend co-operation between the six countries to new fields, in particular foreign policy and defence, but with the development of new kinds of institution. The first kind of development has been strongly favoured by the Commission and some of the governments, in particular that of the Netherlands. The second has been associated mainly with the French Government. Although the Commission and the other governments are also in favour of extending the Community into new fields, they have been suspicious of the kind of institutional means for achieving this which the French have so far proposed.

[1] Indeed it seems that most of the member States opposed a proposal to call the new combined Executive the 'High Commission', even though this would have been a more modest sounding title than 'High Authority'. See F. Dehousse, *L'avenir institutionnel des Communautés Européennes*, Nancy, Centre European Universitaire, 1967, pp. 39–40.

[2] See, for example, *Sixth General Report on the Activities of the Community*, Commission of the EEC, 1963, pp. 295 ff.; *Memorandum of the Commission on the Action Programme for the Second Stage*, 1962, *op. cit.*, p. 10.

At present the activities of the Community are financed from contributions from the member States. Each of the Community institutions draws up provisional annual estimates and sends them to the
Commission which submits a preliminary draft budget to the Council
by September 30th each year. The Council adopts a draft budget by
weighted majority vote, submitting it to the Parliament, which has
the right to propose amendments by October 31st. After discussing
the Parliament's amendments with the Commission, the Council
takes the final decision on the budget by qualified majority vote.[1]
The Commission, supported by some governments and by all committed Europeans, has sought to change this procedure with a view
to giving the Community some independent source of finance.
Article 210 of the Treaty states that: 'The Commission shall study the
conditions under which the financial contributions of the member
States . . . may be replaced by other resources of the Community
itself, in particular by revenue accruing from the common customs
tariff when the latter has been definitively introduced.' In the spring
of 1965 the Commission announced proposals which would enable
revenue from the common customs tariff to be paid direct to the
Community, at the same time as it proposed, as a second means of
providing independent resources, that the levies on agricultural
imports should accrue directly to the Community when the final
stage of the agricultural policy was reached.

At the same time as it made these proposals for giving the Community independent sources of finance (*ressources propres*), the Commission also recommended a new procedure for approving the
annual Community budget. The Council would still make the final
decision on the draft budget, but would have to accept amendments
from the European Parliament if these were passed by a simple
majority of the Parliament's members and approved by the Commission. The French Government objected to the presentation of
these different proposals in the form of a 'package deal', and the
resulting conflict led to a French boycott of the Community between
1965 and 1966. At the end of this boycott it was agreed by the member
governments that any decision on providing the Community with its
own financial resources would be postponed.[2]

[1] *Budgetary Control in the European Economic Community*, Occasional Paper
No. 6, PEP/ London, 1960.
[2] See pp. 275 ff., below.

Another way in which the role of the Parliament might be developed arises from Article 138 of the Treaty which states that: 'The Assembly shall draw up proposals for elections by direct universal suffrage in accordance with a uniform procedure in all member States. The Council shall unanimously decide on the provisions which it shall recommend to member States for adoption in accordance with their respective constitutional requirements.' The Parliament drew up a draft Convention on direct elections in May 1960 which it presented to the Council of Ministers. This proposed a two-stage move to a fully elected Parliament. During the first stage the Parliament was to be enlarged and two-thirds of its members would be directly elected, the remaining third continuing to be nominated by the national Parliaments. The system of election for the directly-elected members could be worked out independently by each member State. A detailed and uniform electoral system for all its members would be worked out by the Parliament during the first stage for implementation during the second.[1] However, despite repeated requests by the Parliament, the Convention has not been approved by the Council. The Commission has consistently supported the idea of direct elections to the Parliament and has argued from the very beginning for an increase in its powers. It has tried actively to include the Parliament in the decision-making process of the Community, for example, by publicizing its own proposals to the Parliament before submitting them to the Council.[2]

While there have been numerous voices in support of increasing the financial and other powers of the Commission, and at the same time making it accountable to a directly elected Parliament, such ideas have been strongly opposed by the French Government. In fact, during the negotiations towards the end of the French boycott of 1965–66 the French were insisting that the Commission's authority 'should be precisely circumscribed and leave no room for discretion or autonomous responsibility.'[3] Among other steps aimed at bridling the Commission the French proposed that its expenditure on information services should be more tightly controlled, and that it

[1] PEP, *Direct Elections and the European Parliament*, Occasional Papers No. 10, October 24, 1960.
[2] See M. Camps, *What Kind of Europe? op. cit.*, pp. 43–4.
[3] M. Camps, *European Unification in the Sixties*, London, Oxford University Press, 1967, pp. 104–8.

should in future refrain from publishing its proposals before they had been considered by representatives of the member States. These suggestions were not fully accepted by the other members of the Community and they were contained in the 'Luxembourg Compromise' of January 1966 only in emasculated form. Following this crisis, however, it has proved impossible to make any progress with steps to increase the powers of the Commission or the Parliament. Indeed, the reverse has been the rule, in that in future a greater number of 'executive' functions has probably been given to joint committees consisting of representatives of national governments rather than to the Commission.[1]

Another way by which the Commission's position might be strengthened would be implementing in practice as well as in theory the provisions of the Treaty regarding majority voting in the Council of Ministers. During the first eight years of the Community unanimity was still necessary for a large number of decisions, but after July 1, 1966, majority voting became, according to the Treaty, applicable in many more cases. In practice, however, voting by a majority has rarely proved to be necessary. More importantly, one of the conditions of the French for ending their boycott was an agreement between the member States that they would endeavour to reach solutions acceptable to each one of them on all matters where 'very important interests of one or more partners are at stake', even if majority voting was provided for by the Treaty. The same agreement also noted that 'the French delegation considers that where very important interests are at stake the discussion must be continued until unanimous agreement is reached'.[2]

As for the other main kind of development towards a political union, extending the treaties to include non-economic sectors, the Commission remarked in 1965 that:

'The immediate consequence of effective economic integration is to pose clearly the problem of extending integration to several other domains of national activity, not excluding foreign affairs and defence'.[3]

The French have always been particularly keen to extend the

---

[1] M. Camps, *European Unification in the Sixties*, p. 206, n 5.

[2] *ibid.*, p. 114.

[3] *Seventh General Report on the Activities of the Community*, Commission of the EEC, 1964, p. 20.

Community in this way, and General de Gaulle even went so far as to make this a condition of his further co-operation in attaining the existing objectives of the Community. He was prepared to consider any kind of development, however, only if it proceeded on different constitutional principles from those adopted up to now. Since 1959 discussions between the Six foreign ministers have been held each quarter. In 1960 General de Gaulle took the initiative of putting forward a plan for extending political co-operation between the member States and this led eventually to the establishment of a committee (the Fouchet Committee) which studied the possibility of following up this initiative during 1961 and 1962. On this committee the French proposed a plan involving regular meetings of a Council of Heads of Governments and of Foreign Ministers on which all decisions would be taken unanimously. Meanwhile Ministers of Defence, Education and Cultural Affairs would also meet regularly. In addition there would be a European Political Commission stationed in Paris and consisting of high officials from the national foreign ministries. Its task would be to prepare and carry out the Council's decisions. The existing European Parliament would be empowered to address questions to the Council and to make recommendations. The Council would reserve the exclusive power to decide unanimously whether or not to admit new members to the Political Community. The other five were not prepared to enter into an arrangement of this kind, and all that came out of the discussions was a bilateral Franco-German Treaty of Co-operation, signed in January 1963.[1]

Any further progress in this direction has been impeded by deadlock between France and her five partners on two major issues. In the first place, there was fundamental disagreement in the field of foreign policy itself, with particular regard to relations with the USA and the admission of new members (especially Britain) to the Community. Second, there was a basic difference over the future development of the institutions of the Community, concerning in particular the roles of the Commission and the Parliament. Thus the Community has been deeply divided on the question of development towards political union. On the one hand, the Commission, usually supported by five of the member governments, and backed by the European movement, is in favour of the Community institutions

[1] Camps, *What Kind of Europe?*, *op. cit.*, pp. 97–102.

developing more and more of the characteristics of a federal system of government, including, in particular, some financial autonomy combined with full accountability to a directly elected Parliament. Meanwhile, it considers an extension of the Community into fields such as foreign policy and defence as being an inevitable consequence of growing economic union. On the other hand, the French régime of General de Gaulle was fundamentally opposed to any institutional development which might threaten to direct political attention away from the existing national governments. While the Commission has itself sometimes been as reluctant as the French Government to take steps towards 'Atlantic Partnership', its motive for caution has been an anxiety to consolidate the union of the Six before embarking on adventures in world politics. However, General de Gaulle's campaign for a 'European foreign policy' seems to have been motivated largely by nationalist ambitions.

'Throughout the long negotiations in the Fouchet Committee and the spasmodic discussions since then it was clear that the French were trying to downgrade and control the Economic Community by capping it with an intergovernmental arrangement ... It has ... been clear for some time that the present French government would accept no system that would now or in the foreseeable future give any effective role to an independent body representing the common interest.'[1]

The preceding review of the objectives of the European Economic Community, as contained in the Treaty and as developed since 1958, makes it quite clear that the economic aspects of European unity cannot be considered apart from the political. In the first place, the founders of the Treaty and the main representatives of the Community itself regarded the Community as more than a merely economic or technical undertaking. Secondly, the main actors in the Community have been quite conscious of the political implications of economic integration. We have already seen in the above review of the Community's various objectives how in one sector after another progress towards economic union necessitates parallel progress in the harmonization of national legislation and policy, and that this can really take place satisfactorily only in a common institutional framework. Thirdly, however, the 'spillover' from economic to political integration (as well as that from negative to positive

[1] Camps, *European Unification in the Sixties, op. cit.,* pp. 225–6.

75

economic integration) has not proved, as many hoped it would, to be an automatic process. In many cases progress towards the Community's economic objectives has been impossible owing to the lack of political unity. One of the main lessons of the history of the Community so far may well be that unification will not proceed without some kind of prompting of a political nature. It is on the political side of its development that the Community faces its most crucial challenge.

CHAPTER 4

THE DECISION-MAKING PROCESS

For the European Economic Community to be more than an industrial customs union it must be dynamic. The creation of a common market is expected in itself to produce some kind of dynamic towards further integration by leading to 'interpenetration' of industrial activity across national frontiers and by involving a measure of collective decision-making. At the same time, the Treaty of Rome expresses the intention of the member States to enter into agreements on common economic and social policies and this implies a substantial amount of political co-operation:

'What (the Treaties of Paris and Rome) provide for, indeed, is the integration not of economic activity as such—the actions of employers, workers, producers, merchants, professional men, and consumers—but of the increasing role played by governments in determining the conditions within which such economic activity takes place. We are not integrating economics, we are integrating policies. We are not just changing our furniture, we are jointly building a new and bigger house.'[1]

However, as we have seen, these supposedly dynamic elements do not seem to be effective without a measure of political initiative. Moreover, it may well be that agreement on common economic and social policies, far from being a precursor of political integration of broader scope, may itself depend on the prior existence of common foreign and defence policies and of a substantial surrender of national sovereignty. We have already seen that the political system of the Community does not compare readily with other systems with which we are familiar, let alone the federal system, into which it is intended to develop. On the other hand, it is equally unlike known international associations. For one thing, there is clearly an element of independent political authority at a Community level. For another,

[1] Walter Hallstein, *United Europe: Challenge and Opportunity*, London, Oxford University Press, 1962, p. 66.

77

there are the repeated declarations of leading Community representatives to the effect that the Community is an evolving political union.[1] A number of distinguished scholars have looked at the institutions of the Community, partly from the constitutional point of view to scrutinize their formal powers, and partly from a sociological point of view to trace their impact on the behaviour of key decision-makers at Community and national levels. This has helped to reveal what kind of political process the Community involves. In this chapter we shall briefly cover this ground again to present an idea of the existing state of knowledge regarding the politics of the Community.

<h2 style="text-align:center">THE FORMAL POWERS OF THE COMMISSION</h2>

The Commission's part in helping to achieve the objectives of the Community is defined in various parts of the Treaty of Rome and has also developed as a result of decisions taken by the Council of Ministers. In the first place, the Commission's institutional character is defined by certain general obligations put upon it by the Treaty. The members of the Commission must carry out their functions 'in complete independence' and 'in the general interest of the Community', and can neither request nor accept instructions from a government or other body. The member States for their part undertake not to seek to influence the members of the Commission in carrying out their functions.[2] Arising out of this and other provisions it is generally accepted as constitutional doctrine within the Community that the Commission has two essential characteristics, one of which is summed up in the term 'independent', and the other in the term 'European'.

The Commission must be independent in that it must treat the views of each of the member States with equal respect—it must be impartial politically and indifferent as to nationality. However, it must also be European, meaning that it must discern the common interest clearly and accurately and promote it energetically. In this sense it must be partisan and protagonistic. Thus the Commission

---

[1] On this point see the controversy between J. Siotis, Some Problems of International Secretariats, *Journal of Common Market Studies*, Vol. II, No. 3, March 1964, pp. 222–51, and D. Sidjanski, A Reply to Siotis's Article, *ibid.*, Vol. III, No. 47, 47–61, 1965.
[2] Treaty establishing the EEC, Article 157.2.

is seen in constitutional terms to be more than a civil service or secretariat, and more than a kind of quasi-judicial, regulatory agency, and as having executive-type functions such as taking initiatives, laying down rules, and generally interpreting and furthering the common interest. We shall go into the full implications of this in later chapters but are concerned immediately with how this character is expressed in the formal responsibilities of the Commission as defined in the Treaty and in Community legislation.

So far the most important formal power of the Commission has proved to be *initiating Community legislation.*

With only one or two exceptions the Council of Ministers can decide on provisions which are at all general in scope or of major importance only if it has before it a proposal to that effect from the Commission. This is the case, for example, with decisions on all measures for formulating the common agricultural policy and putting it into effect, on the details of the common transport policy, and on the means of implementing the main provisions of the Treaty for regulating competition between enterprises. On such questions as these the Commission has an important right of initiative which has been fortified by the fact (already mentioned), that the Council can amend such proposals of the Commission only if it is unanimous.[1] Otherwise it must reject a proposal altogether or accept it.

This means that the Commission is closely involved in the deliberations of the Council of Ministers and that to the responsibility for taking the initiative, is added that of honest broker, or of bringing about agreement between the member States. The Commission can, indeed, submit any number of revised proposals up to the time when the Council reaches its final decision. The Commission has this important duty, partly so that it might provide an element of consistency in Community legislation (in other words to prevent the Council adopting contradictory proposals as a result of shifting political compromise), and partly to provide an assurance to individual states that a majority of the Council could not impose a measure which did grave harm to the interests of any minority (in other words a measure to which the Commission itself was opposed). (What more striking illustration could one have of the Commission's respectively European and independent character.)

[1] See pp. 44–5, above.

79

Another important duty of the Commission, though of a rather different character from the one just considered, is in *implementing Community legislation*. According to the Treaty the Commission must ensure that the provisions of the Treaty and the rules made by Community institutions in accordance with it are observed correctly. In fulfilling this task the Commission is given two particular powers, first, to act as 'guardian of the Treaty' and, second, to make delegated legislation. In all such cases the Commission is empowered to act alone and on its own initiative if necessary. As 'guardian of the Treaty' the Commission may decide that an infringement has taken place on its own initiative or on the complaint of a government, a private person, or a corporation. Having so decided, it can call upon the State concerned to explain itself within a stated time and, if the government does not remedy matters to the Commission's satisfaction (which it does normally in 40 per cent of the cases in any one year), the latter issues an *avis motivé* setting a time-limit within which the State must comply. In about 10 per cent of such cases so far the Commission has had to take the next step, which is to refer the case to the Court of Justice, whose final decision is binding and irrevocable. Most of the cases dealt with up to now have arisen from mistakes rather than wilful breaches of the Treaty and have not, anyway, concerned matters of great substance.[1]

The Commission is empowered by the Treaty to act independently in more than thirty cases, mainly either by making Regulations (124 in one typical year) or Decisions addressed to particular member States (about 250 a year). It is empowered, for example, to make Regulations concerning action to be taken in the case of 'dumping', and Decisions adjusting or prohibiting State aid to a particular sector of the economy. The Regulation adopted by the Community on competition gives the Commission power to authorize agreements between firms which are economically justified. Under the same provision the Commission may hold investigations into the activities of individual firms and impose fines and penalties in certain cases (subject to appeal to the Court of Justice), for failure to comply with its decisions. The most numerous cases where the Commission can make delegated legislation arise under the common agricultural policy. For example, since July 1962 it has had to make about one

[1] S. Holt, *The Common Market, the Conflict of Theory and Practice*, London, Hamish Hamilton, 1967, p. 54–7.

hundred decisions a month fixing the bases on which the levies are worked out under the rules governing agriculture during the transition to a common market. Now that the customs union is finally established and the Community is advancing towards its objectives of common economic and social policies, the exercise of these implementing tasks is expected to become more and more important and to take up a greater and greater proportion of the Commission's time. This is a point of great significance and we shall return to it later.

The Commission has a fourth set of responsibilities requiring it to act as a purely *technical and advisory body*. In some parts of the Treaty (for example, those concerned with common social and economic policies), powers to act are vested in the member States themselves, which are meant to co-ordinate their activities with the assistance of the Commission. In some of these cases, the Treaty confined itself to recommending that joint studies and research be undertaken into particular common problems.[1]

A fifth duty of the Commission is *to act as a diplomatic representative of the Community* in economic relations with third countries. When a State applies for admission to membership, the Commission's duty as defined by the Treaty is simply to give an opinion to the Council, which then decides on the request. The Commission attended the negotiations on British entry between 1961 and 1963, and was called upon for technical assistance. It also carried out exploratory talks before the negotiations for the association of Greece and of Turkey and then actually conducted the negotiations on the basis of general instructions from the Council and with the co-operation of the Permanent Representatives. Similarly, the Commission negotiates on behalf of the member States and under instructions from the Council in tariff and trade negotiations within the framework of the GATT, e.g. the Kennedy Round. In 1959 it was decided that diplomatic missions to the Community from third countries (of which there are now 74 stationed in Brussels) should present their credentials jointly to the Presidents of the Commission and of the Council.[2]

[1] See, for example, Treaty establishing the EEC, Articles 105.2, 108.1, 118, 122, etc.
[2] J. Lambert, M. Palmer *et al.*, *European Unity*, London, George Allen & Unwin for PEP, 1968, pp. 192.

Finally, it can be said that the Commission is given a vague but very important responsibility to act, as it were, as the *conscience of the Community*. This is based partly on some of the general provisions of the Treaty, partly on what has been written and said by leading representatives of the Community, and partly on the implications of certain powers already bestowed on the Commission, including some of those we have already mentioned. In this respect the Commission can be said to have a general responsibility for 'filling out' the provisions of the Treaty, for constantly reminding the other parts of the Community of its fundamental objectives, and for suggesting new paths for the Community to follow. It is not just a passive conscience ensuring that the written and unwritten law of the Community is not breached but also very much an active one bringing the existence of the Community and its objectives to the attention of the world at large and encouraging its development beyond the terms of the Treaty. Needless to say it is in its performance of this role that the Commission has been most controversial, and some actors of the Community believe it should be restricted severely in this respect. However, a full picture of the work of the Commission cannot be obtained unless this rather undefined and undefinable power is taken into account as many of the most important developments in the Community have flowed from it. The Commission described its own responsibilities under this heading of 'conscience of the Community' in 1958, giving this view of the Community institutions:

'Far from being merely the machinery for executing a series of technical measures, they form a dynamic element which will bring about the progressive approximation of national policies and, later, the application of a common policy.' In this process the Commission itself assumed 'a special responsibility' including the 'thinking out and formulating of the main lines of the action to be taken' and was a 'protagonist of the common interest'.[1]

In performing this task the Commission has available, first of all, the right given to it by the Treaty to formulate recommendations or

---

[1] *First General Report on the Activities of the Community*, September 1958, ECC Commission, Brussels, Sec. 8, p. 13. Has the English translator read his Fowler? *A Dictionary of Modern English Usage*, 2nd. edn., Oxford, 1965, pp. 488–9.

opinions on matters coming within the scope of the Treaty, whether the Treaty provides specifically for this or not. Second, the Treaty empowers the Commission to take part in the making of decisions by the Council and also in the activities of the Parliament. Third, it must publish each year a general report on the activities of the Community and has included in its administrative services an active Information Service. Perhaps the best examples of the way the Commission has carried out this function are the various initiatives it has taken in formulating and publishing proposals on future Community action at strategic moments during the Community's development. For example, in 1959 it published proposals to accelerate the implementation of measures for achieving the customs union, in 1962 a programme for the second stage of the Transitional Period, and in 1964, an *Initiative* 1964.[1] Members of the Commission have also commented widely, before the European Parliament and elsewhere, on the need for further development of the Community and its institutions.

From a mere list of these constitutional powers it is now clear that the Commission has a variety of formal duties. It is also clear immediately that they call for different kinds of attitude on the part of the Commission and that they require different degrees of legitimacy for their effective performance. In acting as the conscience of the Community and initiating Community legislation, the Commission seems to be represented in its 'European' guise, as a protagonist of the common interest. As honest broker, on the other hand, it is seen as being strictly 'independent'. Similarly, it demands far less political authority to act as a diplomatic representative of the Community, or as a technical and advisory service, than to act as conscience of the Community. Moreover, implementing Community legislation is quite a different function from initiating it. Although the implementing power gives the Commission some direct executive authority in particular fields of Community activity, this is only within limits prescribed and defined by the Treaties or according to rules laid down by the Council of Ministers: 'Only in a limited sense does the Commission have the margin of decision in changing circumstances

[1] Memorandum of the Commission on the Action Programme of the Community for the Second Stage, 1962, EEC Commission, Brussels; *Initiative 1964*, Community Topics No. 15, 1964, Press and Information Service of the European Communities, Brussels.

that is normally the prerogative of the executive branch of government.'[1]

Yet the fact remains that some of the formal powers bestowed upon the Commission imply a role similar to that of the typical executive branch of government. It is interesting, however, that many other powers normally regarded as vital to the government of a national state are absent. The Commission (like the Community as a whole), has no powers in fields such as foreign affairs or defence, and has no right to the use of force internally or externally. It has no power to *approve* Community legislation (as this rests with the Council of Ministers). As far as the European Economic Community is concerned, the Commission has as yet no power to raise revenue from an independent source of finance. The Commission cannot appeal for support to any majority in a directly elected Parliament nor to any majority of a general electorate; nor can it hold referenda for the same purpose. Its members are appointed by the governments of the member States and their term of office is renewable every four years.

The Commission's responsibility to be European would itself seem to demand some degree of legitimate authority which was independent of the member States. The word 'supranational' is used in the Treaty of the Coal and Steel Community to describe the character of the High Authority,[2] but the expression does not reappear in the Treaty of Rome. All the same, in the case of the EEC, the Commission still shares many of the 'supranational' characteristics of the High Authority—namely the independence of its members as prescribed by the Treaty, and its obligation to pursue the 'common interest'; the fact that it is endowed with formal powers of its own and not simply entrusted with functions by the member States;[3] and, finally, the direct incidence of its powers over the people living in the member countries.[4] On the other hand, its lack of power to make decisions on its own on all the most important questions, and its lack of an independent source of revenue (in theory temporary, but in

[1] R. Mayne, *The Institutions of the European Community*, London, PEP Chatham House, 1968, p. 28.
[2] Treaty Establishing the European Coal and Steel Community, Article 9.
[3] P. Reuter, *La Communauté Européenne du Charbon et de l'Acier*, Paris, Librairie Générale de Droit et de Jurisprudence, 1953, pp. 138–40.
[4] See pp. 25–6 above.

practice persistent), limit the sense in which the term 'supranational' can be applied to the Commission.[1]

Without getting too involved in these problems at the purely legalistic level, we can conclude with some certainty, as a result of this review of the formal powers of the Commission, that the latter is designed only as a partly executive or 'supranational' body.

It is indeed extremely difficult to come to any satisfactory conclusions in the language of constitutional law regarding this extraordinary and complex institutional framework of decision-making. Reactions vary from claims that it is a refreshing departure from antique methods of Parliamentary government, unsuited as these are to the technical twentieth century,[2] to dismissal of the whole system as a Europe of offices.[3] The supreme legislative decision-making body of the Community is, without doubt, the Council of Ministers, but even the Council refuses to fit ordinary constitutional classifications. Strictly speaking, it is neither a legislative nor an executive body, for it consists simply of ministers representing their respective governments and has no means of implementing Community legislation.[4] The main principle of the system seems to be that the agreement of the governments must be obtained before any major action is taken. Meanwhile, this is subject to the important qualification that the governments should reject the conclusions reached by the Commission as to the desirability of such action only for the strongest possible reasons. This is what is implied by the Commission's right to initiate legislation and by the obligation of the Council to amend the Commission's proposals only by a unanimous vote.[5] Thus Community legislation results from a kind of dialogue between the Commission, on the one hand, and the member governments as represented in the Council on the other.

The member governments or their representatives are as we shall see also closely involved in the implementation of Community legislation as well as in achieving most of the more general goals of the Community not so clearly articulated in the Treaty of Rome. The Commission may act alone only when it implements certain

---

[1] R. Lemaignen, *L'Europe au Berceau*, Paris, Plon, 1964, pp. 105–6.
[2] *ibid.*, p. 100–2.
[3] See below pp. 95 ff.
[4] Mayne, *op. cit.*, pp. 29–35.
[5] Lemaignen, *op. cit.*, p. 103.

technical and rather detailed aspects of the Community laws and, in all the more important of such cases, there exists some provision for the intervention of national representatives. Even where no such special provision has been made, the Permanent Representatives and their staff act as national 'watchdogs', and the Commission often finds it necessary to consult them on its own initiative when it exercises its delegated powers.[1] Thus, the decision-making process of the Community consists essentially of an interaction between the Commission and the representatives of the governments of the member States.

THE PROCESS OF 'ENGRENAGE'

The successful way in which the Commission has utilized this inter-action to bring about progress towards Community objectives has been celebrated by most authors on Community institutions. In practice a key element is the process called '*engrenage*', a more or less untranslatable word, meaning in this context 'meshing' or 'inter-locking'. This process consists in the crudest terms in the Commission engaging national ministers and, particularly, civil servants in the decision-making process of the Community. As one commentator puts it:

'In searching for the main key to the fulfilment of the mission confided to it, the EEC Commission unhesitatingly singled out above all else the development of relations and collaboration with the national administrations.[2] Another writer describes the involvement of national representatives as the 'keystone of the Commission's tactics'.[3]

The most significant way in which representatives of the governments have been involved up to now is in the performance of two major functions entrusted to the Commission, namely, the drawing up of proposals for submission to the Council of Ministers, and the

---

[1] For example, in interpreting its powers under Regulation 86 concerning competition between enterprises and in deciding whether violations of the Treaty of Rome have occurred: see L. Lindberg, *The Political Dynamics of European Economic Integration*, London, Oxford University Press, 1963, p. 58.

[2] A. Spinelli, *The Eurocrats: Conflict and Crisis in the European Community*, Baltimore, USA, Johns Hopkins Press, 1966, p. 71.

[3] Lindberg, *op. cit.*, p. 53.

86

engineering of agreement between member States in the Council. But as we have already pointed out, government representatives are involved in the exercise of practically all the Commission's tasks. Already by 1962 one of the writers already quoted declared that 'the involvement of government officials in the integration process has been carried to an extent that few could have foreseen', and that 'a vast bureaucratic system is developing involving thousands of national and Community officials in a continuous decision-making process'.[1] The same author estimated that in any one year just under 18,000 officials might participate in all the committees and working groups meeting before and after the Commission submits its proposals to the Council of Ministers. The Committee of Permanent Representatives itself was serving 'more and more as a clearing house for an expanding coterie of specialised committees, reserving for itself only matters of general, or essentially political, importance'.[2] There are now at least 20 or so permanent specialised groups working under this Committee, and numerous *ad hoc* groups are set up from time to time on particular issues. The Committee itself cannot, of course, formally decide any matter other than its own procedure, and cannot take the place of the Council of Ministers in the legislative process. In practice, however, the quantity of decisions to be taken is so great and the proceedings of the Council are so congested that the role of the Committee has had to be greatly expanded. In order to ease congestion at meetings of the Council itself it has been found necessary to adopt a procedure by which a number of technical and detailed matters can be agreed by the Committee of Permanent Representatives, placed on the Council's agenda as 'Points A', and taken as read by the Ministers, unless some member State or the Commission requests a discussion. In 1964, out of 36 sessions of the Council, 138 questions were so treated out of a total of 192. The Committee now meets more or less on a regular basis, except during periods when Community business is slight. The Commission has come to approve of this expanded role of the Permanent Representatives and has even encouraged it. Regular weekly meetings are held between the President of the Commission and the Chairman of the Committee 'to exchange information and impressions on important current or future business, to discuss difficulties and possible

[1] Lindberg, *op. cit.*, p. 62.
[2] *ibid.*, p. 60.

solutions, and where appropriate to co-ordinate the efforts which the Chairman of the Committee and the Commission will make in their respective fields to bring about any necessary decisions'.[1]

In many ways, however, the growth in importance of the Committee might be regarded as a challenge to the Commission's right of initiative and as a threat to undermine the 'European' element in Community decision-making. The same fear arises with regard to the Commission's consultation of national experts in the preparatory stage of its proposals. The Secretary-General of the Commission has written in this latter respect:

'These experts do not formally commit their governments but, as they are informed of the interests and opinions of the latter, they perform a useful function in guiding the Commission in its search for solutions that are technically accurate and generally acceptable to the six governments.'[2] How far should the Commission go, however, at such an early stage in the decision-making process in seeking solutions of this kind? At least one author suspects that the consultations must sometimes 'degenerate' into negotiations, because the experts are generally the same people who will later give their advice to their own governments when the latter come to decide on the Commission's proposals.[3] How far, at a later stage in the process, should the Commission amend its proposals to the Council as a result of what takes place at meetings of the Permanent Representatives and their staff? These are representatives of national governments, not of the Community, and they are civil servants, not ministers.

On the other hand, the strategy of *engrenage* reflects accurately the 'functionalist' approach which produced the Treaty itself and it satisfies two basic needs of the Commission. In the first place, the Commission feels obliged to draw up proposals which have the greatest possible chance of being accepted in the Council of Ministers. Any failure of the Commission in this regard might seriously retard the development of the Community. At the same time, as we have already seen, it is obliged to act as an honest broker among the

[1] E. Noël, The Committee of Permanent Representatives, *Journal of Common Market Studies*, Vol. V, No. 3, 1967, pp. 219–51.

[2] *ibid.*

[3] P-H. J. M. Houben, *Les Conseils de ministres des communautés européennes*, Leyden, Sithoff, 1964, p. 99.

interests of the member States. In this respect, the Commission behaves very much like any international secretariat, inventing proposals which are designed to bring about compromise between different national interests. The involvement of national officials at an early stage is partly a way of cutting corners towards such compromise, and co-operation with the Permanent Representatives is seen simply as a means of facilitating progress in the Council of Ministers.

At the same time, the *engrenage* is seen by the Commission as a means of fulfilling another major obligation, that of acting as a champion of the common interest, which it seeks to do in this case by infecting national officials with the European idea. The Permanent Representatives, for example, have a dual role: they act as national envoys to the Community, but also in a certain sense as Community representatives and spokesmen in their own capitals. Most of them have served for quite long periods in Brussels; (anything from five to eight years in some cases). Moreover, the regularity and frequency of formal and informal contact betweeen the staff or the Commission and the Permanent Representatives, as well as with other national officials, is now so great that all commentators attest to the way the latter have come to identify with the Community in spite of their basically national loyalty. In addition, contact between the different national administrations of the Six has been intensified as a result of the Community so that already by 1963 it was no longer 'necessary for contacts . . . to be channelled through the Ministries of Foreign Affairs and the other appropriate Ministries: "We just pick up the phone."[1] In this respect the Commission acts in a kind of proselytizing role, taking responsibility for more than just engineering compromise, and seeking to get the agreement of the governments to measures involving further integration. In this it behaves less like a normal international secretariat and far more like a promotional group, or even a political party with a firmly rooted ideology. The immediate object is presumably to ensure that proposals which have a strongly European element can be accepted by the Council of Ministers.

The *engrenage* is not, however, confined to national civil servants and ministers. The Commission has also taken positive steps to involve official representatives of socio-economic groups in the decision-making process. In one sense the Commission might be

[1] Lindberg, *op. cit.*, p. 84.

89

seen as acting rather like a federal government seeking to assert the
public interest against sectional interests (in this case, the member
States), by means of mobilizing the support of the general public
(in this case, social and economic interests in the member countries).
A federal government could set about this by appealing to the people
by whom it was elected in the States themselves, or by rallying its
supporters in the federal Parliament, and thus vaunting its legitimacy.
The Commission cannot do this, as it does not derive this kind of
support from the people in the member countries. On the other
hand, it usually consults Community federations of the main
national interest groups even before it consults national civil servants
and it has, as we have already seen, sought to pursue an active policy
of informing the public and of maintaining direct relations with the
press and other mass media.

It also has the European Parliament. The Commission can rely
on the Parliament's support at almost all times and, as we have seen,
the Parliament has to be asked for its opinion on proposals which
the Commission submits to the Council on almost all occasions
where such submission is provided for in the Treaty. However, the
support of the Parliament is not a very effective sanction since the
latter is not directly representative of the people in the member
States and is, moreover, widely regarded as having a built-in pro-
European composition. The Parliament is usually critical of the
Commission only when it feels that the latter has put forward proposals which are insufficiently European. Thus, the main use made
of the Parliament by the Commission is as a sounding board for its
policies and proposals before the member States or their representatives on the Council have committed themselves. This tactic of
canvassing support for its proposals before decision by the Council
is regarded as an important guarantee that the European view will
not get submerged in negotiations with national officials.

Yet the questions we asked a few paragraphs ago still remain.
How far does the process of *engrenage* compromise the Commission's
role is a source of European initiative? In the answer to this question
lies the key to the adequacy of the decision-making process of the
present Communities. Commentators have tended to differ in the
answer they give. For a long time the most popular answer was that
the present decision-making process was a response to real needs
and was vital to the success of the experiment of European integra-

tion. We shall examine next, therefore, a representative, and at the same time very influential, statement of this view. More recently, however, it has become customary to argue that the process has slowed down, not to say stopped, the process of unification and a similarly important example of this kind of argument will be examined in the section after next.

THE 'LINDBERG THESIS'

One of the earliest works by a political scientist to celebrate the decision-making process in the Community was *The Political Dynamics of European Economic Integration* written by an American scholar, Leon Lindberg. Lindberg was greatly influenced in his turn by Ernst Haas, whose development of the concept of 'spillover' was considered earlier in the present book.[1] Needless to say, therefore, he had reason to incline towards the 'functionalist' approach to unification and set out with the assumption that the Treaty of Rome met the main conditions for sustaining a continuing process of integration between the six countries. At the same time, Lindberg was clearly greatly influenced by the behaviouralist school of American political science,[2] so that much of his analysis is designed to suggest that the Community has had a critical influence on the attitudes and behaviour of various key decision-makers in the six countries. Finally, the study was carried out over the first four or five years of the Community's life and Lindberg himself was clearly influenced by the optimistic, pioneering spirit prevalent in the Community during those early years. This work of Lindberg's has been extremely influential, particularly with American and British political scientists interested in European unification, and his analysis and assessment of the decision-making process in the Community have for a long time been widely treated as orthodox. It is certainly not alone among studies by British and American

[1] See pp. 31–2, above.

[2] 'If political integration, as we have defined it, is going on then we would expect to find a change in the behaviour of the participants.' Lindberg, *op. cit.*, p. 9. Without wishing to enter into an elaborate discussion of political analysis, we would like to suggest here that contrary to the assumptions of much recent research, institutions should be studied in their own right. The group behaviour of human beings is not necessarily a guide to the role of institutions. The role of institutions sometimes affects the behaviour of men. It is, therefore, inadequate to present data indicating changes in the aims and attitudes of groups, unless it can be shown simultaneously that these relate to changes in the roles of institutions.

academic writers to place the Commission at the centre of the
Community process and to apotheosize it and its tactics.

In *The Political Dynamics* Lindberg sets out to test whether the
political conditions which exist in the Community are those necessary
to permit a process of integration between the economies (and
eventually, the politics) of the member States. He suggests that the
arrangements provided by the Treaty of Rome give every opportunity for developing such conditions. First, there is provision for
central decision-making machinery with its own independent source
of initiative. Second, the tasks assigned to these Community institutions are sufficiently important and specific in nature to activate
direct contact between themselves and socio-economic groups in the
member States. Third, the tasks are 'inherently expansive'. Finally,
another necessary condition for integration to get under way—a
feeling on the part of the member States that further integration was
in their own interests—had been present in the Community up to
the end of 1962 (when Lindberg wrote). Furthermore, Lindberg
regarded the progress of the Community up to this time as an almost
unqualified success in that most of the aims specifically laid down in
the Treaty already been achieved (some of them ahead of time),
while others were already in sight of achievement. Moreover, the
role of the Community institutions, and in particular the Commission had been expanded.

There can be little doubt that as far as Lindberg was concerned,
the contribution made to this success by the role of Community
institutions could be taken for granted:

'The great integrative potential of the Rome Treaty lies in its
generality, in the powers granted to the central institutions of the
ECC to fill out the Treaty and in so doing to "legislate" for the Community as a whole'.[1]

Lindberg wished to draw attention, not so much to the actual
content of Community policies or the output of decisions by the
Community institutions, as to the method by which decisions had
been taken. The important thing, he stressed, was the extent to which
support for and opposition to the Commission's proposals could be
channelled through Community, rather than national, procedures.
At the same time, the aim of the institutions, and in particular of the
Commission itself, had been "upgrading the common interest", a

[1] Lindberg, *op. cit.*, pp. 278–9.

concept borrowed from Haas and intended to contrast with the search for a 'minimum common denominator' and with 'splitting the difference', objectives commonly associated with 'ordinary' international secretariats. In 'upgrading the common interest', the parties re-define their conflict so as to work out a solution at a higher level. In an international community this level could be reached by an expansion of the role of some central international agency. But an essential element is a final decision which binds the parties to a significant step towards further union.

Four aspects of the role of the Commission in the Community decision-making process were singled out by Lindberg as being of particular importance. First, the Commission is required to reduce the intensity of conflict by 'isolating issues and identifying common interests' in order to bring about unity among the member States. Secondly, the Commission has to interpret its own role in such a way as to ensure that its own competence can be increased. Thirdly, the Commission must compensate for its existing lack of competence by promoting consensus among the member States. Fourthly and finally, it must include national policy-makers in the decision-making process at a Community level. After making a series of case studies of major decisions taken by the Community in its first four years, Lindberg concluded that on the whole the Commission had done each of these things adequately and that this explained the success of the Community so far. Crucial, in his view, had been the Commission's central tactic of 'co-opting' national administrations and interest groups by the process of *engrenage*. This tactic satisfied the first criterion mentioned in that it helped to avoid major conflict, the second in that it gained support for the Commission, and the third and fourth in that it engaged national civil servants and interest groups in the decision-making process. Lindberg was particularly impressed by the 'restructuring of political action' which was brought about as a result of this *engrenage* between Community and national policy-makers. He was conscious of the threat to the Commission in the development of the Committee of Permanent Representatives as a Community institution and admitted the cumbersome nature of the decision-making process with its plethora of committees and working groups. But he still maintained that the influence of the Commission had not diminished and that the main decisions which had been taken had all sought to 'upgrade the common interest'.

93

'There is nothing to prove that the system has had negative effects for long-range political integration. . . . The system developed in response to definite needs . . . it is eminently rational from a political point of view and . . . it represents a positive adjustment to the environment on the part of all Community institutions, and particularly the Commission.'[1]

It is easy to find fault with this analysis, in view of the fact that it was made in 1962 before a number of catastrophes hit the Community—in particular, the first French veto and the French boycott of Community institutions. In fact, Lindberg was quite aware that a number of eventualities could undermine the process of integration which he believed to be firmly under way: in particular, any feeling on the part of one or more member States that further integration was no longer compatible with its own interests. At any rate we are not concerned at this point with whether or not Lindberg's analysis is accurate as a description of the Community today. Rather we are interested in his *methodology* and in the way he identified certain criteria of successful integration. How valid is his suggestion that the *engrenage* was the key to the success of the Community up to the time of his writing? In his research Lindberg was almost exclusively concerned with the relationship between the Commission and other actors, mainly the Permanent Representatives and other national civil servants. This is partly because he wants to find evidence of 'restructuring of political action' as a direct result of the Community's existence (Haas's criterion of political integration), and partly from his concentration on changes in individual attitudes and behaviour (consistent with his behaviouralist approach). He pays far less attention to the consequences of the Commission's tactics on its nature as an *institution*, or for that matter, to the general *institutional* conditions which might favour or impede further integration. He does deal briefly with the internal organization of the Commission and warns that this body can be effective only if its members and officials are able to keep the European or common interest to the fore. He stresses that the need to maintain a geograph-

[1] *ibid.*, p. 65. Writing again in 1965 Lindberg noticed that, following the de Gaulle veto, much of the early 'romanticism' about the Community had evaporated and that the decision-making process had become more cumbersome. However he clearly felt that in its essentials it was still intact: L. Lindberg, Decision-Making and Integration in the European Community, *International Organisation*, Winter 1965, Vol. XIX, No. 1, pp. 56–80.

ical distribution between officials of different nationality might lessen this ability and mentions the growing administrative tasks of the Commission as a possible future source of anxiety.[1] But, while he tells us that one of the Commission's key tasks is to 'upgrade the common interest', he tells us little about the conditions which are necessary for this *within the Commission itself*. We are left wondering what kind of organization the Commission should be to meet his criteria, yet, as we shall see, this omission on his part could be crucial.

Furthermore, Lindberg saw little threat in the process of *engrenage* to the Commission's capacity to act as a 'protagonist of the common interest'. He was, in fact, the first to make use of the concept of 'co-optation' in the context of the Community Method, borrowing it from a sociologist working in the field of administrative theory, Philip Selznick. In Selznick's hands 'co-optation' referred to the tendency of organisations to adapt to a potentially hostile environment by recruiting, and thus neutralising, potential antagonists. This is certainly analogous with what the Commission seems to have done in involving the national experts and Permanent Representatives so closely in the decision-making process of the Community. However, Lindberg does not follow through Selznick's own use of this concept, which suggested that such a process is invariably damaging to the vitality and independence of the organization concerned.[2]

These criticisms of the 'Lindberg Thesis' are designed to help our own later critique of the Community, but there are other and more basic criticisms, such as his over-estimation both of the Commission's success in appealing for support beyond the national governments and of the 'inherently expansive' nature of the tasks assigned to the Community institutions in the Treaty of Rome. We shall also have cause to comment later on Lindberg's tendency, typical of many other writers in explaining the process of unification, to exaggerate the part played by the Commission at the expense of the member States.

[1] Lindberg, *Political Dynamics, op. cit., pp.* 278–9.
[2] P. Selznick, *TVA and the Grassroots: A Study in the Sociology of Formal Organization,* Berkeley, California, 1953.

THE 'SPINELLI THESIS'

It is sometimes all too easy to forget that there were a number of campaigners for a united Europe who did not regard the Treaty of Rome and what followed from it as a major victory for their cause. Certainly the vast majority of commentators have started from the assumption that there was something inherently and inevitably right in the Community system established in 1958 and that the main attention of all good Europeans should henceforth be concentrated on participating in and supporting this venture. One dissident in this respect is Signor Altiero Spinelli, who between 1943 and 1962 led the Italian section of the European Federalist Movement which he had helped to launch. Spinelli, who is regarded by many of those tied up in the present Community as a sort of 'wild man' of European federalism, is, in complete contrast to Lindberg, essentially a practising politician and man of action. His concern has always been to prescribe positive action rather than simply to record events and at first sight his written work does not seem to be of great value or interest to the political scientist. It is certainly not possible to find much detailed empirical analysis in his main work, *The Eurocrats*, published in an American edition in 1966. Nor does this book contain much sophisticated theoretical work. However, the appearance is deceptive, and Spinelli's writing contains a number of insights of great importance, which may be accessible to the student grounded in the turgid and presumptuous style of American political science only after several readings (or after meeting face-to-face with the man himself).[1]

In brief, Spinelli's argument is that the movement for European unity will fail unless it can harness a mass political movement mobilized in support of European federation. The Community system is just one of many different possible systems which could have been evolved by Europeans after the war. But the system which has been established is deficient in that it has turned out to be a 'Europe of offices' and represents the building of Europe as an essentially 'bureaucratic undertaking'. Spinelli does not deny that, given the limitations on its powers in the Treaty of Rome, the

---

[1] See, for example, the author's own review of *The Eurocrats*, which picks out the lack of academic sophistication in the book but misses most of its insights! *Government and Opposition*, London, Summer 1968, Vol. 3, No. 3, pp. 389–91.

Commission has done well to evolve a method of decision-making which not only preserves an independent European element, but also helps 'Europeanize' a large number of national officials and representatives of interest groups. He congratulates the Commission in this respect for its tenacity and its loyalty to the European idea.

'Moving into the complicated region of measures only vaguely delineated in the Treaty, the Commission has made itself the most important and enduring centre of effective integrated European activity presently existing. It does not have the strength to make it possible for the Community to surmount the possible decisive and determined resistance of governments, but it has shown that it can surmount many hesitancies of governments and can translate into specific united European actions the general and naturally passive Europeanism of the governments and public opinion of the six countries.'[1]

Where Spinelli differs from Lindberg and from most other academic analysts of the Community Method is in arguing that this policy of co-opting civil servants and interest groups has proved far from sufficient. He condemns the Commission for failing to mobilize sources of support which are truly independent of the national governments. First, the Commission is criticized for failing to face the French Government head on over the issue of its own role in the Community system, (Spinelli wrote before the proposals of spring 1965 on financing the common agricultural policy). According to Spinelli, the Commission should have emphasised 'systematically' in every proposal it made in accordance with the Treaty what powers should be taken from national authorities and assigned to the Commission itself, and by what explicit procedure this should be achieved. Secondly, it is accused of not taking full advantage of the European Parliament in that it has given prominence in drawing up its proposals to direct consultations with national civil servants and interest group representatives, in spite of the fact that the Treaty stipulated in most cases only that the Parliament and Economic and Social Committee should be asked for their opinions. The process by which the Commission amends its proposals while they are before the Council of Ministers is a relatively secret one and the Parliament, once it has given its opinion on the Commission's original proposal, is henceforth excluded from the final negotiations. The Commission

[1] Spinelli, *op. cit.*, p. 70.

D

97

is also accused of having been 'systematically deaf' to Parliamentary amendments of its projects. Thirdly, the Commission is criticized for not developing 'any methodical policy' towards the political parties in the member countries parallel to its encouragement of Community-level interest groups and for not recognising the potential as sources of support and 'instruments of democratic action' of the various voluntary European movements and committees of action.

The Commission's failure in these respects is far more important to Spinelli than its success in maintaining the process of *engrenage*, for the latter gives it no real sanction against the national governments. He stresses that this process is a motor of further integration only in so far as the member States continue to co-operate with it and continue to show good-will towards the Community. Here is a very pungent rejoinder to Lindberg's argument that one can rely to a very great extent on the conversion of national civil servants and of the representatives of interest groups to provide the process of integration with its own motive power. Do not these elements in fact work essentially within a framework already laid down by the national governments? Is not their influence limited to technical aspects of national policy-making and to the application rather than the resolution of decisions? To overcome the inertia, or even the opposition, of governments, is not much more than this needed, and should not one's attention be directed to political parties and other movements, and to creating directly responsible institutions at a Community level?

It may well be that many of Spinelli's criticisms of the Commission are based on an exaggerated assessment of the possibilities open to it in dealing with the national governments.[1] No doubt however the main purpose of these criticisms is really to show the weaknesses of the Treaty of Rome and of the 'gradualist', 'functionalist' approach to integration. In order to test Spinelli's propositions about weaknesses of the decision-making process, it would be necessary to carry out extensive research on the *methods* by which the attitudes of governments are changed, as well as on the extent to which they

[1] For example, the Commission tried dramatically to extend its powers in its famous proposal of spring 1965 concerning the financing of the common agricultural policy, but with equally dramatic results: the French Government boycotted the Community for nearly twelve months. See pp. 275–83, below.

have changed under prevailing political circumstances.[1] As we shall see in a later chapter, more recent commentators who are pessimistic tend to support Spinelli's view. We have not carried out this kind of research in the course of the present study and have no definitive conclusions to offer, although a suggestion that the present Community has reached a major crisis in its development through its failure to find a strong political base will form part of our conclusions. For the purposes of our immediate study of the role of the Commission, however, there are two particular ideas we can draw from the 'Spinelli Thesis.'

The first of these is a clearer impression than Lindberg ever gives of the need for the Commission to provide in itself 'the ideas, the drive, the creative imagination' which provide the impetus of further integration.

'If the Commission for any reason . . . is inhibited and does not act, either because it has not found the happy formula, or because it lacks energy, or because it is blocked by a Council veto, all co-operation on the part of the national bureaucracies ceases.'[2] This challenge is all the greater because of the very fragility of the system of decision-making which the Commission has helped to bring into being. If the *engrenage* is to function, and particularly if it is to result in further integration, then the Commission must provide 'an ever-increasing output of spirited energy, indoctrination, and propaganda to convince innumerable centres, which by their nature depend on national leadership, to remain under its sole European direction'.[3] This leads us straight into the question of whether the Commission is the right sort of organization to perform this role.

Indeed, the second idea we intend to take from Spinelli makes a positive answer to this question extremely unlikely. For he refers again and again to the Commission's conscious desire to create a 'bureaucratic Community' and diagnoses this as an inherent tendency on the part of the Commission. Its members and officials, he fears, are obsessed primarily with the problem of setting up a new administration and of getting it accepted:

'they are inclined to regard as a positive rather than a negative factor the absence of real political activity'.[4]

---

[1] In *Political Dynamics* Lindberg carries out the second of these procedures, but not the first.
[2] Spinelli, *op. cit.*, p. 97.   [3] *ibid.*, p. 98.   [4] *ibid.*, p. 72.

Spinelli sees the Commission's sponsorship of federations of interest groups at a Community level as endemic of its conception of the EEC as: '. . . a Community founded on a consensus of economic interests, with Community offices and their regulations, rather than on a popular consensus and hence with political institutions'.[1]

The same bureaucratic attitude is said to explain the Commission's alleged neglect of the European Parliament:

'The attitude of defending [the Commission's] own independence suspiciously before Parliaments, regarded as creators of disorder, is a normal reflex on the part of all public administrators, and it is natural that it should be manifested also in the European administration.'[2]

The link between the study of European unification and that of comparative politics could not be illustrated more aptly. Even if we assume favourable attitudes on the part of the member governments it is clear that no long-range forecast of the future prospects of the Community can sensibly exclude some assessment of the role of the Commission as an institution. It is clear, however, that such an assessment will have to be conducted from a functional point of view, seeing the apparent pointlessness of considering the Commission purely in terms of its formal, constitutional powers. The Commission's main function in the Community decision-making process is to provide political impetus and leadership towards European goals. Yet the Commission's formal powers are not those normally associated with political leadership. Indeed, the Commission seems to have interpreted its function of political leadership in an unusual way, namely by 'co-opting' national civil servants into the decision-making process. What we need to determine, therefore, is what are the Commission's functions in the political system of the Community and on what conditions does the effective performance of these functions depend. Is the Commission a political leadership, or is it a 'bureaucracy', or is it in some ingenious way both?

[1] Spinelli, *op. cit.*, p. 121.
[2] *ibid.*, p. 167.

THE ROLE OF THE COMMISSION

CHAPTER 5

THE CONCEPT OF BUREAUCRACY

When compared with other bodies on a purely legal, constitutional basis the Commission of the EEC does not seem to fit into any familiar classification of institutional types. Its formal powers fall some way short of those normally associated with the executive branch of a federal government: it has had up to now no power to raise revenue of its own; it is not based on any electoral or Parliamentary majority; above all—it lacks authority to make decisions on its own in all but the most detailed matters. Yet it is entrusted with functions which go far beyond those normally associated with an international secretariat or civil service. Its formal powers to make the proposals upon which Community legislation is based and to act as 'conscience of the Community' give considerable practical relevance to these functions.[1] Thus, the language ordinarily used to describe international or federal organizations does not seem to be of much value in the case of the Community.

At the same time, definitions of the political role of the Commission which concentrate on social and economic developments or the behaviour of individual participants also seem to be inadequate.[2] Thus we have been forced to search for some suitable definition of the role of the Commission *as an institution* in the process of political unification. We have already seen the Commission criticized in this sense for behaving like a 'bureaucracy',[3] and in the first part of this

---

[1] See pp. 78–86 above.
[2] See pp. 30–39 and 91–95 above.
[3] See pp. 95–100 above.

book we examined theories of unification which stressed the role of political leaders or *élites* in achieving effective political unions.[1] We have also seen that the Commission is intended to be the main source of political leadership in the Community and as such is expected to represent the Community as a whole. Therefore, though revealing many of the features of a 'bureaucracy' or 'civil service', the Commission can be just as easily seen as representing a federal political leadership in embryo. In fact, we shall assume that the key question about the role of the Commission is whether or not it is a 'bureaucracy'. We shall also assume that in so far as it is a 'bureaucracy', then the Commission will be unable to ensure the political leadership which is required to bring about an effective political union of Europe. This is no mean task, for the term 'bureaucracy' used in this sense begs a number of questions, and it will take the whole of this chapter to unravel them. In this sense, the present chapter might be regarded by those purely interested in European unity as a digression into certain aspects of sociology and political theory.

We shall distinguish here three possible uses of the term 'bureaucracy'. First, there is what might be called the *constitutional* use of the term to refer quite simply to a distinct part of the State, namely, the machinery of public administration, including, for example, departments staffed by civil servants, public corporations and government agencies. Secondly, the term is used in *sociology* in the theory of organizations, particularly in order to analyse the exercise of power and authority and the effects of functional specialization. In this sense it usually refers to a general type of organization rather than to a particular set of institutions. Thirdly, it can be employed in *political science* in analysing different types of political system. In this usage, it has been employed to describe a whole political system which reveals certain general characteristics, but it might also be used to refer to particular functions performed by the government of a political system. These uses of the term 'bureaucracy' are closely related to each other, but great confusion can result from failure to distinguish them carefully.

[1] See pp 35–9 above.

'THE ADMINISTRATIVE STATE'

When used in a *constitutional* sense to refer to the central administrative apparatus of the state, or 'the Administrative State',[1] the term 'bureaucracy' is used in a largely neutral, descriptive manner. The bureaucracy in this sense is a definite list of organizations and institutions. This can, however, be a very misleading use of the term if it is employed too readily to contrast the administrative parts of government with the more overtly political parts. Indeed, there is a vast literature showing the tendency in practically all known types of political system for the 'Administrative State' to 'encroach' upon the 'territory' of other parts of the system, such as political executive, legislature, etc., and to acquire the latter's functions, such as political leadership, representation, etc. The Civil Service of modern, western industrialized democracies is seldom completely confined to the implementation of legislation under the instruction or active surveillance of political executives or ministers, but finds itself invariably involved in national policy-making and in exercising wide discretion in the management of public affairs.[2] Some writers have even gone so far as to describe the Civil Service as acting as a kind of pressure group with a collective but distinct goal of its own which it seeks to promote in competition with other groups.[3]

This leads straight to another problem in the *constitutional* use of the term which is that not all sections of 'the Administrative State' are the same, even in legal, constitutional terms. Thus it is very often necessary to distinguish the 'administrative class' consisting of officials at a relatively high level in the hierarchy from the public servants performing more routine and specialized tasks at lower levels.[4] When reference is made to the bureaucracy performing a political role it is clearly the former type of official which is meant. Yet both types, (and no doubt others, too), people the 'Administrative State'.

[1] The expression comes from F. Morstein Marx, *The Administrative State*, University of Chicago Press, 1957, see particularly pp. 154–87.

[2] *ibid.*; see also C. J. Friedrich, *Constitutional Government and Democracy*, New York, Ginn, 1950, pp. 386–410.

[3] F. Morstein Marx, The Higher Civil Service as Action Group, in J. La Palombara, *Bureaucracy and Political Development*, Princeton University Press, 2nd edition, 1967, pp. 62–95.

[4] J. La Palombara, An Overview of Bureaucracy and Political Development, in J. La Palombara, *op. cit.*, pp. 6–8.

For these reasons the definition of bureaucracy as the 'Administrative State' threatens to confuse more than to clarify and we shall not adopt it for the purpose of this book. Indeed, as we have already begun to see, the Commission of the EEC cannot really be classified according to legal, constitutional criteria and from a review of its formal powers it is not clear whether it is a bureaucracy in the constitutional sense or not. This use of the term is, of course, quite legitimate, in so far as it simply denotes a list of organizations, but its weakness is that it is not very useful. It does not describe the functions of the organizations to which it refers, (the 'Administrative State' might not administer), and it glosses over important distinctions between their various parts. The reason it seems desirable to distinguish the bureaucracy as a particular set of institutions from other parts of the state is no doubt that in western, democratic experience the 'Administrative State' is supposed to bear a special relationship to other parts of the constitution. Thus in most constitutional theory the Civil Service departments and other organs of administration are regarded as forming 'the arm of public policy', this policy being established by political leaders and representative assemblies.[1] The impartiality, permanence, and discipline of the career civil servant are designed to underpin the strictly instrumental character of the administration. In practice, however, such a rigid constitutional separation of powers rarely serves to describe the behaviour of real political institutions.

BUREAUCRACY AS A PROBLEM OF ORGANIZATION

The study of organizations and of their crucial importance in modern life has become one of the main concerns of academic sociologists and has also led to the development of whole new disciplines of applied knowledge, such as the 'science of management'. Organizations appear in varied aspects of society and include such diverse collectivities as political parties, government departments, churches, hospitals, universities, voluntary associations, and so on. The term 'bureaucracy' has been widely used in the study of organizations, but in different ways. Generally, however, it is given a teleological sense. An organization is based essentially on purposeful activity

[1] F. Morstein Marx, The Higher Civil Service as Action Group, *op. cit.*, pp. 62–6.

and 'bureaucracy' in the *sociological* sense usually refers to certain characteristics which affect the ability of organizations to achieve their purposes. This use of the term, therefore, differs completely from the constitutional use just considered.

The value of sociological treatment of the concept of bureaucracy is greatly limited from the point of view of comparative politics for a number of reasons. First of all, it has been concerned almost entirely with studying single organizations, particularly business firms, and the validity of comparing these with single political institutions is far from clear. Moreover, because of its concern with single organizations, the sociological approach to bureaucracy produces a kind of 'micro-theory', which is very interesting at the level of individual and group behaviour and is often very useful to managers of real organizations, but which does not often deal with the effects of different types of organization on society as a whole, or on whole political systems. Secondly, there are two quite different approaches to the phenomenon studied. From one point of view, bureaucracy is regarded as a highly effective type of organization and from another (including the popular, vulgar sense of the term) it represents all that is commonly deplored in day-to-day experience of organizations:

'It evokes the slowness, the ponderousness, the routine, the complication of procedures, and the maladapted responses of 'bureaucratic' organizations to the needs which they should satisfy, and the frustrations which their members, clients or subjects consequently endure.'[1] Yet a third difficulty is that modern students of organizations seem to try to avoid using the term 'bureaucracy' altogether and to concentrate on finding means of overcoming the limitations of human rationality in order to create effective organizations. This 'decision-making' approach is of even less value for the student of political systems, in that it normally tends to take the existence of organizational purposes for granted. Politics is concerned above all with the setting of such purposes.

We have only a passing concern here with the sociological study of organizations, but some aspects of the 'micro-theory' of bureaucracy are of considerable interest for our main study, particularly when these are transposed to a 'macro' level of the political system

[1] M. Crozier, *The Bureaucratic Phenomenon*, London, Tavistock Publications, 1964, p. 3.

as a whole. In fact, sociologists do seem to be referring to the same thing in their various approaches to bureaucracy, even though these do require considerable unravelling. The main disagreement has concerned its consequences for organizational effectiveness, and whether or not all organizations must necessarily be of this type. This disagreement will in itself be quite revealing for our main study.

The most generally accepted characterization of bureaucracy is the 'ideal-type' devised by Max Weber. Unlike most of the authors whom we shall consider in this section, Weber was concerned with the general significance of organizations for society as a whole and his 'ideal-type' bureaucracy was an abstraction from the characteristics which seemed to make large, complex organizations so effective, and thus so pervasive, in modern societies. Thus Weber's 'classical' treatment of bureaucracy has become the basis of most sociological investigation into the nature of real organizations. According to Weber bureaucracy is ideally represented by an administrative system in which everything is sacrificed to the rational pursuit of specified goals. There is, for example, a clear division of labour and this enables a high degree of specialization. At the same time officials are recruited purely on the basis of their technical qualifications and not as a result of personal influence. A rigid hierarchical or 'pyramidical' structure is established and authority is clearly circumscribed at each level. Indeed, in order to expedite co-ordination and to ensure continuity in decision-making there is a uniform system of rules to govern all individual official decisions and actions. Officials are expected to avoid making personal considerations in their treatment of colleagues and clients and all transactions take place on a formal, emotionally detached basis. Employment in the organization constitutes a career, promotion is based on merit or on seniority, and the sole form of remuneration is in the form of a salary and a pension after retirement.[1]

It is interesting to note that these characteristics are practically identical with those ideally associated in western, democratic experience with civil services and other administrative agencies at the level of the state. Impersonality, anonymity and hierarchical

[1] Max Weber, *The Theory of Social and Economic Organisation*, translated by A. M. Henderson and Talcott Parsons, London, Oxford University Press, 1947.

106

discipline are normally regarded as essential prerequisites of sub-servience to political leaders on the part of the administration. The coincidence is significant for it illustrates a common element in both approaches which is to regard the bureaucracy as being strictly instrumental. In the study of organizations this 'classical' bureaucracy represents a rationalization of the collective, purposeful activity for which organizations are designed:

'It is superior to any other form in precision, in stability, in the stringency of its discipline, and in its reliability. It thus makes possible a particularly high degree of calculability of results for the heads of organizations and for those acting in relation to it. It is finally superior both in intensive efficiency and in the scope of its operations, and is formally capable of applications to all kinds of administrative tasks. . . . For bureaucratic administration is, other things being equal, always, from a formal, technical point of view, the most rational type. For the needs of mass administration today, it is completely indispensable. The choice is only that between bureaucracy and dilettantism in the field of administration.'[1]

Students of organization who have succeeded Weber have been concerned mainly with disproving his thesis that bureaucracy is the most effective type of organization. The main proposition of these later students is that the 'classical' bureaucratic administration is productive of certain unforeseen or 'unintended' consequences. These consequences are described in sociological jargon as 'dysfunctions', and are said to 'feed back' into the organization and prevent it from achieving its stated goals or 'intended' results. These dysfunctions are practically all said to result from the very rational, mechanistic character of bureaucracies, overlooking as it does the essentially irrational nature of most actual human behaviour. Two examples of such dysfunctions are worth illustrating here, the first related to the impersonality and regularity of bureaucracy, and the other to the degree of specialisation entailed by it:

(1) Bureaucracy depends on the maintenance of a rigid, hierarchical structure of authority and of uniform, impersonal procedures for regulating individual behaviour. Thus great emphasis is placed on

[1] Max Weber, *The Theory of Social and Economic Organisation*, p. 337.

the formal rules and regulations of organization and these come to be observed in their own right, as ends in themselves. These, and the formal definition of roles and status, serve as protective devices to individuals within the organization, who come to value conformity as a means of controlling their environment:

'Adherence to the rules, originally conceived as a means, becomes transferred into an end-in-itself; there occurs the familiar process of displacement of goals, whereby 'an instrumental value becomes a terminal value'. Discipline, readily interpreted as conformance with regulations, whatever the situation, is seen not as a measure designed for specific purposes but becomes an immediate value in the life-organization of the bureaucrat. This emphasis, resulting from the displacement of the original goals, develops into rigidities and an inability to adjust readily.'[1]

In one sense this process helps to maintain the organization, but in another sense it creates problems for it, for example, by worsening difficulties which result from arbitrary treatment of clients. Such difficulties only serve, however, to reinforce the original need for control and officials revert defensively to the formal rules even more than they did before.[2]

(2) For the sake of co-ordination at the top of the organizational pyramid there is usually a clear delegation of authority to lower levels in a bureaucracy and this delegation is based on specialization of function. This results in departmentalization and tends to lead individuals to identify with departmental or 'sub-goals' at the expense of the goal of the organization as a whole. This in turn leads the departmental units to seek to increase their own power and thus to intensify even further the root-cause of the original problem, the delegation of authority.[3]

In contrast with its treatment by Weber, bureaucracy in the hands of these authors becomes a clinical problem: a threat to the efficiency of an organization and a challenge to its management. In this sense, of course, it can no longer be regarded as rational, even in the limited,

[1] R. K. Merton, *Social Theory and Social Structure*, Glencoe, Illinois, Free Press, 1957, p. 199.
[2] *ibid.*; see also J. G. March and H. Simon, *Organisations*, New York, Wiley, 1958, pp. 37–40.
[3] P. Selznick, *TVA and the Grassroots*, Berkeley, California, University of California Press, 1949; March and Simon, *op. cit.*, pp. 40–4.

formal sense of 'rationality' employed by Weber.[1] Because of the 'dysfunctions' it produces, bureaucracy cannot be regarded as conducive to effective organization. Thus many theories of organization have abandoned the concept, except as representing something to be avoided, and have concentrated on finding a new 'rationalization' based either on study of human behaviour within organizations (the study of informal organization)[2] or on study of the nature of communications (the study of decision-making).[3]

This has not, however, succeeded in somehow 'spiriting away' bureaucracy as a problem of organization. Indeed, recent study of informal aspects of administrative organizations, in particular of the effects of human attitudes and behaviour of different kinds of power structure, has suggested that bureaucracy may well be an inevitable consequence of organized activity towards specified goals. The very instrumental, delegative nature of an administrative organization seems to demand such characteristics as rigid hierarchy, specialization of functions, conformity and so on—at least, that is, in certain cultural environments. When imposed on collective human activity these characteristics produce bureaucratic 'dysfunctions'. What is worse, these 'dysfunctions' seem to engender a 'vicious circle' in that an administrative organization is unable to learn from its mistakes and accordingly fails to adjust.[4]

Nevertheless, the clinical study of organizations has thrown some light on how these consequences might be avoided. To this end, three problems in particular have been highlighted. First, it has been found that a distinction needs to be drawn between 'pro-

[1] In the 'ideal-type' Weber uses 'ratonality' in the sense of the most effective adaptation of means to given ends. There is, of course, a much wider sense of 'rationality' on a higher level according to which the ends of an organization themselves would be judged. See B. Gross, *The Managing of Organisations*, Vol. II, London, Collier–MacMillan, 1964, pp. 752–4. Weber was himself aware of the limitations of the narrower, 'formal' rationality and of the existence of a broader, 'substantive' rationality, according to which his ideal-type of bureaucracy could be seen as a horrifying sign of increasing 'materialism', see, R. Bendix, *Max Weber, An Intellectual Portrait*, New York, Doubleday, 1960, p. 464.

[2] See, for example, P. M. Blau, *The Dynamics of Bureaucracy*, University of Chicago Press, 1955; A V. Gouldner, *Patterns of Industrial Bureaucracy*, Glencoe, Ill., Free Press, 1954; C. Argyris, *Executive Leadership*, New York, Harper, 1953, etc.

[3] See, for example, March and Simon, *op. cit.*; H. A. Simon, *Administrative Behavior*, 2nd edn, New York, MacMillan, 1957, etc.

[4] M. Crozier, *op. cit.*, pp. 175–236.

grammed' and 'unprogrammed', or 'routine' and 'critical' decision-making. This distinction is based partly on a more fundamental distinction between statements of fact and statements of value, and partly on a distinction between 'static' and 'dynamic' adaptation to change in the growth and development of organizations. Programmed or routine decisions certainly involve problem-solving and search and involve adapting to change, but they are essentially repetitive and 'reproductive'. They do not involve search for new criteria of organizational conduct. They are concerned above all with questions of efficiency, and assume that goals are settled and the main resources and methods for achieving them available. Unprogrammed or critical decisions, on the other hand, involve the exercise of creative intelligence and invention; they require adaptation to new situations, and affect the 'key values in the organization'.[1]

Secondly, a number of writers have drawn attention to the way in which the effect of different systems of administration varies according to the functions of the organization concerned. For example, much attention has been paid to the needs of economic enterprises working in the field of technological development, where great demands for inventiveness and flexibility are made upon them. Implicit in this stress on comparative analysis of organizations has been an assumption that different methods of organization can be related to variables such as the degree of continuity and of specificity of organizational goals. For example, the more mechanical, the more technical, the more specialized the work of an organization, and consequently the more precise its goals, the greater will be the need for a 'classical' bureaucratic type of administration.

Thirdly, there has been increased interest in the power structure of organizations, for example, in status systems as preventing adaptation to change and in individual motivations and commitments as 'displacing' the goals of the organization. In this respect much has been learned about the behaviour of individuals within organizations, their tendency to identify with informal groups, to hold preconceived notions of organizational goals, and so on.

Two examples of such treatments of the subject seem to be particularly interesting from the point of view of our main study. First, in the works of Selznick the problem of bureaucracy is stated

[1] March and Simon, *op. cit.*, pp. 136–50, 173–94; P. Selznick, *Leadership in Administration*, New York, Harper & Row, 1957, pp. 29–37.

fundamentally as a challenge to the leaders of an organization to support its goals or ultimate purposes:

'The effective leader continuously explores the specialized activities for which he is responsible to see whether the aims taken for granted are consistent with the evolving mission of the enterprise as a whole.'[1] The leaders are charged with ensuring that the social structure of the organization truly embodies its purposes, for example, by instituting appropriate policies for recruitment and training and critically reviewing whether rigid procedures for decision-making have been imposed 'prematurely'. They are also responsible for defending the organization's integrity by ensuring that the inter-action between informal groups within the enterprise, as well as its relationship with groups outside, are such as to sustain its own commitment and purpose. In all this the leaders' task is above all the creative one of setting goals and infusing the organization with the necessary sense of purpose to achieve them: a leader must be 'an expert in the promotion and protection of values'.[2]

Any failure by the leadership in this regard produces a displacement of goals with similar effects on the organization as the bureaucratic 'dysfunctions' familiar to students of organizations. Indeed, Selznick treats the whole attempt to achieve 'rationality', in the sense of adapting means to given and established ends, as constituting a 'cult of efficiency'. By fixing attention on 'maintaining a smooth running machine', this 'cult' 'slights the more basic and more difficult problem of defining and safeguarding the ends of the enterprise'. At the same time it stresses techniques of organization that are essentially neutral, and therefore available for any goals, rather than methods peculiarly adapted to a distinctive type of organization or stage of development.[3] In this sense, bureaucracy seems to represent a preoccupation with the routine of day-to-day administration and a consequent neglect of purposes.

A similar stress on the importance of organizational leaders is reached at the end of a British study by Burns and Stalker, but by a rather different route and with a somewhat different emphasis. This is a detailed, empirical study of a number of British firms in various technological industries. The aim is to test whether there is

---

[1] Selznick, *Leadership in Administration*, *op. cit.*, p. 81.
[2] *ibid.*, p. 28.
[3] *ibid.*, pp. 134–5.

any noticeable relationship between particular styles of management and success or failure in economic activity where a high rate of technical innovation is essential. The main conclusion is that:

'The effective organization of industrial resources, even when considered in its rational aspects alone, does not approximate to one ideal type of management system, but alters in important respects in conformity with changes in extrinsic factors. These extrinsic factors are all, in our view, identifiable as different rates of technical or market change.'[1]

This change can be brought about either by new scientific discoveries or by the assertion of new demands on the enterprise. Organizational effectiveness is also a function of the political and status systems within the enterprise and of the nature of its leadership. Taking all these variables into account Burns and Stalker identify two distinguishable 'poles' of management system, which they represent respectively as 'mechanistic' and 'organic'.[2] The mechanistic system is found to be poorly adapted to dynamic situations where the organization is called upon to react to frequent change by innovating.[3]

Burns' and Stalker's mechanistic system is very similar in its essentials to the 'classical' bureaucracy of Max Weber. It is characterized by specialized differentiation of tasks; precise definition of rights and obligations attached to each role; a hierarchical system of control, authority and communication. In the organic system, which is adapted to unstable, changing conditions, tasks cannot be so easily broken down into specialisms, and there is continual re-definition and adjustment of individual tasks. Commitment to the concern is spread more or less evenly throughout the organization, sanctions are less hierarchical in origin and tend to be self-imposed out of a feeling of shared values. Consultation rather than command is the main way of solving disagreements and exchanging information. In responding to change, mechanistic firms met with difficulties.

---

[1] Tom Burns and G. M. Stalker, *The Management of Innovation*, London, Tavistock Publications, 1961, p. 96.

[2] *ibid.*, p. 122. The two systems of management are not dichotomous: Burns' and Stalker's empirical researches show that firms can be plotted along a line from one pole to another, most of them possessing features belonging to both systems.

[3] Vice-versa, the organic system is said to be unsuited to stable situations where routine activity is called for.

Existing managers were made to feel insecure by the challenge to their status when new departments were created or the existing structure was reconstituted.[1] Under similar circumstances, however, the organic firms faced fewer problems of status, in so far as the location of leadership was settled mainly by consensus or on the basis of professional or technical capability.[2] This system was effective, however, only in conjunction with a 'common culture' within the firm which aided its adaption to changed conditions:

'In exploiting human resources in this new direction, such concerns have to rely on the development of a 'common culture', of a dependably constant system of shared beliefs about the common interest of the working community and about the standards and criteria used in it to judge achievement, individual contributions, expertise, and other matters by which a person or a combination of people are evaluated. A system of shared beliefs of this kind is expressed and visible in a code of conduct, a way of dealing with people.'[3] Burns and Stalker suggest that the maintenance of such a code of conduct is one of the main tasks of leadership in organizations, but stress that this might well involve some abdication on the part of the leaders themselves in order to develop the right kind of human relationships between different strata of the organization.[4]

It is clear that Selznick's administrative 'leaders' and Burns' and Stalker's 'organic firm' cannot in any meaningful sense be regarded as examples of bureaucracy. Rather they are means of adapting organizations to conditions in 'the real world'. Without inspired, or at least energetic, leadership, or without a common culture, the organization becomes a bureaucracy. The 'ritualism', personal withdrawal and conservatism found to be ingrown, organic features

---

[1] Tom Burns and G. M. Stalker, *The Management of Innovation* pp. 96 125. It is not possible in this short space to do justice to Burns' and Stalker's detailed representation of these two systems of management. Readers are strongly recommended to refer to the original.

[2] *ibid.*, pp. 856: 'It was claimed that nobody on the staff had a title except the managing director; at least, nobody had a definite function to which he could keep . . . It was also an explicit rule of the firm that any member of the top management group could be consulted or asked for a decision by any junior.'

[3] *ibid.*, p. 119.

[4] *ibid.*, see in particular pp. 121–7, 139–40, 209–51.

of administrative organization[1] are probably best seen as substitutes for personal leadership or a common culture (or for any other means or relating the organization to its purposes).

The point which has become increasingly evident in studies of organization is that rationality, in the sense that the 'classical bureaucracy is 'rational', cannot be a sufficient criterion for assessing organizational effectiveness. In the same way, efficiency, in the sense of minimizing scarce inputs for a given quantity of output, long regarded by management scientists as the overriding aim of organization,[2] cannot constitute an organization's 'goal' without producing absurd results. The purposes of an organization are multifarious, ranging from satisfying customers, contenting employees and rewarding shareholders, to producing goods and services, investing in its own growth, observing the various codes imposed by society without, and so on.[3] Some writers go so far as to define 'administration' as being concerned with all these various purposes.[4] We prefer here the more limited sense of the term by which it refers to the performance of delegated, defined tasks, the taking of routine, programmed decisions, and the maintenance of organizational codes and practices to provide continuity and consistency.[5] Administration, in this sense, is certainly an inadequate concern for the managers of an organization. The more dominant a concern it becomes, the more bureaucratic (including the sense of bureaucratic 'dysfunctions') we can expect the organization to become. In other words, the management of organizations can be seen as a kind of politics including as it does representative functions, such as satisfying the various groups of people concerned with the organization, (shareholders, customers, employees); the determination of ends and values; responsiveness to changing environmental circumstances; and so on. The personal and organizational qualities demanded by this role are different from those required for the role

[1] See Crozier, *op. cit.*, pp. 186–7 and elsewhere, *passim.*
[2] See, for example, L. Gulick and L. Urwick, *Papers on the Science of Administration*, New York, Institute of Public Administration, 1937; B. Gross, *op. cit.*, Vol. I, pp. 128–48.
[3] Gross, *op. cit.*, Vol. II, pp. 467–501.
[4] *ibid.*
[5] This narrow definition of 'administration' runs counter to the current trend in American studies of organization, but permits greater clarity when one is dealing with 'macro-theory' at the level of the whole political system, as we shall do in the main body of this work.

of administrator, as we have defined it. However, the administrative function depends on the managerial function, without which it becomes an ingrown, ritualistic, self-justifying, activity.

BUREAUCRACY AND THE POLITICAL SYSTEM

We are concerned in this section mainly with recommending a use for the term 'bureaucracy' in the study of political systems, rather than with analysing existing uses. As we have just seen, most of the sociologists who have written on the subject have treated bureaucracy as a problem affecting single organizations; or, if they have taken a broader perspective, they have been concerned with the general effects of bureaucracy on human behaviour or society. Most students of politics seem to have used 'bureaucracy' in the constitutional sense by which it refers to the organizations which make up the 'Administrative State'.[1] Little attention seems to have been paid to bureaucracy as the administrative function of the political system—by whatever specific set of people or institutions this function is performed. However, if we transpose the findings of sociological writers on bureaucracy to the dimension of the political system as a whole, they acquire important new meaning At the 'micro' level of business enterprise and government agency, bureaucracy is seen as a threat to the vitality and effectiveness of management. Can the same threat be said to exist to government itself at the 'macro' level, and, if so, in what form?

To many political writers 'bureaucracy' at the level of the whole political system refers to a spread throughout the system of bureaucratic characteristics, such as hierarchical lines of command, functional specialization, and so on. Thus bureaucracy may be found in political parties, legislative chambers, and so on, as well as in the executive branch of government itself. However, we would suggest that this is really the same as the sociological use of the concept to refer to certain characteristics which might be found in any kind of organization. We suggest that the real complement at the level of the *political system* to the administrative function studied by sociologists as the source of bureaucracy in organizations is public

[1] See, for example, J. La Palombara, *op. cit.*, p. 6–7; F. Mostein Marx, *The Administrative State*, *op. cit.*, pp. 54–72, etc.

administration—the implementative, delegative part of the central government. This may not always be identical with the civil service, for the latter may perform other functions and commonly does so, particularly in developing countries.[1] However, in practice, we may expect to find that in western, democratic experience, public administration is predominantly the task of permanent officials employed by the state. The constitutional norms of impersonality, impartiality, and discipline which are so often applied indiscriminately to civil services of modern, democratic states, were formulated primarily with this function of public administration in mind. The people and institutions who are responsible for performing this function constitute the state bureaucracy and they rely on other parts of the governmental apparatus to relate them to the purposes of government. Without the alliance of these other parts, public administration will probably be the victim of consequences analogous to the various bureaucratic 'dysfunctions' reported by sociologists.

Let us pause to consider some of the characteristics we can expect the State bureaucracy to possess in relation to the other parts of government. The administrative function depends on delegated authority and in this respect the bureaucracy develops a self-consciously defensive posture. The bureaucracy has no means of legitimizing itself, for example by direct appeals for electoral support, and its survival and self-expression come to depend on glorifying the legal orders and instructions from which its authority is derived. Left to itself, the bureaucracy displaces the goals of the State with these programmed, delegated objectives, which have become for it the sole repositories of institutional identity. Thus, derived standards and forms of behaviour can be maintained long after the circumstances which brought them into being have changed. The bureaucracy itself has no means and no wish to change them.[2] This leads to a second characteristic which might be called the conservatism of bureaucracy and its inability to adapt by its own resources to fluctuating, changing conditions. This is reinforced by the need for stress on hierarchy, resulting in emphasis on formal

[1] See the contributions by F. Morstein Marx, S. N. Eisenstadt, and Fred. W. Riggs to J. La Palombara, *op. cit.*, pp. 62–167.
[2] This is presumably what J. P. Nettl meant in *Political Mobilization*, London, Faber & Faber, 1967, pp. 339–43.

rules and regulations. Those working at lower levels have no interest in resisting the formalized, hierarchical system for their attachment to the organization is based purely on the earning of a fixed monetary reward and on the expectations of security of tenure. Indeed, they are more likely to criticize those higher up the organization for departing from the formal regulations, which are seen as a defence of the employee's 'stake' in the organization.[1] This all results from the fact that the bureaucracy cannot logically have a will of its own without usurping the function of other parts of the government. In order to do this, however, it would first need to acquire the essential characteristics of these other parts, a step which would change its own nature irrevocably. Some new bureaucracy would then have to be found in its place to perform the administrative function of the polity. Finally, we can expect the bureaucracy to seek to avoid identifying itself with objectives based on evaluation and to seek to present itself as neutral and impartial.[2] This disqualifies it, of course, from exercising governmental functions other than the purely administrative.

These related characteristics of natural defensiveness, conservatism, and 'affected neutrality' are analogous at the level of government to the 'dysfunctions' identified by sociologists at the level of single organizations. Thus, 'bureaucratization' of the whole political system can be seen as a result of dominance by the administrative function. Bureaucracy is compatible with effective government only in so far as the other parts of government can assert themselves in their respective roles. There must be political leadership, representation of interests, and so on. Alternatively, it is conceivable that there might be such a prevailing consensus of values, such a 'common culture', surrounding government that the delegative, hierarchical and formalistic qualities of bureaucracy are unnecessary. This would represent at a governmental level conditions analogous to those found in Burns' and Stalker's 'organic firm'. However, it is most

1 Crozier, *op. cit.*, pp. 203–7.
2 Selznick, *Leadership in Administration, op. cit.*, pp. 134–41; March and Simon, *op. cit.*, pp. 137–71. Though, in fact, it may not be 'neutral and impartial', seen as part of the political system. It may by its general inertia 'sabotage' the programme of a 'radical' party newly in office (see, for example, S. M. Lipset, *Agrarian Socialism*, University of California, 1950), or help to entrench a 'conservative' party already in office. The point is that the bureaucracy can have no views of its own—it must support the prevailing 'system'.

unlikely that in societies of any complexity or development such conditions of government could be found, at least for any period of time.

What political study there has been of the role of bureaucracy, in the sense of the people and institutions performing the function of public administration, has been confined largely to developing political systems in the new nations of Africa, Asia, and Latin America. The general conclusion of many such studies seems to bear out our own assumptions. Thus the State bureaucracy seems unable to substitute effectively for the roles of political representatives and leaders in the government of many such countries.[1] This is in spite of the fact that public administrators have been increasingly called upon to perform such roles in practice. In western, industrialized countries it has been known for some time that the administrative function cannot be clearly differentiated in practice, owing to the increasing complexity and technicality of modern government and perhaps in part also owing to the failure of conventional democratic processes to produce legislative representatives and executive leaders who are capable of managing the government machine. Some observers have gone so far as to consider this development inevitable, and one that may well be a necessary condition for economic growth. It is also seen by some as a vital means of compensating for 'ineffective' political processes, such as party competition, 'government by assembly', and so on.[2] These attitudes need to be carefully examined, in view of what has been postulated here. According to the assumptions we have made about the role of bureaucracy in the political system, any demise on the part of conventional forms of political representation and leadership should be regarded pessimistically from the point of view of the effectiveness of government.

The Commission of the EEC is endowed with formal powers which are similar in many ways to those normally associated with the administrative function in a national political system. It is, meanwhile, expected to grow into a kind of federal government of a united Europe and even during the long and indefinite transition

---

[1] Fred W. Riggs, *Thailand: the Modernization of a Bureaucratic Polity*, Honolulu, East-West Center Press, 1967, and A Paradoxical View, in J. La Palombara (ed.), *op, cit.*, pp. 120–67; J. P. Nettl, *Political Mobilisation, op. cit.*, pp. 337–80.
[2] See pp. 329–36 below.

towards this stage is expected to impel other parts of the Community by the exercise of various forms of political leadership. Is this a case of bureaucracy being asked to substitute for the roles of other parts of government? If so, what does the experience of the Communities tell us about this process? These are far-reaching questions to which the ensuing empirical study of the role of the Commission will hope to supply some possible answers.

A prime objective will be to test the assumptions we have made here about the nature of the administrative function in general in the context of the decision-making process of the Community. We would expect to find that, in so far as the Commission has acquired other functions than the administrative and performed them effectively, then it has not been a bureaucracy in the sense understood here. On what has it depended in order to perform the functions of political leadership—can the conditions of this be identified in terms of organizational characteristics and relations with other parts of the Community? If such conditions can be identified, how reliable are they and how long are they likely to prevail? In identifying such conditions we shall need to examine closely the nature of the people who make up the Commission's organization and the principles according to which they are recruited and employed. This is our immediate task. Following this we shall examine the role of the Commission in some chosen examples of the political process of the Community at work, in order to establish what are its relations with other parts of the Community and to see how the members of its organization behave in the decision making process. Finally, we shall try to gain a general view of the functions which the Commission has acquired and of the functions which it must acquire if it is to succeed. This will enable us to assess the real potential of the Commission as part of the Community and as part of the process of European unification.

CHAPTER 6

THE FRAMEWORK OF AN
ORGANIZATION

This and the next chapter deal mainly with the attempts of the Commission of the European Economic Community before the merger of the three Community Executives on July 1, 1967, to found a multi-national, independent civil service. This attempt was not abandoned with the merger and can be considered as being still in progress. However, in view of their special importance to our main theme the effects of the merger and the events which have followed it will be dealt with separately in a later part of the book. We have limited consideration of the attempt to found a European Civil Service to the experience of the EEC Commission partly for convenience, in that it will save us making a number of detailed and minor exceptions to our account, but also because the EEC is by far the most important and wide-ranging of the three Communities.

In general, however, the same basic problems in the field of recruiting and managing personnel have faced each of the three Community Executives. The High Authority obviously had a longer history of personnel administration than either of the other two Executives: a Statute of Service for its officials was adopted in 1956. There were some differences, particularly regarding the pay and conditions of service of officials, between this Statute and that later adopted for the EEC and Euratom. Even though the two newer Communities shared the same Statute there were differences of interpretation and application, mainly because of the highly specialised nature of the work of Euratom and the large number of professional scientists and engineers employed there in comparison with the EEC. However, these differences need not detain us here. In the new combined Commission there are more former officials of the EEC Commission than of either of the other two Executives.[1] The new provisional Statute of Service which has been adopted

[1] At the time of the merger the staff of the EEC Commission numbered 2,970.

120

in the merged Commission differs in no major respect from the Statute previously applying in the EEC and Euratom.[1] So, in general, what is said here about the methods and principles of personnel administration in the former EEC Commission will continue to hold—for the time being at least—for the new combined Executive.[2]

The merger was itself seen as an important step towards a common goal pursued by each of the three Executives—namely, the establishment of a unified, independent, multi-national career civil service in Brussels. Quite apart from utilitarian arguments that the Community Executive should be served by a reliable and competent staff, the creation of a European Civil Service was valued in its own right as an important step towards political unification. Its emergence could be regarded as an essential prerequisite of the evolution of federal political institutions. Thus, to those who saw the Commission of the EEC as the embryonic federal executive of a united Europe, the staff of the Commission obviously counted for much more than a mere international secretariat and was seen as an embryonic federal civil service. So the symbolic importance to committed Europeans of the Commission's personnel administration was much greater than the utilitarian or operational significance of this seemingly mundane aspect of the Commission's work.

By the same token, however, to those who shared General de Gaulle's conception of the future development of the Communities, namely that the Commission's power *vis-à-vis* the national governments should not be increased, and that the Commission should act more as an ordinary international secretariat than as a kind of federal executive, the growth of a European Civil Service had a very different meaning. To those who regarded the Commission essentially as the servant of the member governments, the notion of a self-contained, zealous body of 'Eurocrats' was not inviting. Indeed, the French Government has argued for some years now that the Commission should recruit its staff from national civil servants on periods of secondment from their national posts. Therefore, in its

[1] *Journal Officiel des Communautés Européennes*, 11th year No. 156, March 4, 1968, pp. 1–7.

[2] Certain member governments have recently pressed for a complete revision of the existing Statute of Service, with a view to substituting secondment of national officials for a career civil service as the basic principle of recruitment of Community personnel.

attempt to establish an independent career service, the Commission of the EEC did not meet with unanimous support, and this was, to a large extent, a result of disagreement and uncertainty regarding its proper role in the Community. A major object of this part of the book will be to see how far the Commission succeeded in its attempt to create a European Civil Service. In the rest of this chapter we shall depict the background to the Commission's task. This task was carried out against both favourable and unfavourable background, corresponding respectively to the legal framework of personnel administration (sponsored mainly by the Commission itself) and the political framework in which this legal basis had to be applied. In the next chapter we shall go on to examine how the Commission's policies of recruitment and career management have wored out in practice.

CRITERIA OF A CIVIL SERVICE

The Treaty of Rome itself did not lay down any instructions or guide-lines regarding the Commission's internal organization or recruitment and employment of staff. Article 162 simply instructed the Commission to determine its internal rules of procedure so as to ensure the proper functioning of itself and its services under the conditions laid down by the Treaty. Article 212 stated that the Council of Ministers voting unanimously would decree a Statute of Service for Community officials 'in collaboration with the Commission and after consultation with the other institutions concerned'. (Following the fourth year after the entry into force of the Treaty, this statute could be amended by the Council by qualified majority vote on a proposal from the Commission and after consultation with the other institutions concerned.)

All that the Treaty laid down in detail was the procedure for appointing the members of the Commission themselves and their conditions of service. The key articles here were numbers 157 to 161 inclusive. The Commission was to be composed of nine members, chosen on grounds of their general competence and 'whose independence could be fully guaranteed', (this number could be varied by the Council voting unanimously). Commissioners had to be nationals of the member States of the Community and no more than two of them could share the same nationality. (In practice,

122

France, Germany and Italy were represented by two Commissioners each, the Netherlands, Belgium and Luxembourg by one each.) As we have already noticed, the members of the Commission were bound by certain obligations and duties, namely: to act in complete independence and in the 'general interest of the Community'; not to solicit or accept instructions from any government or other body; to abstain from any act 'incompatible with the nature of their functions'; not to exercise any other professional activity, whether paid or not, during their term of office; and, finally:

'to accept from the date of their installation a solemn undertaking to respect, both during their tenure of office and when it is over, the obligations which attach to their office, notably the duty to show integrity (*honnêteté*) and discretion (*délicatesse*) about accepting certain appointments or certain benefits after relinquishing their posts'.

If any member of the Commission should cease to fulfil the necessary conditions attaching to his office or should commit a 'serious offence', he could be dismissed by the Court of Justice at the request of the Council or of the Commission. In such a case the Council acting unanimously could provisionally suspend the individual concerned and provide for a replacement until the Court produced a verdict.

The members of the Commission were to be appointed by means of 'a common agreement of the governments of the member States'. Their term of office in the EEC Commission lasted for four years and was renewable. In the case of death, voluntary retirement, or dismissal, the Commissioner concerned was to be replaced for the remainder of his term of office, but the Council might decide by unanimous vote that there should not be a replacement. The salaries, pensions and other benefits of the members of the Commission were to be fixed by the Council by a majority vote.[1] The member governments also acted by common agreement to select a President (and in the case of the EEC Commission two Vice-Presidents) from the members of the Commission. The terms of office of the President and Vice-Presidents lasted for two years and were renewable. Except when the membership of the Commissions was being renewed generally the Commission was to be consulted on the selection of its President and Vice-Presidents.

[1] Treaty establishing the EEC, Article 154.

123

In essentials, the Commission was organized on much the same principles as a national government, with the nine Commissioners themselves playing the part of ministers and their staff that of civil servants. From the outset each member of the Commission was entrusted with a special Community activity—agriculture, competition, etc.—and correspondingly nine departments or Directorates General were established, each in turn divided into Directorates and sub-divided into Divisions. In order to facilitate co-operation between the different Commissioners, (the Commission being a collegiate body), the responsibility for each Directorate General, while laid primarily on the Commissioner entrusted with the activity concerned, was in principle also given to two other Commissioners, the three forming a group of which the Commissioner primarily responsible acted as chairman. In addition, an Official Spokesman was appointed with a small staff, and the Commission shared with the Executives of the other Communities responsibility for the three common Services: the Legal Service, Press and Information, and the Statistical Service. Apart from the officials serving in these different departments and services, there were also private offices attached to each Commissioner on the pattern of the French ministerial *cabinets*. The strength of each *cabinet* was officially restricted to two (although the President soon had a private office of four). Their appointment is the personal prerogative of the Commissioner himself.

However, to call the staff of the Commission 'the European Civil Service' implies not only a similarity between them and the civil servants of a national government, but also some commonly accepted view of the role and function of a national civil service. In actual fact there are different interpretations of what a civil service is or should be—even within the national context.

The following standards of personnel administration are normally laid down for the 'classical' type of civil service. There is free selection based on competitive examination of merit or technical ability. High posts are filled from within the service, recruitment being confined to the lowest grades. Promotion is by seniority and/or merit. Supervision and control are centralized, usually by delegating responsibility for personnel administration to a specialized agency within the service. These features are often embodied in a set of fixed rules given legal force. Membership of the service normally

124

constitutes a lifetime's career and, in the course of this career, the official should not be prejudiced by any 'subjective' elements, such as political or other personal views, or by race, sex, or place of origin, but should be judged purely by 'objective' tests of his technical ability, merit, seniority, and competence.[1] It must be stressed, however, that these standards are purely normative; in most west European countries it has proved difficult to meet them all in practice.

In the six countries of the Community central personnel agencies within the civil service generally took a long time to set up and have remained weak relative to individual departments or to the political heads of the service. In Germany, indeed, there is little or no delegation of personnel matters to independent organs within the administration: the majority of candidates for the public services are selected by individual ministries in the different *Länder*.[1] Nor is there in Italy any single body to prepare and administer entrance examinations.[3] In both France and Belgium the drawing up of the general statutes of service did not take place until after the second world war, and in Belgium it did not succeed either in centralizing and regularizing personnel administration or in 'depolitizing' the civil service.[4]

It is a convention in making appointments to the German federal civil service to maintain an equilibrium between officials coming from different *Länder*.[1] In most countries where there is a confessional element in politics a distribution between different religious denominations must be maintained and the Six are no exception to this. There are cases in France, Belgium, Germany and the Netherland of particular ministries becoming the 'fiefs' of particular reli-

[1] This 'classical' type of civil service is based on Weber's ideal-type of bureaucratic administration. See pp. 106–7 above. The Weberian 'ideal-type' is still being used by authors to typify the 'classical' civil services of France and Germany. See, for example, F. Heady, *Public Administration. A Comparative Perspective*, New Jersey, Prentice-Hall, 1966, pp. 40–5.

[2] B. Chapman, *The Profession of Government*, Allen & Unwin, 1959, pp. 77–9.

[3] J. C. Adams and P. Barile, *The Government of Republican Italy*, Houghton, 1961, p. 106.

[4] For Belgium, see the report of the *Commission mixte d'enquête sur la réforme des administrations de l'Etat (1952)*, *Moniteur Belge*, May 12, 1952, and for attempts at centralization in France and elsewhere, see R. Grégoire, *The French Service* Brussels, International Institute of Administrative Sciences, 1964, pp. 102–12.

[5] Chapman, *op. cit.*, pp. 84–5.

gious groups.[1] In Italy and France, as in most other European countries, a certain proportion of posts are reserved by law for particular types of candidate (for example, war veterans). In all the six countries a candidate's political leanings can influence his career, whether, as in France, by gaining him entry into a ministerial cabinet, or simply by the intervention of political heads of ministries in the selection process.[2]

Although in France promotion is highly institutionalized on the basis of merit and seniority, with arrangements for official participation by personnel representatives, in Germany it tends to rest almost entirely on the choice of the political and official heads of the relevant department. In the Netherlands there is limited promotion from within the service and the higher posts are often filled by direct recruitment from outside. In both Italy and Belgium prospects of advancement rest on performance in an examination rather than on the reports of superiors or on length of service.

Recently, more and more doubts have been thrown on the value of the 'classical' rules of selection and advancement in the civil service. It is now regarded as unusual in practice, and even undesirable in theory, for the selection and advancement of personnel to be completely impersonal or for control to be completely centralized. In particular, the classical type of selection does not take account of the vital political role of higher officials in government departments. Selection according to 'objective' criteria may not be possible in the case of such officials, who are engaged in making policy and in negotiating with private groups on behalf of the State. Problems also arise from the practice of specialization. Modern administrations often depend on highly skilled, and professionally oriented, technicians. Specialization of functions within the organization tends to make these technicians caste-conscious. Moreover, the formal rules of the organization do not succeed in obtaining conformity from such officials, whose personal loyalties are to their profession or to fellow experts rather than to the organization.[3]

As we have seen, by testing the effect of bureaucratic methods of

[1] Chapman, *op. cit.*, pp. 284–5.
[2] For the French experience see Gregoire *op. cit.*, pp. 353–8, and B. Gournay, *Introduction à la Science Administrative*, Paris, Colin, 1966, pp. 272–3.
[3] For a review of findings on this subject, see P. M. Blau and W. R. Scott, *Formal Organizations*, Routledge & Kegan Paul, 1963, pp. 80–4.

administration in certain existing organizations, sociologists have found that the rationality of these methods is undermined by informal and personal factors. Such tendencies clearly undermine the vitality of an organization and its ability to adapt to change.[1] In order to survive, organizations have to find alternatives to the formal precepts. Thus, in the French civil service, an *élite* of senior officials, forming the *Grands Corps*, has been deliberately separated from the rest of the service partly with a view to making available a group of 'personalities capable of imposing the necessary reforms on the administrative units that need them'.[2] A similar solution in the case of the EEC Commission has been the deliberate recruitment of devoted Europeans at the highest levels. By their zeal and their commitment to the goal of integration these officials are intended to maintain the Commission's vitality.

Thus we may expect to find that the 'classical' type of civil service, providing for objective standards of selection and advancement, centralization of control, and life-long careers, is not always compatible with the circumstances in which civil servants find themselves. Moreover, the characteristics of this type of organization may well be injurious to the dynamism and adaptability of an institution.

THE POLITICAL FRAMEWORK

In developing a policy for the selection and careers of its officials the EEC Commission had to observe a number of obligations of a more pressing and immediate nature than the 'classical' standards of a career civil service. These obligations may be grouped together somewhat loosely under the term 'political', using the term rather widely here to include not just matters of policy, or of party or international politics, but also personal factors and even the technical requirements of administration. One of these obligations was in fact written into the Statute of Service for Community officials. Another arose directly from the formal relationship between the Commission and the Council of Ministers. A third was determined by technical aspects of administration. The fourth was political in the narrower sense, arising from the interest of member governments in the administration of personnel.

[1] See pp. 107–10 above. M. Crozier, *The Bureaucratic Phenomenon*, Tavistock, 1964, pp. 97–8.

(1) *Distribution of Posts by Nationalities*

In practice, the distribution of posts among nationals of the member States had by common agreement, to be roughly proportionate to member States' budgetary contributions.[1] Article 27 of the Statute of Service of the Community required officials to be recruited 'on the widest possible geographical basis among the nationals of member States'.[2] The Commission was under strong political pressure to maintain this distribution and this was a fundamental limitation on its freedom to appoint to posts. Its credibility as an international institution depended on the maintenance of such a distribution—at least in the higher posts (category A) and at least for the time being. In this respect, however, its position was similar to that of most international administrations.[3]

The Commission was somewhat sensitive about this aspect of its personnel policy. It was rather reluctant to give exact figures for the distribution of posts among the different nationalities. In answer to a question from a member of the European Parliament in 1960 asking for such figures, the Euratom Commission and the High Authority of the ECSC gave fairly full replies, but the EEC Commission was prepared to say only that posts were distributed 'approximately' to the scale of 25 per cent each for French, Germans, and Italians, and nationals of the Benelux countries. It did, however, supply the following Table:[4]

DISTRIBUTION OF NATIONALITIES IN THE STAFF OF THE EEC COMMISSION ON NOVEMBER 10, 1960
(percentages)

	Germans	French	Italians	Belgians	Dutch	Luxembourg
Category A	24	25	23	13	11	4
Category B	23	23	23	13	12	4
Category C	24	20	18	26*	4	8

* The disproportionately high Belgian figure for Category C reflects the need to recruit a disproportionately high number of French-speaking Belgian secretaries, given the difficulty of attracting French secretaries to work in Brussels.

[1] These are fixed by the Treaty of Rome, Art. 200.1 at 28 per cent for France, Germany and Italy, 7·9 per cent for the Netherlands and Belgium, and 0·2 per cent for Luxembourg.

[2] In the selection of staff for promotion, however, consideration of nationality would be in conflict with the Statute.

[3] Cf. Art. III (3) of the United Nations Charter.

[4] European Parliament *Debates* (1960), Reply to Written Question No. 62.

In answer to a rather curt supplementary question asking for fuller figures, the Commission revealed that the distribution was maintained with more or less equal rigidity within the different grades of category A:[1]

NUMBER OF OFFICIALS IN CATEGORY A ON DECEMBER 31, 1960

	Germans	French	Italians	Belgians	Dutch	Luxembourg
Grade A1	2	3	3	1	2	0
Grade A2	12	9	6	8	6	2
Grades A3–8	103	103	100	51	45	17

This position was fairly closely maintained in 1963, according to figures released in answer to another Parliamentary question.[2]

NUMBER OF OFFICIALS IN THE EEC COMMISSION ON JUNE 30, 1963

	Germans	French	Italians	Belgians	Dutch	Luxembourg	Others
Grade A1	2	3	2	0	2	0	0
Grade A2	14	11	6	8	6	2	0
Grades A3–8	117	119	100	58	47	18	2
Category B	79	82	79	50	42	17	0
Category C	146	123	88	208	41	15	0
Category D	12	13	29	33	6	6	0

The following figures, relating to the distribution by nationality of officials in category A of the three executives (EEC and Euratom Commissions and ECSC High Authority) combined, were released by *Le Monde* on January 19, 1968.

	Germans	French	Italians	Belgians	Dutch	Luxembourg	Others
Grades A1–3	125	131	82	51	63	16	5
Grades A4–8	455	349	472	247	152	58	34

The need to maintain this rough overall distribution meant that in most cases, before a post might change nationality, a reciprocal

[1] European Parliament *Debates* (1961), Reply to Written Question No. 104.
[2] *ibid.* (1963), Reply to Written Question No. 32.

change elsewhere had to be arranged. Such a procedure induced a certain rigidity and conservatism in those responsible for appointments—for any departure from convention in one case could lead to enormous complications in maintaining the overall distribution. This held true for all higher levels of the service, although often not where clerical, secretarial, and manual staff were concerned. The distribution was maintained as far as possible throughout all branches of the service (though not within small subdivisions of the administration).

(2) *Distribution of Posts by Grades*

The Council of Ministers, as the budgetary authority, retained effective power to determine both the total number of posts to be filled by the Commission in any one year and also the distribution of those posts in categories and grades. The Commission's difficulties in obtaining budgetary approval for an adequate number of posts became a familiar feature of Community politics. The Annual Reports of the Commission repeatedly complained that the number of new posts approved by the Council for a particular year were insufficient for the increasing work of the Commission. The Commission had just as much difficulty in getting approval for new posts at the particular grades it would have liked.

This meant that, although some personnel performed tasks and functions which could have qualified them for higher posts, the higher posts had not been made available in the Community budget. This made it difficult for the Commission to pursue a progressive policy with regard to promotions. It also led to embarrassment in the grading of individual officials.[1] For example, while the Commission was able between 1959 and 1967 to more than double the number of established posts in category A (roughly equivalent to the British administrative class), this increase comprised almost entirely new posts at lower grades, and there was a major bottleneck for promotion at grade A4 (which is more or less equivalent to the British grade of Principal). For similar reasons, it proved extremely difficult to get promotion from category B (equivalent to the British executive class) into category A.

[1] See, for example, appeals, to the Court of Justice, *Receuil de Jurisprudence de la Cour de Justice:* Affaires 109/63, 13/64.

(3) *Specialization*

The possibilities of promotion and transfer from within were also limited by the very specialized functions which were associated with many of the higher posts in the administration. Thus, the Commission often found it necessary to go outside to fill such posts while recognizing that, according to classical standards of a career service, they should have been filled from within. The Commission justified the filling of such posts from outside on the ground that it had little scope for finding sufficiently experienced and qualified personnel inside, in view of the small numbers of its ranks compared with normal national administrations. The incumbents of such high posts were, moreover, often required to have intimate knowledge of national systems, which, it was thought, only actual experience of those systems could provide. The need to fill posts was often very urgent and the new incumbent had to be ready to begin work immediately, preparing policy drafts and negotiating with national representatives in highly specialized subjects.[1]

Some people were sceptical about these arguments and suggested that the Commission exaggerated this difficulty. They stressed that, in so far as the Commission insisted on appointing to high posts in the service from outside, this held up progress towards a truly 'Europeanized' administration. Outside recruits probably found it difficult to adjust to the European setting, yet this adjustment was just as important a requirement in high-ranking Community officials as specialized qualifications or experience of service in a national administration.

(4) *Reserved Posts*

Member governments and individual Commissioners took a close interest in the selection and preferment of officials. Certain posts in the service might in practice be reserved for particular types of candidate, on grounds such as nationality or party political affiliation. It is very difficult, if not impossible, to produce evidence of the

---

[1] Some posts seem to be restricted to a very small field of candidates. One advertisement (chosen at random) for a post (at grade A5 and A4) in the Social Affairs Directorate General called for the following qualifications: university degree or equivalent professional experience, thorough knowledge of national legislation concerning the redistribution of labour, *and a good knowledge of German systems of administration regarding professional retraining, reinstatement, and recoversion* (our italics).

number of posts so reserved or of how the practice varied at different levels of the administration. It was generally agreed, however, that such reserved posts did exist at all levels, particularly the highest ones in category A, although the reservations might not always have proved successful in face of competition from other candidates.

By a common understanding, Directors General (A1 officials at the head of Directorates General roughly equivalent to the British Permanent Secretary) were appointed according to the same distribution between nationalities as Commissioners themselves. This meant that the French, Germans and Italians claimed two each, and the Benelux countries a total of three. Each Director General had to be of a different nationality from the Commissioner responsible for his Directorate General. Up to the end of 1966 only one post of Director General—that for Administration—had changed nationality, and this was when a Belgian replaced a Dutchman in 1965.

Appointments which were made at the top levels sometimes had to reflect the political situation in member countries. As we have already said, some member governments insisted in their own administrations that appointments to high posts (and in some cases to all posts) were based on party political, interest-group, or religious affiliation—and they liked to take a similar interest in the appointment of their own countrymen to the ranks of the Commission.

Sometimes, however, the Commission chose to reserve posts for reasons other than the need to take account of the demands of member governments. Certain posts, by the very nature of the functions attached to them, might require a candidate of a particular nationality or political allegiance. This could mean anything from giving a senior official a secretary who spoke his own language to ensuring that the Director General of Social Affairs was a Belgian trade unionist. Whatever the reason, the existence of 'reserved' posts was not denied—and it often led to considerable delays and difficulties in filling posts, because of the need to find the 'right' candidate.

THE LEGAL FRAMEWORK

Although fundamental to the work of the Community institutions arrangements for recruiting, employing and paying officials, their conditions of service, and their rights and obligations were not embodied in an agreed legal framework until four years after the Treaty of Rome came into force. And even when this basis was finally agreed upon by the Council of Ministers in 1961, as the Statute of Service of the EEC and Euratom, the final document was the result of considerable amendment and compromise and was to present many difficulties of interpretation.

Until the Statute came into force, all officials of the Commission were appointed on the basis of individual contracts. Some foundations of a career service had already been laid in the ECSC, which adopted its own Statute of Service in 1956, but the laying of administrative foundations was not a priority of the leading actors in the new Community. In the first years of the Commission's life, administrative arrangements were essentially *ad hoc* and pragmatic.

Uncertainty regarding the status of the increasing number of officials assembled in Brussels and failure to decide the future of the new administration led to difficulties with regard to paying officials and securing their career prospects. A former Commissioner has described cases, in the early years, where the smallest financial regulation regarding the payment of salaries would necessitate 'months of correspondence between the six financial administrations'.[1] Some officials did not have fixed salaries at all and were paid on account. The cause of the uncertainty was largely reluctance on the part of national representatives to accept the level of salaries and benefits in force in the ECSC. That Community's Statute of Service was clearly to form the basis of an EEC and Euratom Statute (particularly in view of the foreseen amalgamation of the three Communities). Yet there was much criticism in member States of the level of salaries and other payments in the ECSC and many were reluctant to be as generous in the case of the newer Communities.

In March 1960 the Council of Ministers decided that a Statute for the EEC and Euratom should come into force by July 31, 1960.[2] By September of that year, however, the Council was able to approve a draft only for certain aspects of the proposed Statute and could not agree on provisions for auxiliary and other special staff who would not be included in the main body of the Statute. The outstanding provisions were finally adopted in draft by the end of

[1] R. Lemaignen, *L'Europe au Berceau*, Paris, Plon, 1964, p. 70.
[2] *EEC Bulletin*, 3rd Year, No. 3, 1960, Commission of the EEC, Brussels.

February 1961, but the Parliament and Court did not render their opinions, as was required by the Treaty, until October of that year. The Statute finally came into force on January 1, 1962.[1] It applied to all officials appointed to permanent posts under its provisions in any of the institutions of the EEC and Euratom, including, with some exceptions, the staff of the Economic and Social Committee. It had the status of Community law, and officials could appeal to the Court of Justice against abuse or non-enforcement of its provisions.

The Statute was executed by means of general dispositions decreed by each institution (Commission, Parliament, Court, or Council) for its own officials. The Joint Legal Service advised on the drafting of such dispositions and also defended the institution concerned before the Court of Justice in suits arising from the Statute. In interpreting the provisions of the Statute the members of the Legal Service were guided mainly by the aims and intentions of those who drafted it, but account was also taken of the law and practice in member countries and an attempt was made, not without difficulty, to synthesize this into a set of 'international laws' regarding the administration of personnel.

The Statute provided for a Personnel Committee (one for each institution) to represent the interests of the personnel and to ensure permanent contact between administrative and staff sides. The Committee was empowered to bring to the attention of the official authority of its institution any difficulty of general significance relating to the interpretation and application of the Statute, and could be consulted by the authority on any such difficulty. It had to be consulted before general dispositions were decreed.[2] There was also provision for a Statute Committee, composed in equal numbers of representatives of the institutions and representatives of the Personnel Committees, which could both suggest revisions of the Statute and also render opinions on the general dispositions by which it was implemented.[1]

There was no noticeable feeling among officials at the Com-

---

[1] *Statut des fonctionnaires et le régime applicable aux autres agents de la CEE et de la CEEA*, *Règlement* No. 31 (CEE), 11 (CEEA), *Journal Officiel des Communautés Européennes*, No. 45, 1962, pp. 1385–1460.

[2] *Statut des fonctionnaires*, *op. cit.*, Arts. 93 and 110.

[3] *ibid.*, Articles 10 and 110.

134

mission concerned with administration or representation of personnel that the Statute or its interpretation favoured any one particular national system of personnel administration. It followed the French *Statut des Fonctionnaires* very closely indeed in the provisions regarding discipline and competitions for posts, but elsewhere features common to all or most of the national staff regulations were incorporated, along with some which were original and which were designed to meet the special circumstances of a Community civil service.

The main difficulty in applying the Statute was uncertainty regarding the future role of Community institutions. In particular, the decision to establish a permanent, independent career service on the same broad principles as those laid down in the Statute of the ECSC had important political implications. It was expected to underpin the independence of the Commission, in that officials would not depend on their national governments for promotion or for their future careers. It thus appealed to those who favoured speeding up the application of the Treaty of Rome and enhancing the authority of the Commission.[1] However, towards the end of the procedure for drafting the new Statute, the French Government's representatives began to argue in favour of a system whereby officials served the Commission on secondment from their national administrations. Such a system, it was argued, would do more to 'Europeanize' officials than the creation of a career service, by giving a greater number of officials experience of service in Brussels. Moreover, it would make service with the Commission more attractive to civil servants, whom it would otherwise be difficult and expensive to compensate for lost career prospects and lost pension rights at home. In spite of the adoption of the Statute of Service, the French, along with some other governments, continued to practise the system of secondment for at least some of their officials serving with the Commission.

Meanwhile, as we have seen, there have been numerous practical obstacles to treating those in the service of the Commission exactly like the officials of a national civil service. For one thing, contrary to normal national experience, there was no firm basis of legal

[1] See, for example, Resolutions in the European Parliament calling for a speedy drafting of the Statute, December 17, 1958, and June 30, 1960; and Debates on the Draft Statute, October 16 and 19, 1961.

precedent by which to interpret the provisions of the Statute (excepting some cases in the Court arising from the Statute of the ECSC), nor was there any substantial tradition of administrative practice from which to borrow. In many respects, therefore, the Statute should be seen as a manifesto rather than a legal ordinance. Its proper implementation depended largely on the extent to which those who applied it shared the assumptions and aims of those who conceived it. The literal meaning of its provisions, or even their meaning as interpreted by lawyers, was not always a reliable guide to what was done in practice. An added difficulty was that, in so far as it was a manifesto, it was the manifesto of a coalition of interests and opinions and as such would bear different interpretations and suit different aims. This empirical element was quite consistent with other aspects of the Community system, and in view of this we would not expect legal provisions to do more than provide a framework within which a continuing process of negotiation and experiment could take place.

Yet in principle, the Statute set up the framework for the establishment of a European career civil service, independent of the member States and acting in the sole interests of the Community. Besides prescribing fixed scales of salary with incremental steps equivalent to different grades of the service, it provided for a contributory scheme of social security for established officials covering them and their families against accident, sickness and death. In addition, an established official with at least ten years' service had the right to a service pension which was due to him at the age of sixty. (For thirty-three years' service the pension was 60 per cent of the salary prior to retirement.) Officials contributed 6 per cent of their basic salary to a pension fund for which provision was also made in the Community budget. Officials were expected to reside at or near their place of work, which for officials with the Commission usually meant Brussels.[1] All Community officials were immune from paying tax on their salaries and emoluments to their countries of origin or residence, and paid a special Community tax which appeared on the receipts side of the Community budget.

According to Article 7.1 of the Statute, the Commission had to grade each official 'in the sole interests of the service, and without consideration of nationality'. Conversely, under Title II an official's

[1] *Statut des fonctionnaires, op. cit.*, Articles 72–6, 77–84, 57–60, respectively.

first obligation was to carry out his functions and conduct himself 'having solely in view the interests of the Communities, without soliciting or accepting instructions from any government, authority, organization, or person extraneous to his institution'. The provisions concerning incompatibility were very strict. Other than for services rendered before joining the staff of the Communities, or in the course of military or national service, an official might not receive any honour, decoration, favour, gift, or remuneration from any source other than his institution without special authorization.[1] Special permission was also needed from the Commission before he might exercise any outside activity or undertake any commission, whether paid or unpaid, and such permission might not be given if the activity or commission were prejudicial either to the official's independence or to any activity of the Communities.[2]

The chapter in the Statute concerning recruitment was also quite explicit where independence was concerned:

'Recruitment must aim to ensure for the institution the assistance of officials who possess the highest qualities of competence, performance and integrity, recruited on the widest possible geographical basis among the nationals of member States of the Communities. Officials are chosen without distinction of race, creed, or sex. *No post may be reserved to the nationals of a particular member State.*'[3]

Candidates had to satisfy a number of conditions commonly demanded in the administrations of Western European countries, such as guarantees of moral and physical fitness. They had also to be nationals of one of the member States (unless special exception was made), in possession of their rights as citizens, and able to give proof of a profound knowledge of one of the languages of the Com-

[1] *Statut des fonctionnaires, op. cit.*, Art. 11.
[2] *ibid.*, Art. 12.
[3] *ibid.*, Art. 27 (our italics). Individual decisions to fill posts have occasionally been challenged in the Court of Justice partly on the grounds that the posts concerned were 'reserved' for a particular nationality. Such claims have never been found proven or upheld. Indeed, the Court has maintained that, whereas nationality cannot be a decisive factor in making an appointment, it can be an additional consideration where the candidates are of equal merit. This is particularly so where a candidate of a particular nationality is favoured in order to maintain the overall distribution of nationalities in the service (or the 'geographical equilibrium' as it is called). See, for example, *Receuil de Jurisprudence de la Cour de Justice, op. cit.*

munities and of a satisfactory knowledge of another one in so far as this was required by the duties assigned to them.[1]

The services of the Commission were divided into four classes or 'categories', in line with the divisions adopted in the civil services of most western European countries. Entry to each category demanded a particular level of educational attainment or equivalent professional experience. Category A officials (corresponding to the British administrative class) had to have a university education or its professional equivalent; those of category B (corresponding to the British executive class) needed to have had secondary education up to the age of university entrance; and those of category C (corresponding roughly to the British clerical class) had to have reached the level of the first major school examinations (taken at the age of about sixteen). Category D officials needed only primary education supplemented by technical training and were the manual employees of the service: the doormen, chauffeurs, cleaners and so on.[2] Each category was divided into grades (eight for category A and five each for categories B and C) and each grade into echelons (ranging from two to eight for any one grade) corresponding to different levels of salary. After two years' service in one echelon, promotion to the one above was automatic, bringing with it a fixed increase in salary. The appointing authority decided whether to promote from one grade to another but had to base its decision on the official's seniority, his merits, and on the reports of his superiors.[3] Appointment to a higher category could take place only after a competition (*concours*).

A particularly French aspect of the Statute of Service was the division of grades into separate *carrières*.[4] Within his *carrière* an official might be promoted without having to take on new functions. When the Statute was being drafted, many protagonists of a European career service (in particular, the committee of the European Parliament which reported on the draft Statute) felt that the *carrières*

---

[1] *Statut des fonctionnaires*, *op. cit.*, Art. 28.
[2] Translators and interpreters were placed in a separate cadre, divided into eight grades.
[3] *Statut des fonctionnaires*, *op. cit.*, Art. 45.
[4] This division was similar in principle to the division of the British civil service into different levels, such as Assistant Principal, Principal, Assistant Secretary, and so on.

provided were too narrow in range.[1] In category A, for example, there were only two *carrières* within which an official could rise to a higher grade (namely, those of Administrator and Principal Administrator), and even so these two *carrières* each comprised only two grades (A7–A6 and A5–A4 respectively). Movement between grades other than these involved taking on new functions.

The main reason for this restriction was really budgetary in that the member States were reluctant to afford the Commission much discretion in augmenting its officials' salaries or status. As far as possible, they wanted to ensure that the Commission would be able to promote officials to a higher grade only by increasing their functions. Within these limits, however, the Commission might of course make what promotions it wished, depending on the qualifications of the candidates and above all, depending on the number of posts provided in the budget by the Council of Ministers.

Article 28 provided that entry to the service must be by general competition, exceptions being made only for grades A1 and A2 and for some posts demanding specialized qualifications.[2] Competitions (both internal and external) might be held on the basis of written qualifications, or by examination, or both; they were assessed by a jury, set up by the appointing authority in the institution concerned and including a representative of the personnel.

The Statute laid down in Articles 29–34 that a post might be filled from outside the service only after a series of other possibilities had been explored; namely, internal promotion or transfer, a competition within the institution, and finally, transferring an official from another institution of one of the three Communities.[3] Article 31 provided that a certain proportion of all new appointments must be made at the lowest grade of a category,[4] in order to make sure that a substantial proportion of higher posts were filled by promotion from the lower ranks and that recruitment from outside was confined as far as possible to the lowest levels. In this way

---

[1] See Debates in the European Parliament, October 16 and 19, 1961, and Report of the Budget and Administration Committee, Document 66 (1961–62).

[2] *Statut des fonctionnaires, op. cit.*, Art. 29.2.

[3] *ibid.*, Art. 29.1.

[4] One-half of posts vacated and one-third of posts newly created in the case of grades A1–3, and two-thirds of posts vacated and one-half of posts newly created in the case of other grades.

139

an official could hope to work his way up the service to the higher grades as in any career service.

Thus, in most essential respects, the Statute of Service provided the legal framework for a 'classical' career civil service.[1] Most of the provisions normally expected in such a document were present: official representation of personnel; arrangement for automatic advancement of salary; promotion by seniority or merit and the reports of superiors; the right to a pension; provisions for recourse against arbitrary decisions; limitation of recruitment to lower grades and to candidates possessing fixed qualifications assessed by an independent jury.

Why was the drafting of the Statute of such significance? In many ways this is a question which only an Englishman could ask, for in Britain there is little or no history of legislation on the status of civil servants.[2] On the other hand, in each of the six member countries of the European Communities the status and role of civil servants over a wide area (pay, conditions, grading, discipline, recruitment, and promotion) is legally documented and is enforceable in administrative courts. This difference between administration according to public law, and administration according to unwritten standards, is one of the most striking differences between British practice and that of the Six.[3] Given the accepted conventions in the Six, the formulation and enactment in the EEC of a Statute of Service for officials was of great psychological and legal importance. To the dedicated European it was an essential step towards European integration and an escape from the uncertainties of the early years. However, unless the provisions of such a document were applied in the right spirit, they would remain purely normative and lack prescriptive force. In the next chapter we shall see how far the Commission succeeded in building on the legal foundations laid by the Statute.

[1] An extremely useful analysis of the background to the Statute and of its general nature is D. Rogalla, Zum Beruf des Europa-Beamtes, *Zeitschrift für Zolle und Verbrauchsteuern* (Bonn), XXXXII, Nr. 5, May 1966. For a comparison of the Statute with similar provisions in national and other international organizations, see P. van de Meerssche, *Het Europees Openbaar Ambt*, Louvain University, 1966, pp. 103–13.

[2] See H. W. R. Wade, *Administrative Law*, Oxford University Press, 1961, pp. 233 ff.

[3] The present author had some difficulty in making officials in Brussels understand that, though he taught Public Administration, he was not a trained lawyer.

CHAPTER 7

THE 'EUROPEAN CIVIL SERVICE'

In this chapter we will attempt some fairly simple and very rough tests of how far the Commission of the EEC managed to provide careers for its officials. Three kinds of information will be useful for this purpose. First, we may assume that the more the Commission went outside the service to recruit staff, the more it was influenced by factors such as the specialization of functions and the need to reserve certain posts, and the more it was prevented from developing a system of careers by the need to maintain a distribution between nationalities. Conversely, we shall be interested in the extent to which promotion within the service became a normal part of the officials' expectations. This will also show how far the Commission was hindered by its lack of control over the distribution of posts by grades. A second aspect which will be worth examining is the background of officials in the highest posts, their length of service, and the rate of turnover of staff. We shall where possible give figures and estimates for all grades in the services, but we are primarily interested in posts where policy-making functions are carried out (in other words, category A). Thirdly, an important aspect of a 'classical' type of career service is institutionalized procedures for personnel management and the existence of a specialized branch for this purpose. In the last section of this chapter we shall examine how far the Commission went in this direction.

THE STAFF OF THE COMMISSION 1958–67

The posts available to the Commission in 1958 were by gentleman's agreement distributed among the different nationalities of the Six in proportion to each country's contribution to the Community budget. Lists of potential candidates were drawn up for each nationality by the Commissioner or Commissioners concerned, with the help of close personal and political friends and assistants,

141

and by others in national administrations and elsewhere who had been closely involved in the negotiation of the Treaty of Rome. The candidates came mainly from government departments and from other international institutions (in particular those of the ECSC), but also from business and industry and from university and other professional occupations. The main qualification for inclusion was to be 'pro-European'. Involvement in some aspect of European integration either as a national representative or an international civil servant was one obvious criterion for this. A second qualification was the possession of sufficiently specialized experience and ability. A third qualification also had to be borne in mind, but was less important in the early years than it was to become later, namely, the need to satisfy different social and political groups at home. While in the first few years a number of posts had to be filled on a temporary basis, there was really no difficulty in filling the initial lists of candidates. The tenure of posts was quite stable up to 1962 and a good number of those holding posts at the top three grades, A1, A2 and A3, at the end of 1966 had joined the Commission in the first few years. One has the impression that most of those who were appointed in this period served because they were committed to the new venture rather than in search of career advantages with the Commission, or even of later advancement in some other career at home.

Since the Statute of Service came into force on January 1, 1962, the Commission seems in fact to have filled only a small proportion of posts from outside. The figures are given in the Table opposite. Only 3 per cent of appointments made to category A posts and 2 per cent to category B posts were filled by general competition in the period from January 1, 1962, to April 24, 1967; about 7 per cent of category A posts were filled by the special procedure provided in Article 29.2 of the Statute (but in fact, the majority of these were for grades A1 and A2 to which promotion is seldom possible). Overwhelmingly, therefore, posts seem to have been filled either by promotion or transfer from within or by internal competition.

However, an important qualification must be added to these figures. The actual staff of the Commission included numbers of auxiliary personnel, recruited on an entirely different basis from established personnel, but permitted to enter internal competitions

APPOINTMENTS MADE SINCE JANUARY 1, 1962
(up to and including April 24, 1967)

Category	Under Article 29–1/a (Promotion or transfer)	Under Article 29–1/b (Internal Competition)	Under Article 29–1/c (Transfer from another Community institution)	By (General 'External' competition)	Under Article 29–2 (Special procedure)	Total
A	260	275	5	18	44	602
Linguists	116	147	10	29	—	302
B	199	286	2	11	6	504
C	522	737	30	67	1	1,357
D	33	57	—	—	—	90
Totals	1,130	1,502	47	125	51	2,855

Figures supplied by the E E C Commission.

for established posts. An auxiliary agent was appointed by renewable contract, lasting in the first instance for one year or for the period of absence of the official he replaced. He had his own system of grading and his own salary scale, and did not contribute to or benefit from the pension scheme provided in the Statute. The only conditions he need satisfy for appointment were that he must normally be a national of one of the member States, in possession of his civic rights, have observed the law regarding military service, and be able to offer guarantees of moral and physical fitness. Auxiliaries did not vote for representation on the Personnel Committee, but had their own separate staff representation.

According to the Statute, an auxiliary could be appointed for only one of two purposes: to carry out functions for which no post had been provided in the budget; or to replace an official who was temporarily unable to perform the functions assigned to him. He might not, however, replace an official of grades A1 or A2, but might replace any other grade A official, if the latter occupied 'a very specialized post'.[1] In practice, most of the contracts of auxiliaries lasted for much longer than one year. The auxiliaries were appointed for three different reasons: first, to fill posts which, in the Commission's view, could not be filled quickly enough by any other method—in other words, because the Commission regarded these

[1] *Statut des fonctionnaires: régime applicable aux autre agents, op. cit.*

143

posts as being too 'specialized' to be filled from the existing establishment, while it would have taken too long to appoint someone new
to an established post; secondly, to compensate for the limited
number of established posts provided in the Community budget;
and thirdly, simply to avoid the drawbacks of the procedure for
recruitment to established posts as laid down in the Statute.
In 1963 there were no less than 568 auxiliary staff working
for the Commission (equivalent to a quarter of the total
strength). In practice a substantial number of these acted as
permanent staff, performing functions of a continuing and
permanent nature.

The recognition of auxiliary personnel as 'officials' in the sense
of the Statute of Service, and their right to admission on this basis
to internal competitions, has been upheld by the Court of Justice.[1]
The Personnel Committee opposed the Court's stand and pressed for
an amendment of the Statute. The Committee's main argument was
that, unlike established personnel, auxiliaries did not have to be
recruited by external competition, hence their admission to internal
competitions represented a misinterpretation of the intentions, if not
of the letter, of the Statute. In particular, the admission of auxiliaries
with university degrees into internal competitions for category A
posts was a threat, at the time when the Statute came into force, to
the career expectations of many category B officials. Between 1962
and 1965 the Personnel Committee repeatedly called for a smaller
number of auxiliary personnel and for the filling of vacant posts by
the transfer or promotion of established officials.

Towards the end of 1966 the recruitment of auxiliaries in grades
A3–8 was stopped and the prolongation of existing contracts made
more difficult. On March 31, 1967, the number of auxiliaries stood
at 412: 84 category A, 48 translators, 141 category B, 130 secretaries,
and 9 category D. New recruitment of auxiliaries was restricted
to replacements for temporarily incapacitated officials (for example,
women secretaries during pregnancy). This diminution in the
recruitment of auxiliaries was an important concession towards
the supporters of a career service.

A further concession would have been to limit their recruitment,
with certain exceptions, to the lowest grades of a category. As stated
in Chapter 6, Article 31 of the Statute required that a certain pro-

---

[1] *Recueil de la Jurisprudence, op. cit.*, 1964, Affaire 16/64.

portion of new appointments must be so made, but this was not observed in practice. The lowest grade of category A (A8) was, in fact, never the normal entry point for category A officials. In 1965 there were less than two dozen officials at this grade. Appointment to A8 was extremely rare, partly because of the poor salary and prospects, but also because the functions performed at this level were not in much demand. The Commission needed far more the service of experienced and specialized personnel capable of performing highly elaborate tasks and of holding positions of responsibility. Even the number of officials in grades A6 and A7 was in 1967 less than half that in grades A4 and A5.

The Personnel Committee argued that Article 31 should be applied in practice and that recruitment from outside should fill only the lowest grades in categories A and B. At the same time, it called for a system of general competitions, held on an annual basis, *ad hoc* competitions for specific posts being abolished. Exceptions to this rule, said the Committee, should apply only to a limited number of posts demanding highly specialized qualifications, of the sort which could not normally be found within the service (such as engineers, medical practitioners, architects, etc., should they ever be needed).

The table on p. 143 shows that, out of the total number of appointments made from the beginning of 1962, 43 per cent in category A were promotions or transfers. A further 46 per cent were the result of internal competitions, but this does not necessarily indicate promotion in the ordinary sense, both because a substantial number of these appointees were auxiliaries and also because the Commission normally resorted to an internal competition to appoint a candidate who did not fulfil the regular conditions for promotion (that is, if he lacked the seniority required and was not in the grade immediately below the post to be filled). In each Directorate General, an average of between 25 and 45 per cent of the officials in 1967 had received a promotion since 1962.

Promotion at the highest levels was very slow indeed. At the end of 1966, of the eighteen Directors General appointed since the Commission was set up, nine were selected by the Commission in 1958 (of whom five remained for eight years or more), five were appointed by the Commission from outside the service at a later date (including one who had previously served with the Commission in a lower post), and only four were promoted from within the service. Meanwhile nearly sixty appointments to the rank of Director were made between 1958 and the end of 1966. Under a quarter of these Directors were promoted from a lower rank, many of them from a Commissioner's cabinet rather than from a Directorate General. On the past record Heads of Division had in normal times about an 8 per cent chance of promotion. In addition, they had a negligible chance of transfer to some other part of the service or into a cabinet.

The real bottleneck was at grade A4. There were in 1966 about 170 officials at this grade, but not more than a handful of them stood any chance of promotion to Head of Division in the foreseeable future. An A4 official was, moreover, paid at the top of his scale only about the same as a British Assistant Secretary (who has about a one in three chance of going higher). Even the Personnel Committee felt that an exception should be made of the highest grades (A1–3) on the ground that there were bound to be fewer posts available at these levels. In a career civil service, however, promotion to the highest grades should be a reasonable possibility, and this is not yet the case in the administrative services of the Commission.

At lower levels the situation did improve in 1965 and 1966 when a start was made to institute a system of 'automatic' promotion within *carrières* (that is, promotion without a change of functions). This system was introduced in 1965 when 102 promotions were made from the lowest to the highest grades in the ten *carrières* of the service; at the 1966 annual review there were 104 promotions, and in 1967 ninety-six up to July 1st. Promotions are made from a list drawn up by Joint Committees on the basis of seniority, competence, performance, and good conduct. Most officials enjoying such preferment in the years concerned, however, were in the lower grades; only a handful of promotions from A5 to A4 took place. If this system is to do much to ease promotion the Commission will have to stop advertising posts at the top grade of a *carrière*. This practice, which limits the number of posts available for promotion, was not abandoned with the institution of promotion within *carrières*. In fairness to the administration, however, it must be noted that no appointments were made in 1966 at grades A4 or A6. The Personnel Committee argued that if reservation of

146

posts could be confined to exceptional circumstances then not only posts at the top grade of a *carrière*, but also those at the bottom, might be filled only by promotion from below. Similarly, the Committee wanted to abolish internal competitions except for movement between categories, for which a general reserve of candidates for promotion should be created each year. By these means it hoped to increase the opportunities for promotion and for full careers.

The Commission could well plead that it faced particular difficulties owing to its dependence on the Council of Ministers for allocation of posts. However, the main reason for the slowness of promotion in many parts was the stress on specialization. The need to maintain a distribution between nationalities, and the reservation of posts for particular types of candidate, also contributed. The number of internal competitions, and the fact that there were enormous delays in finding candidates for some of the higher posts (in spite of applications from lower-ranking officials) suggested that there was no shortage of posts relative to the number of candidates at these top levels. However, while the Commission sought the sort of qualifications from candidates that it did, it proved impossible to satisfy the career expectations of its officials. There seemed to be a lack of compatibility here between the immediate needs of the Commission and the normal criteria of a career service.

Being unable, therefore, to offer numbers of its officials in the most important grades the normal expectations of a civil service career, the Commission had to rely on other means of attracting staff. The chief of these means was commitment to the cause of European unification and to the Commission's part in it. In addition, however, the Commission relied on seconded civil servants from the national administrations, who often saw service with the Commission primarily as a means of furthering their own careers at home. There were, of course, a number of individual officials who did not fit exactly into one or other of these categories, and who served the Commission partly out of commitment and partly for material expectations, whether these were to be derived from the rewards of a European career or from those of an existing career with a national civil service. At the same time, a number of well-known 'committed Europeans' have served with the Commission on secondment from a national post, not because they are sceptical as to the case for a European Civil Service, but simply because this was the only way they could work for the Commission without sacrificing the rights associated with their career at home. The nature of his service with the Commission, therefore, may not always say very much about a particular official's role or attitude. However, it is worth noting the differing types of service on which the Commission relied.

First, there are the officials who took up their appointments before the Statute came into force, in the early days of the Commission's life, joining at the outset no doubt primarily out of a commitment to the Commission itself. At the less high grades, such as A4 and A7, such officials have not enjoyed very promising career prospects. A small number will have found their way up through a few grades, perhaps jumping two or three at a time by means of an internal competition. The majority will have had to be content with regular increments in salary earned by seniority. Most in the top three grades will have joined the Commission after leaving public service careers in their own countries. None will have been recruited to the service by a general competition as provided under the Statute, though some will have reached their present positions by taking an internal competition. For the more highly placed of these officials it would probably still be possible to find attractive jobs in a national civil service. Many in lower ranks, however, would now find such outlets cut off. The majority will have settled in Brussels and made the service of the Commission their career. In the higher grades a good number of this intake must be reaching retiring age, and this particular supply of 'committed Europeans' is obviously in the process of drying up.

A second type of official is illustrated by those who have served for short periods (four to five years) on loan from their national administrations. The nature of this kind of service can vary from the formal type popular with the French (whereby the official retains his post in the home civil service and in many cases continues to enjoy promotion by echelon in his absence) to the informal arrangements preferred by the Germans, whereby the official resigns his previous post and is regarded as being on leave.[1] The French have

---

[1] For the legal position of officials from the German civil service, see D. Rogalla, *Zum Beruf des Europa Beamtes, op. cit.*

actively encouraged young officials to serve for four or five years in Brussels and have not facilitated the departure of officials for permanent careers with the Commission. There have been criticisms of this French system of short-term secondment (known as *roulement*) on the ground that it infringes the spirit of the Statute. However, a number of committed 'Europeans' argue that the Commission should employ civil servants on loan from national administrations, and the practice of 'lending' officials has not been confined to the French. The Italians seem to have largely followed a similar practice. Some Germans from the Foreign Office in Bonn serving in high posts with the Commission have eventually left after a certain period to take up ambassadorships, or other posts overseas, with their national government. There is a difference, however, between the French system of *roulement* (that is, a deliberate system of sending officials to Brussels for short periods) and the German 'lending' of officials. In the latter case it is—theoretically—left to the official himself whether or not he tries to return to his national administration, and no formal assurances are given regarding the post to which he might return. In both cases, it is always stressed that no official can receive instruction from the national government for which he worked previously or be under any obligation to return to its service.

These officials have entered the Community service by a variety of means—often as auxiliaries later established by internal competition. It is estimated that at any time they have not constituted more than twenty per cent of the whole of category A. Nevertheless, short period secondment continues to be a vital means of obtaining the service of public officials with the required degree of specialization, attainment, and experience.

Finally, there are officials who have joined the Commission since or just before the Statute of Service came into force, who either had no previous ties with a national administration or broke these off on joining the Commission. The number of officials in this category has increased gradually in number and has been much advertised by the Commission as the basis of a future European Civil Service. Increasingly, in fact, new recruits have come from a business or academic—rather than a public service—background. A good number have come from graduation or postgraduate work at university. Recruiting people of this type is of course an ideal way of avoiding the difficulty of encouraging national civil servants to leave good promotion prospects and favourable pension rights at home. It is also a way of ensuring that officials of the Commission are truly independent and have no ties with national governments. Typically, the officials who have entered category A in the last five or six years are young specialists—university-trained economists, agronomists, and so on (often with a postgraduate as well as a graduate qualification)—whose loyalty is primarily to their specialism. In so far as they have joined the Commission for a decent job, rather than out of commitment to any cause or in the hope of later advancement in a national civil service, they are the nearest thing to real 'European civil servants' so far.

However, the extent to which the Commission could attract young men and women at the beginning of their careers was greatly limited. Recruitment to the lowest grade was very restricted, as we have already mentioned. The prospects of promotion between A7 and A4 were slight. The Commission had no training programme for new recruits, and no means of adapting officials in one part of the administration for service in others. There was, however, a system of six-months' probationary service open to university students who might or might not later choose to apply for posts with the Commission. Yet there was still no European service in the sense of easy movement from one part of the administration to another; even movement between Divisions of the same Directorate General was often difficult. The emphasis on specialized techniques in the higher posts resulted in compartmentalism, and individual parts of the service were very self-contained.[1]

THE INSTITUTIONAL FRAMEWORK

A significant stage in the development of any public administration is reached when selection and administration of personnel are entrusted to a special organ within the administration itself. This can take the form either of delegation from outside (usually from a political source, such as a Minister or a Parliament) or of centraliza-

[1] The estimates made in this Section are based partly on figures published by the Commission, and partly on unpublished material. The turnover of personnel at the highest grades of the service can be observed in the annual organigrams of the administrative services published at various intervals in the EEC Bulletin. Figures for the total strength at different grades are shown in the Community budget published annually in the *Journal Officiel*.

tion from the individual sectors of the administration (which will previously have managed their own staff directly). The object of a transfer of functions like this is to limit political or personal influences on the appointment of personnel, and to establish and maintain objective standards of recruitment and advancement within the service. Occasionally, the organ concerned is also responsible for such matters as discipline, pay, pensions, and so on; but more often the powers delegated may be distributed between different bodies, some of which may already be regular departments of the administration (such as the British Treasury) and some not (such as the British Civil Service Commission).

Effective delegation (or centralization) of personnel administration to specialized organs implies a high degree of unity and consensus both within the administration itself and among those to whom it is responsible. In what might be termed the more highly developed systems of public administration, this kind of delegation has already taken place, at least formally, and in many of the civil services of western Europe and North America one can expect to find specialized organs responsible for aspects of recruitment and personnel administration (for example, the Civil Service Commissions of Britain and the United States, or the *Direction de la fonction publique* in France). The participation of personnel representatives on joint bodies of consultation and advice (such as the *commissions paritaires* in France) is a normal concomitant of this delegation, especially on questions of discipline and promotion.

In the administration of the six member countries of the EEC the extent of this delegation of personnel management varies greatly. In this section we shall observe just how far the making of appointments and administration of careers in the EEC Commission has been entrusted to agencies within the administration. This could serve as some guide to the stage this administration had reached in developing into a career service or bureaucracy of the 'classical' type.

(1) *Bodies Responsible for Selection and Appointment*

When responsibility for the different services of the Commission was divided between the nine Commissioners in 1958, that for administration was regarded as too important to be entrusted to any one Commissioner. As a result it was entrusted to a body called

151

'The Meeting of the Presidents', consisting of the President of the Commission and the three Vice-Presidents. In practice, this meant that any initiative or leadership on administration questions had to come via the President himself. The Directorate General concerned (DG IX) was divided into three Directorates: personnel (including recruitment, promotion, salaries and so on), domestic affairs (furniture and equipment, library and documentation, etc.), and budget and finance. In 1966 budget and finance was hived off to form a separate service. In spite of this, at the time of the merger of the Executives DG IX remained the largest single unit among the Commission's administrative services, comprising more than twice as many officials as the largest of the other Directorates General.[1]

However, although DG IX bore the nominal responsibility for administration, it was perhaps the weakest and least autonomous of all the Directorates General; less real power has been delegated from Commission staff here than anywhere else, largely because of the political factors discussed in the previous Chapter. There was very little delegation even in the formal distribution of responsibility. The Statute of Service did not specify which particular organ of each institution should be responsible for executing its provisions, but referred only to 'the authority vested with power of appointment'. On June 18, 1962, the Commission decreed that, with certain exceptions, it would exercise the powers of this authority itself.[2] In fact, the Commission became the authority for executing all provisions concerning officials of category A, and only certain minor duties were delegated to the Director General of Administration. Most of these delegated duties were pure formalities, such as opening the procedure of a competition, or drawing up the advertisements of, and forms of application for, vacancies, or drafting the lists of candidates fulfilling the necessary conditions to apply for entry (under Article 28 of the Statute). Some duties were more than purely formal, but applied only where officials of category A4 and below were concerned, such as giving permission for the appointment of an official who was not the national of a member State. In 1966, in face of severe difficulties in filling posts due to the

[1] Even allowing for the fact that its staff included many interpreters and translators as well as technical personnel of lower or intermediate ranks.

[2] Published in No. 16 of *Informations au Personnel*, October 19, 1962. Some of the acts of delegation mentioned in the following paragraphs took place at later dates but in each case they were announced in the same way.

cumbersome nature of the recruiting procedure, special powers were delegated to the Director General to decide whether or not to move from one procedure to another under Article 29 of the Statute, and to decide on the constitution of juries for competitions for posts of A4 and below. (These special powers could be exercised, however, only in consultation with the chairman of the group of Commissioners responsible for the Directorate General or Service where the vacancy occurred.)

Similar powers were delegated concerning category B officials, but otherwise provisions regarding these officials were to be carried out by the Meeting of the Presidents. Only where officials of categories C and D were concerned (that is, at the level of secretaries, clerks, and below) was DG IX given the full powers of an appointing authority. In short, the Commission retained responsibility for personnel administration in the policy-making grades and even in the higher grades concerned purely with preparatory or executive work.

The lack of delegation was even more marked in the ways these powers were actually exercised. Though not recognized formally in the distribution of responsibilities for personnel matters, two bodies were of outstanding importance in this field. First, the cabinet of the President of the Commission, which was officially charged with advising and assisting the President on all matters for which he was responsible, including, of course, personnel and administration. In fact, the President's cabinet took a close interest in administrative matters and was extremely influential in determining administrative practice in the whole service. (In the new combined Commission, which met first in July 1967, personnel and administration matters were entrusted to one of the Vice-Presidents, M. Levi-Sandri. It will be interesting to see whether M. Levi-Sandri's cabinet achieves the same authority in administrative matters as did President Hallstein's cabinet in the Commission of the EEC, strengthened as it must have been by the very fact of being the President's cabinet.)

There was conflicting evidence as to the importance of the President's cabinet with regard to individual appointments and promotions. Some considered it very great, others no greater than that of the cabinet of any Commissioner serving on one of the bodies responsible for making appointments (such as the Meeting of the Presidents or the Commission itself). In the last resort all individual appointments had to be approved by the 'appointing authority' itself, so that, in the case of categories A and B at least, no single person or body could have had any continuously overriding authority.

The other vital organ in administration was a body which, until the merger of the Community executives, had no official existence at all, namely, the 'Meeting of the Heads of Cabinets'. This body could be instructed by the Commission to make preparations for its meetings. It consisted of the heads of the cabinets of each of the Commissioners, and was the venue where many questions concerning personnel and administration received preliminary, and sometimes perhaps even decisive, consideration. Its role was enhanced by the fact that many decisions of the Commission were taken by what is known as the 'written procedure'.[1] The Commissioners normally discussed personally and in full session any appointment to grade A1, 2, or 3. For grades A4 and below, however, it was more usual for the written procedure to be used. The Commission itself was always extremely overworked and the co-ordinating and preparatory role of the cabinets, and in particular of the Meeting of the Heads of Cabinets, was thereby increased in importance. In many individual top-level appointments the role of this latter body must have been crucial. (With the merger of the executives the Meeting of the Heads of Cabinets has received official status—a sign of its real, even though formally unrecognized, importance in the past.)

Another important organ, again with no official status, was the Administrative Committee (*Comité Administratif*) consisting of all the Directors General and the chiefs of the common Services. This Committee formed a sort of second-tier authority below the first tier of the President's cabinet, the Meeting of the Heads of Cabinets, and the Commission. Below this second tier there was a third tier consisting of the representatives of the personnel, sitting on the Personnel Committee. This Committee, as mentioned in Chapter

---

[1] According to the written procedure members of the Commission are sent draft decisions, together with the relevant dossiers, and asked to submit any reservations or objections, within a fixed period. If they do not submit any reservations or objections, the proposal is deemed to have been accepted at the end of the specified time limit. The role of the cabinets, and of the Meeting of the Heads of Cabinets in particular, is clearly a key factor in the successful functioning of this procedure.

Five, had the right to be consulted on certain matters and to issue statements on questions affecting personnel. In addition, it shared representation with the Heads of Directorates General and Services on a number of joint bodies concerned with personnel administration.

The most important of these was the Statute Committee which had met about thirty times up to the end of 1966. In addition, each Community institution had a Joint Committee (*commission paritaire*), consisting of four representatives of the personnel and four of the administration, plus a Chairman appointed by the institution itself who could participate in a decision only if it concerned a question of procedure. A Joint Committee (that in the EEC Commission met about twenty times a year) could be consulted by the appointing authority or by the Personnel Committee on any general question. It had to be consulted on a number of questions arising out of the Statute, in particular on the advertisements for competitions for posts, on each of which it rendered an opinion, having the right to call for the advertisement to be republished.

These Joint Committees enabled representatives of the personnel to air their views and grievances with high-ranking officials of the administration and gave both sides the opportunity to examine ways of improving the management of the service. However, the power of decision in all important administrative matters rested with the Commission itself or with the Meeting of Presidents—meaning generally in practice the Meeting of Heads of Cabinets or the cabinet of the President.

The personnel were represented on the juries for competitions. A separate jury was usually appointed for each competition held, and consisted of four or five members: one representative of the personnel, not more than two from the Directorate General or Service where the vacancy occurred and the rest from DG IX. These juries were intended to be independent agencies for ensuring objectivity in selection and appointment. However, they fell short of this in a number of ways.

Their task was to list candidates in order of merit, the final appointment being made by the appointing authority.[1] However, the authority need not follow the order laid down by the jury and often did not do so. Moreover, competitions were usually held to

[1] *Statut*, Art. 30.

fill only one post at a time. Thus, whenever the authority had a particular candidate in mind, on grounds other than his merit as assessed by the jury, it had every opportunity to appoint him. The Personnel Committee argued that competitions for entry should be held annually—or at some other fixed interval of time—and should be used to create a reserve of successful candidates for each category. Candidates could then be assigned to posts by a committee representing both staff and official sides.

The role of the juries was also limited by the fact that, before they drew up their lists in order of merit, they had to eliminate candidates who did not meet the conditions laid down in the advertisement for the competition.[1] Though DG IX drew up these advertisements, the Directorate General where the post was vacant was able to determine the particular kinds of qualifications and experience stated as conditions of appointment. Very often highly specialized and particularized qualifications were demanded, and, in particular, the requirements regarding linguistic qualifications were sometimes designed to favour candidates of a particular nationality. However, after some criticism by the Joint Committee, successful attempts were made to regularize the form of these advertisements. The competitions often took place only on the basis of written qualifications (*titres*) and not by examination. The Personnel Committee would have liked all competitions to comprise both the presentation of qualifications and the taking of an examination, both written and oral, with a choice of subjects in the written examination. Further recommendations of the Personnel Committee were that juries should have a fixed membership for different categories and even for different languages, in order to limit even further the opportunity for favouring particular candidates, and that juries should always include some members from outside the service. The recommendations of the Personnel Committee aimed to render the system more 'objective' and to limit personal, political, and national influences. To the administrative side, on the other hand, the best guarantee against such influences was the collegial nature of the Commission as the main appointing authority. This was, however, a rather clumsy guarantee and limited the delegation of responsibility—a serious failing in view of the extent to which the Commission was already overworked.

[1] *Statut*, Annexe, III, Art. 5.

(2) *Procedures of Selection and Appointment*

In the case of selection and appointment from within the service the appointing authority had a wide discretion in effecting promotion and transfers, wider, in fact, than that of some national administrations.[1] According to Article 45 of the Statute, it was limited only by the need to consider the seniority and to assess the merits of the candidates and to take account of the reports of their superiors. Moreover, up to March 31, 1963, the Commission was given a special dispensation by the Council of Ministers (under Article 108 of the Statute) to promote candidates who did not fulfil the necessary conditions regarding seniority. In the first few years of the Statute's application there were a number of appeals to the Court of Justice against decisions to promote particular candidates, mainly attacking the way the Commission had exercised its discretion.[2] The Court generally upheld the Commission's discretion, but ruled that due regard must be paid to the written qualifications of the candidates and particularly to the reports of superiors.[3]

As far as individual appointments were concerned—whether from inside or outside the service—the actual distribution of responsibility reflected the overriding practical importance of the 'political' factors discussed in Chapter Five. Appointment to all policy-making posts, and even to some others, was a political matter engaging principally the interests of the Commissioners and/or their closest advisers. For this purpose informal national groups were said to exist within the Commission and its Services, and posts were distributed by a process of horse-trading. A national group wishing to get a particular candidate promoted or recruited had to get the acceptance of other groups. It was sometimes even possible for a candidate opposed by the Commissioner of his own nationality to get appointed to a post on the basis of the support of other parties.

However, particularly in the higher grades, the governments of

---

[1] In the French civil service, for example, all promotions from one grade to another must be based on an examination of merits and of reports by superiors carried out by joint committees, which can hear the officials concerned. On the other hand, in Germany promotion is normally left to the discretion of superior officers.

[2] Five were upheld, and three withdrawn.

[3] For example, see *Recueil de la Jurisprudence de la Cour de Justice 1963*, Affaire 97/63.

member States were usually involved and appointments often required much travelling and telephoning back and forth between the various capitals. The Benelux and Italian Governments were normally concerned not only with ensuring that their own candidates got on, but also with the political background of the candidates of their nationality who were appointed, and usually wished to vet candidates from this point of view. The change in party control of the Foreign Office in Bonn in 1965 led to demands that more officials from the Social Democratic Party should get German posts at the Commission, and there have been some well-known cases of non-Gaullist Frenchmen failing, after consultation between Brussels and Paris, to get posts which their superiors in the administration originally intended. It was widely felt among officials, however, that the influence of 'political' or national factors was decreasing as time went on and as an *esprit de corps* developed at the Commission. For the lower categories, as we have seen, a substantial amount of delegation to DG IX did take place (although the overall national distribution still had to be watched and some personal choice in the case of secretaries was still permitted). Moreover, promotion from one grade to another within a *carrière* became an easier and more regularized process. Committees of promotion, including personnel representatives, were set up for each category, and began to meet annually to draw up lists of suitable candidates. These committees, which could hear the candidates and their superior officers in person, based their lists on a combination of seniority, merit, the reports obtained by candidates, and the views expressed by candidates' superior officers, the rating given in the reports of superiors being by far the most important criterion.

The procedure of rating (*notation*) was itself also regularized to some extent. In all forms of bureaucratic administration this procedure is of great importance. The more it is regularized and the more reports are taken into consideration by those responsible for the preferment of officials, the less will the official depend for career purposes on influences outside the administration, or, for that matter on informal groupings within. Article 43 of the Statute of Service formed the basis of the system of *notation*:

'The competence, performance, and conduct in the service of each official, with the exception of those in grades A1 and A2, form the subject of a periodic report made at least every two years.'

THE EUROPEAN CIVIL SERVICE

The conditions of the *notation* had to be laid down by general dispositions of the institution concerned. The report was communicated to the official being rated, who had the opportunity to attach any observations which he might consider useful and to express any wishes regarding transfer to other parts of the service. Article 9 of the Statute also provided for a Committee of Reports, appointed from the superior officials of the institution concerned, responsible among other things for harmonizing the rating of personnel in different parts of the service.

Two sets of reports containing ratings of personnel were made by the Commission—in 1963 and 1965. No Committee of Reports was set up, but an *ad hoc* Committee of *notation*, consisting of representatives mainly of Director General rank and chaired by the Executive Secretary of the Commission, reviewed the 1963 reports and made recommendations for conducting the second series. Although invited to send representatives, the Personnel Committee boycotted the meetings of this Committee, as it considered its existence a breach of the Statute. The Personnel Committee was most disappointed with the 1965 rating. It was particularly concerned that no appeal to an impartial body other than the Commission, the Meeting of the Presidents, or the Director General of DG IX was available to officials, and that there was no proper means of ensuring consistency in the methods of rating employed in different parts of the service (language problems clearly played a part in the way different *notateurs* used the prescribed criteria). However, a system evolved whereby the Commission could receive written complaints from officials who felt they had been unfairly or wrongly rated, following which the Commission could invite the Directorate General concerned to reconsider its assessment.

The Personnel Committee's grievance concerning rating was really part of a more general one regarding the weak position of DG IX *vis-à-vis* the other Directorates General. The Commission was reluctant to give it the authority to develop uniform standards for the whole administration and to ensure equal treatment for officials in different parts of the service. The development of reporting by superiors as a basis of advancement was an important step towards a European career civil service. However, though the standard of reports could vary from one part of the service to another, while no institutional channel for appeal against rating existed progress would be impossible. Furthermore, it was still felt that factors other than seniority and the reports of superiors were being used as a basis for promotion.

The Personnel Committee argued that committees of promotion should be set up for movement between as well as within *carrières* and that there should be a greater degree of delegation to the Directorate General for Administration, or to some other internal specialized agency. The Committee suggested that the merger of the three Community executives should be used as an opportunity to take responsibility for recruitment and career management away from the President of the Commission and to give it instead to, say, a senior official working directly under the Commission. It was clear, however, that the point had not been reached where power to select and administer personnel could be institutionalized in this way. (The only noticeable change accompanying the merger is the transfer of special responsibility for the Directorate General of Administration to one of the Vice-Presidents of the Commission.)[1]

Both the Commissioners themselves and the member governments clearly insisted on retaining influence over individual appointments. The official's career thus depended to a large extent on factors other than objective tests of ability and performance carried out by his official colleagues. It is impossible to measure the extent of that dependence; suffice it to say that the general feeling at the Commission was that, while it was decreasing significantly, it still existed. This confirms the view that the Commission's administrative services were increasingly acquiring features of a classical type of career civil service even though they did not fully conform to that type at the time of the merger in 1967.

ASSESSMENT AND CONCLUSIONS

From the analysis presented in this and the previous Chapter it is clear that the EEC Commission was unable to meet all the normal standards of the 'classical' type of career civil service, despite the Statute of Service for its officials approved by the Council of Ministers in 1961. In order to get candidates it wanted into the higher posts, it had to 'bend' the formal rules of procedure; it also had to

[1] For the changes brought about by merger, see pp. 264–71 below.

meet a series of special commitments and obligations more or less 'political' in nature.

This made it difficult to maintain the full complement of staff provided in the budget without considerable delays in some cases and without sometimes disappointing officials 'technically' qualified for promotion. Although still served by a generation of devoted Europeans, who entered in the early years of the EEC, and although many officials have entered the service with the intention of cutting off ties with other institutions, the administration has never become fully self-sufficient or self-contained in terms of staff.

Some bias was bound to be shown in the selection and advancement of particular individuals in an agglomeration of officials from six different nationalities speaking four different official languages. It would indeed have been quite remarkable if 'subjective' influences had been eliminated, for that would make the service unique, even in comparison with the national civil services of the six member countries. Indeed the personnel representatives at the Commission accepted that the geographical equilibrium in selection of personnel should be maintained (it was after all implied in the Statute of Service). Their main objection to other 'weaknesses' of the service as a career service was that they had made it difficult to provide reasonable careers and had threatened the independence of the service. However, most of those interested in personnel administration at the Commission accepted that certain departures from the classical standards of a career civil service were not only inevitable, but desirable.[1] They based this attitude on experience of their own national administrations.

It was understood at the Commission that the highest posts in the service could not really be regarded as a normal part of the official's career (although promotion to these grades from within would certainly never have been excluded). This was largely because there can never be more than a small number of posts available at these levels. However, it also seemed to be widely accepted that the more responsible positions were bound to be filled with some reference to the appointee's political views or to his nationality, or to other factors besides merit or 'technical' ability. The functions

---

[1] The Commission certainly had no greater difficulty than other multi-national administrations. See, for example, S. D. Bailey, *The Secretariat of the United Nations*, New York, UN Study No. 11, 1962.

POLITICS AND BUREAUCRACY

associated with responsible positions in such a service (meaning at
the Commission most of those at grades A1–3 and some at A4, in
other words, roughly equivalent to British Assistant Secretary level
and above) involve an ability to defend one's views in public or
in negotiation with career politicians and representatives of interest
groups. They also demand a good deal of 'political feel' in the formulation of policy. This is particularly so in view of the Commission's
role in the Community system and the importance of negotiation
and bargaining in the decision-making process. It is also underlined
by the Commission's dependence on the support of member States
and their representatives for sustaining progress in the development
of the Community. As in most national civil services, it is impossible
to distinguish between politics and administration at these levels
and access to them cannot therefore be based purely on 'objective'
criteria.[1]

Another apparent consequence of the Commission's role in the
Community system was the emphasis on specialized qualifications
in selecting officials. The staff side considered that this emphasis
had been too great. However, there were certain very good reasons
why the Commission could not make certain appointments on the
basis of general qualifications. The typical function of a high-ranking
official was to work out policy proposals in conjunction with
officials from member States. Sometimes direct knowledge and
experience of a particular national system were necessary. Always
the Commission official had to have technical accomplishment and
professional standing similar to those of his national counterparts.
In the same way, when the Commission acquired a new responsibility for regulating some economic or social activity, which was
formerly the concern of the governments of member States, its
officials might have to take on executive functions of a very complex
and highly developed nature. The Commission simply did not have
the numbers of staff from which it could train enough specialists
of its own in every relevant field. Thus, in many cases it was forced
to recruit directly from outside for many top posts, by one means or
another, and thus limit the opportunities for promotion and transfer
from within. A high degree of specialized attainment, combined with

[1] We refer in this paragraph, of course, not only to the posts in the personal
offices or cabinets of individual Commissioners, but also to those at the top levels
of Directorates General and Services.

162

experience of other institutions, would, under the circumstances in which the Commission functions, seem to call for a more flexible system of selection and advancement than that found in the 'classical' type of career service.

On the other hand, there have been some significant steps towards the foundation of an independent administration in the Community. The first was the adoption of the Statute itself, which (in spite of ambiguities and compromises) did imply a commitment to found an independent European civil service. Some of the more blatant loopholes for evading the Statute have been stopped (such as the recruitment of auxiliaries to carry out permanent tasks), and some important measures have been taken to implement it in the spirit as well as in the letter (for example, arrangements for a series of annual promotions within *carrières*). An important development is the active role of the personnel representatives. They form a pressure group within the administration, anxious to outdo the official side in finding means to 'Europeanize' the service further. Moreover, the personnel and official sides began eventually to meet on a more regular and more intimate basis for the discussion of questions of principle. They were able to agree on some vital common objectives. Fundamentally, both sides were convinced that the service must be permanent in nature, that mobility between different parts should be encouraged, and that it should offer a life-long career to the main body of officials. With these aims in view it was agreed that general competitions should only be used to recruit annual reserves of suitable candidates (rather than to fill specific posts), that only the lowest grades in each category should be filled from outside, and that training schemes should be developed to encourage mobility within the service. Most people at the Commission confirmed that the criterion of nationality was less and less important in effecting appointments, and that it was becoming more and more difficult to exert influence whether from within or from outside to secure the appointment of candidates who did not fulfil the necessary standards or meet the approval of their official superiors.

Thus the representatives of the personnel of the EEC Commission seem to have stressed the need for more bureaucratic elements in personnel administration. This is not surprising, and is a typical attitude for staff representatives in any such organization. The classical rules of 'objectivity' and impersonality, and firm assurances with regard to careers, are always particularly appealing to lower-ranking officials, who normally depend far more on the organization than those in the higher grades. The Personnel Committee's concern with establishing a 'classical' type of career service sprang largely from its very ambition that the European civil service should become a reality. However, our account has shown that it was impossible in practice to go very far towards bureaucratizing the administrative services of the Commission in the prevailing circumstances. This need not detract from the 'Europeanism' of the Commission. Indeed it may not be in the interests of the Commission or of European integration to bureaucratize the administration much further. The European civil service might benefit by disregarding some of the 'classical' rules regarding the status and conditions of public officials.

At the same time, some departures from the 'classical' rules may not be beneficial at all. As we have seen, alongside the desire to appoint good 'Europeans' there was also a necessity to take account of other 'non-bureaucratic' factors such as the interests of member governments. Departure from the classical methods of selection and advancement took the form, not only of the advancement of the Commission's own candidates, but also of a more flexible policy all round, so that a candidate's nationality, and even his political views, were taken into account in making appointments. This in itself was neither unusual nor unduly alarming, but there must be limits to the influence of national governments on appointments, if the principle of an independent service is to be preserved. Some participants in the Communities—the regime of de Gaulle was chief among them—do not regard the Commission's staff as an embryonic federal civil service and they fear its independence and sense of common purpose. The practice of seconding officials to the Commission for fixed periods, or *roulement*, has been encouraged by the French authorities (although at least part of their justification for this has been, as we saw, that as many national officials as possible should get the opportunity to serve in Brussels).

A proper assessment of the effects of the procedure of *roulement* must be postponed until we have gained some fuller idea of the role of officials in the decision-making process. In fact, the policy according to which the Commission has recruited and employed its staff is so closely involved with its role in the Community system,

THE EUROPEAN CIVIL SERVICE

that the first question leads directly into the second and cannot really be assessed separately. Indeed, the history of the EEC Commission's attempt to found a European Civil Service offers an interesting case study of the environmental pressures on the Commission's organization.

CHAPTER 8

SOME CASES OF DECISION:
(1) THE KENNEDY ROUND
NEGOTIATIONS

The two detailed case studies which are described in this and the next chapter are presented in the form of illustrations of some points we have to make at a general level. They are not particularly *typical* of the work of the Commission, on the contrary there are rather unusual features about both of them; but then it is premature, as we shall suggest later, to regard any particular kind of activity as typical of the Commission's work. In neither case is the Commission found in what is probably so far its most publicized role, namely, that of making proposals to the Council of Ministers for decision on common policies in accordance with the Treaty. The most well-known and most interesting case of this, no doubt, is the formulation and adoption of the common agricultural policy and this has already been studied in detail by other scholars.[1] We chose to avoid any repetition of the already considerable empirical work done on this aspect of the Community. However, our choice was to some extent a positive one and for the following reasons.

First of all, these cases both show the Commission acting in the field of positive integration, first, by carrying on important tariff negotiations on behalf of the Community, and second, by dealing with a particular problem of regional development. Second, they are quite different from each other in a way which provides a contrast we particularly wanted to present. The Kennedy Round negotiations constituted a major issue which occupied the Commission and the Council of Ministers repeatedly at the highest level for almost the whole four years. The regional problem, on the other hand, concerned only one small part of the Commission and prob-

[1] L. Lindberg *The Political Dynamics of European Economic Integration* Stanford, California, 1963, pp. 219–82; *M. Camps What Kind of Europe?* London, 1964, pp. 20–35; M. Camps *European Unification in the Sixties*, London, 1967, passim; L. Lindberg, Decision-making and integration in the European Community, in *International Organisation*, Winter 1965, pp. 60ff.

ably hardly even got to the attention of the ministers of the six countries at all. The first case was of great international interest and affected vital interests in all the member countries of the Community, while the second was probably not heard of at all outside the Community and concerned only two member States directly. Yet the true nature of an institution, we suggest, is to be found by looking at the way it approaches a relatively detailed, minor operation and not just at the way it reacts to major crisis. Moreover, so much stress has been placed on the Commission's tactic of playing off the different national interests against each other as a means of 'upgrading the common interest', that we decided it was important to compare a case of this kind with one where only one or two member States were involved and where the conventional tactics could not be employed.

Besides, there were a number of peculiar features which fascinated us in these two cases. The Commission's conduct of the Kennedy Round negotiations has been widely celebrated as a major advance in European integration and we were interested to discover how the Commission was able to act on behalf of the Community as a whole at a time when in other respects the latter was seriously disunited. Moreover, it is exactly this kind of role which the Commission must perform increasingly if the Community is to move from the customs union stage to that of a full economic union. The regional case, on the other hand, is generally regarded in Community circles as having been a failure on the part of the Commission. We wanted to know what 'failure' meant in this context and we were surprised to find that the Commission had seemingly had little effect on a problem which provides an obvious illustration at a very simple level of why integration is necessary.

The generalizations made in this book about the role of the Commission are not based on these two studies alone, but also on interviews with officials in various parts of the Commission and on extensive scrutiny of published evidence regarding all aspects of the Community's development. However, the two cases studied here in depth do bear out our general findings about the role of the Commission, and also throw considerable doubt on conventional accounts of the decision-making process in the Community.[1] In both cases we shall briefly review the background and history of the

[1] See pp. 78–100 above.

167

problem concerned and then analyse in turn the Commission's role in solving it and the way the Commission itself was organized for this purpose. The aim of analysing the Commission's internal organization is not to suggest in either case that this determined the Commission's role, but we shall argue that the Commission's role and its internal organization were closely related.

The studies are based partly on published documentary sources and partly on interviews with officials of the Commission and with others who were directly involved. In the case of the Kennedy Round, the actual negotiations were, of course, conducted in secret and most of our references to events during the course of them and to the various policies and statements of the different actors involved are based on press reports, (particularly those of *Agence Europe*), and interviews. The subject matter of this case study is extremely technical and we have not attempted in this short study to explain fully all of the complicated, and often tedious, issues involved. When we discuss the internal organization of the Commission, we rely almost entirely on interviews with the officials concerned carried out between September 1967 and June 1968. Naturally the names of none of these officials has been revealed, and although it has been extremely difficult to do so in such a direct account as this, we have attempted as far as possible to conceal the identity of any individual official to whom reference is made.

A BRIEF HISTORY OF THE NEGOTIATIONS

The immediate initiative for the Kennedy Round negotiations came from the United States administration of President Kennedy and formed part of the President's 'Grand Design' for Atlantic partnership. They came, therefore, as a challenge to the Community to support its professed aim to be an outward-looking, liberal enterprise.[1] In this respect they were closely linked, both at the beginning and (as we shall see later) at the end, with the question of British entry to the Community. Indeed, it was when the first British attempt to join the Community ran aground in the early part of 1963 that the Kennedy Round became the main instrument of this sector of United States policy.

This was, therefore, an action of major world political signi-

[1] See pp. 66-9 above.

ficance in which the main roles would be performed by the United States and the Community. It affected more than the conduct of relations *between* these two parties. The US initiative clearly presented the Community with a major test of its *internal* cohesion and of the effectiveness of the type of integration which the Community represented. The Commission itself, and particularly its first President, Walter Hallstein, was a vehement supporter of the idea of Atlantic partnership. On the other hand, General de Gaulle had just embarked on a series of measures, the first being the veto of British membership of the Community, which were to reveal his unabashed hostility to the idea. There was also a challenge to the internal political unity of the United States in that President Kennedy had to find means of carrying with him the isolationist and protectionist elements of American politics, including those in the US Congress. The first step was the passing on October 11, 1962 of the Trade Expansion Act which empowered the President to negotiate reciprocal linear traiff cuts within the framework of GATT (General Agreement on Tariffs and Trade). However, this mandate was to expire in June 1967.

The presence of these highly fissionable political elements meant that the negotiations often hit the world news headlines during the four years of their progress and at times the negotiations seemed bogged down in the sordid diplomatic squabbles typical of negotiations between powerful nation states. However, this tended to conceal the fact that in economic terms the Kennedy Round was probably the most ambitious attempt to liberalize conditions of world trade ever undertaken, certainly under the aegis of GATT. For example, up to this time GATT had largely been concerned with more modest reductions of industrial tariffs, whereas the Kennedy Round aimed at an across-the-board reduction of 50 per cent and was to include agriculture and non-tariff barriers as well.

Given the political difficulties already mentioned, however, even at the start of the negotiations hopes were not particularly high. The target of linear reductions of 50 per cent in industrial tariffs which was spoken of by the leading participants in the beginning was not really expected to achieve in practice cuts of more than about 25 per cent on average.[1] In the specially difficult case of agriculture,

[1] S. D. Metzger, *Trade Agreements and the Kennedy Round*, Coiner Publications, Fairfax, Va., 1964, pp. 103–10.

expectations were equally sober, but most of the leading participants set out with the aim of producing some sort of common solution to the problem of food shortages in the under-developed countries. One author indicated in the early stages of the negotiations that 'success' would indicate some lowering of the Community's common external tariff and a liberalization of agricultural quotas; maintenance of an important share of their existing markets by the British Commonwealth and the members of EFTA (that is, in spite of the formation of the EEC); maintenance of African exports of tropical products to western Europe and of Japanese products to the USA and western Europe.[1]

In fact, the Kennedy Round probably achieved more than this, although most economists believe it is still too early to make a realistic assessment of the results. Agreement was reached on most of the essential issues in the negotiations on May 15, 1967, and the final completing convention was signed on June 30, 1967. The 50 per cent target was achieved in the case of a number of tariff points and the average reduction of industrial tariffs was probably as much as 35 per cent. The Commission itself believed that in most cases the customs tariff of the Community was so much reduced as 'to be no longer capable of acting as a significant obstacle to trade'.[2] The Economist remarked that, 'When the cuts are made the European Common Market will be far more like an enlargement of the relatively free trading Germany of Professor Erhard than it will be like the protectionist France or Italy of pre-Common Market days'.[3] In addition to these reductions in industrial tariffs, agreement was reached on an international code concerning anti-dumping policy. On the other hand, a Community plan for a world agreement on cereals was rejected by the United States, while the GATT partners accepted a greatly watered-down scheme for revising the world reference price of wheat and for providing food aid to the developing countries. Quota and tariff reductions were agreed for a number of other agricultural products but the achievement here can only be described as modest.

The US initiative was first taken up under the auspices of GATT in

[1] S. D. Metzger, *Trade Agreements and the Kennedy Round*, pp. 103 ff.
[2] Tenth General Report on the Activities of the Community, 1967, EEC Commission, para. 313.
[3] *The Economist*, Vol. CCXXIII, p. 813, May 20, 1967.

May of 1963 when preparatory talks were held between the main partners at ministerial level. An immediate dispute arose, mainly between the US and the Community, as to the way the negotiations were to be conducted. The main bone of contention was the question of 'disparities' between the USA and the Community—the name given to cases where the US tariff was much higher than that of the EEC, so that a linear cut would leave the former highly protective whilst rendering the latter ineffective. The United States set out insisting on conducting the negotiations on the basis of a linear reduction of equal percentage across the board. The Community was just as adamant that, while such a linear reduction of tariffs should be the ultimate objective, there should be simultaneous reduction of the disparities between the duties attached to single products. A compromise was reached by May 23rd and the partners agreed to meet again the following year to open the negotiations. Meanwhile a special sub-committee of GATT continued to meet throughout the next twelve months in an attempt to solve the outstanding problems concerning procedure. When the negotiations proper finally opened on May 4, 1964, the basic hypothesis of a multilateral linear reduction of 50 per cent in industrial tariffs was accepted and a series of committees and sub-committees was set up in each main sector including agriculture where the rules of procedure were not yet agreed.

The ensuing negotiations lasted for the next three years. The main landmarks can be illustrated by the following outline of the course of the negotiations:

May 4, 1964	Submission of exceptions lists and agreement on a timetable for the agricultural sector.
May and June 1965	Partners presented their offers on cereals and compared positions.
September 16, 1965	Date for submission of main agricultural offers (including cereals)—not met by the Community.
March–August 1966	Community deposited offers in key industrial sectors and in agriculture, including plan for a world agreement on cereals.

November 1966   Partners other than Community presented warning lists.

January–May 1967   Final stage, negotiation on crucial items.

May 15, 1967   Agreement reached on all main outstanding items.

After some common position had been found on the question of disparities, the next major difficulty was that of agriculture. Here the US administration hoped that liberalization of trade in industrial products would be balanced by some guarantee of US exports to the Community. On this question the administration was hard pressed by farming pressure groups in the United States. On the Community side, however, farming interests were equally adamant that European agriculture should not be sacrificed for the sake of freer Atlantic trade in industrial goods. Moreover, the Community was particularly handicapped in negotiating on the agricultural side by the fact that many aspects of the common agricultural policy had not been agreed by the time of the formal opening of the Kennedy Round. In the summer of 1964 the United States tried to tie progress in the industrial sector with the deposition of offers for the main agricultural products. However, the Community was quite unable to meet this deadline, owing in particular to failure to agree its own internal common cereals price. Eventually the United States agreed to drop their demand and to continue the industrial negotiations in exchange for agreement on a timetable for dealing with agricultural products.

When agricultural negotiations were taken up again in May 1965 the Commission was able to present its own outline plan for a world cereals agreement. From the beginning the main feature of the Commission's position on agriculture had been that any new international agreement should include some form of market discipline, to be provided in this case by binding the levels of support (*montant de soutien*) given by each partner to its farming community. This would be achieved by measuring the difference between a world reference price and the income ensured to the farmer. This difference would be fixed by international agreement and any in-increase in support would have to be re-negotiated on the same basis. This reference price would be revised every three years, according to the Community's plan, on the basis of a general

172

negotiation of conditions in agricultural trade. At this stage, however, the negotiations only took the form of a confrontation of different positions. It was at this time that the French government opened its boycott of Community institutions which lasted from July 1965 round to the following February, and meant that the Community negotiators in Geneva were more or less hamstrung throughout this period. The date for the final deposition of agricultural offers came and went without the Community being represented at the negotiations.

Once the boycott was over, however, the Community was able to take up where it had left off and formally deposited its plan for a world cereals agreement in June 1966. Between this date and the final weeks of the negotiations the issue rested on three main points: first, the level of the self-sufficiency rates (*taux d'auto-approvisionnement*) for exporters and importers which would be agreed as part of the Community's plan; secondly, the level of the new world reference price for wheat; and thirdly, the relative amount of food aid to be contributed by each GATT partner. The United States' demands on the first of these points proved to be too much for her partners (including both the United Kingdom and the Community) and the final settlement was limited to a renewal of the existing agreement on world prices including a slight increase in the world reference price (thus increasing the amount of discipline in world markets) and a programme of food aid of which the Community would contribute 23 per cent and the USA 42 per cent.

In addition to this major problem of cereals, a number of other agricultural products were subjects of particularly heated negotiation between the USA and the Community, for example, poultry, tobacco, fruit and vegetables, and sugar. Moreover, on many such products the Community had to consider not just its position *vis-à-vis* the United States, but also the interests of a number of other countries in the Third World. In some cases concessions were being exchanged on these products right up to the last minute as part of the construction of a final settlement. In about a dozen or so agricultural products the United States challenged the Community right up to the last day of the negotiations to increase its offer. While the United States negotiators were trying to appease politically important producer groups at home, the Community wished to protect similar producers in the six countries, who in some cases were of crucial importance to particular regional economies.

While special rules were insisted upon (particularly by the Community) in almost the whole of the agricultural sector, the negotiations in the industrial sector proceeded generally on a multilateral and linear basis. Here too, however, there were important exceptions: first, in the special treatment of disparities, as we have already seen, and, second, in that each partner was invited to submit an 'exceptions list' of items requiring special treatment on account of their particular economic importance in the importing country. It was feared for a long time that the Community would produce a large exceptions list which might result in a more or less permanent stalling of the negotiations. However, by the time the closing date for submission of exceptions arrived, a formula was found whereby the Community was able to produce a list divided into three parts containing respectively, 'full', 'partial' and 'conditional' exceptions.[1] On this basis, the negotiations were able to proceed.

Another general exception to the overall procedure of linear reductions in tariffs, and one which was fought for resolutely by the Community, was that non-tariff barriers to trade should be considered as part of the negotiations. This led, for example, to discussion of anti-dumping measures. But the crucial issue in this respect was the American Selling Price for chemicals (ASP). On depositing its own exceptions list the Community had announced that it was willing to include chemicals in the linear package only on condition that the United States abolished its system of imposing a special duty (raising the price of the imported chemical up to the American Selling Price) on the sale of imported chemical products in the United States. This practice, which had the equivalent effect of a tariff, was regarded by some as an infringement of the spirit of GATT. In 1966 the United States offered to transform the Selling Price into an equivalent *ad valorem* duty and to apply to this the hypothetical linear reduction of 50 per cent. In the view of the Community, (as well as in that of the United Kingdom and Switzerland), such an offer would still leave a considerable disparity between the relative levels of protection and was not acceptable. Ultimately, on the initiative of the Community a formula was agreed which proved acceptable to all parties and which involved abolition of ASP together with reductions of more than 50 per cent in the Ameri-

[1] For the full exceptions list see *The Economist*, November 21, 1964, p. 897

can tariff on certain items. At this point, however, the United States negotiators revealed that they expected special concessions to be made for the abolition of the ASP apart from those made for the reduction in the tariff on chemicals. They argued that ASP was compatible with the United States' legal obligations under GATT and that consequently its removal should be compensated by some equivalent concession. The Community found this new position (which resulted from pressure from the US Congress) totally unacceptable and the resulting disagreement threatened to upset the whole negotiations right up to the last minute. In the end the Community accepted the American principle of dividing their offer into two parts (*découpage*): a reduction in tariffs and abolition of ASP. In this way the Community, the United Kingdom and Switzerland finally agreed to accept a settlement with the USA whereby the latter's partners would cut their tariffs on chemicals in two stages: the first (of 20 per cent) to take place immediately, and the second (of 30 per cent) to follow the abolition of ASP by the American Congress. Meanwhile the USA would in any case cut their tariff by 50 per cent.

It must be remembered of course that, while the confrontation between the USA and the Community dominated the negotiations, another important set of exchanges took place between the Community and members of EFTA. One particular problem facing the EEC was its relations with the Scandinavian countries and Switzerland. These countries had entered the negotiations with a 50 per cent offer across the board, without exceptions, on the condition that they expected to receive adequate reciprocity. In November of 1966 these, along with a number of other countries, drew up individual assessments of the results of the bilateral contacts they had made so far and came to the conclusion that the Community's reciprocal offers were quite inadequate in a number of respects. Some countries posted 'warning lists' to the Community threatening to withdraw their original offer in certain products unless the Community improved on its current position. From December 1966 onwards the Community seemed to be making a special effort to conciliate the Scandinavians and Switzerland and to elicit their support against the United States. As far as the Swiss were concerned, special arrangements were made for them in the settlement concerning chemicals. In the case of the Scandinavian countries the

175

Community made concessions in various sectors in the final months of the negotiations.

We have dealt only with the main points of difficulty in the negotiations and in particular have neglected the problems raised in connection with under-developed countries and with the negotiation of an agreement on anti-dumping measures, as well as many other aspects of the negotiations. However, our emphasis on relations between the USA and the Community is not entirely misleading. Our account has already revealed that the Community was called upon to take a number of important decisions in the course of these negotiations and that, apart from this, a number of important initiatives came from the Community side. One underlying assumption of this account, and one which now needs to be articulated and explained, is that the Community could be treated for the purposes of the Kennedy Round as one unit.

PREPARATION OF A COMMUNITY POLICY

For a long time it seemed as if the difficulties of the Six in finding a common position would wreck the negotiations completely. Certainly, as we have already seen, the Kennedy Round was not only a challenge to the internal cohesion of the Community on domestic matters; it was part of a concerted challenge to the Community's attitude to third countries. In this latter respect a division between France and the other five member States on policy towards the United States became increasingly evident from 1964 onwards, while the 1963 veto of British membership was already widely interpreted as a foretaste of French hostility to 'Atlantic partnership'. Between the end of 1963 and the spring of 1965 relations between France and her partners in the Community gradually worsened. The French boycott of the Community which began in July 1965, while arising in the immediate context of the Commission's ambitious proposals for financing the common agricultural policy, was simply the climax of a trend which had been developing for some years past.[1] The Kennedy Round was caught up in this political storm, which shook the Community in 1965 and 1966, and which left seemingly permanent damage. French willingness to go through with the negotiations was never certain up to the autumn of 1966.

[1] See Camps, *European Unification in the Sixties*, op. cit., pp. 29-80.

At the same time the Six were divided in their economic interest in the Kennedy Round. The Germans sought major gains in freer Atlantic trade on the industrial side and at an early stage suggested that agriculture might well be left out of the negotiations altogether. The French reckoned on having far less to gain in industrial terms and saw the negotiations primarily as a political means of resisting the pretensions of the United States. In so far as they sought any positive results from the negotiations, they were to subject the Americans to greater discipline in agricultural trade and to use the need for a common position on agriculture in the Kennedy Round as a lever to force the Germans to accept the Community's own common agricultural policy.

The Commission was in principle and officially wholeheartedly in favour of the negotiations. President Hallstein had paid a number of visits to the USA in 1962 and 1963 and these were thought to have been aimed at giving President Kennedy positive encouragement in his initiative. However, the Commission's stand was also determined by the need to preserve the unity of the Community and to show itself capable of protecting the member countries' essential interests. Very early on, the Commission took its stand on three basic principles. The first of these was that disparities should be given special consideration and should be negotiated on the basis of generally accepted and automatically applicable rules. The second was that non-tariff barriers should be included in the negotiations as well as tariffs. And the third was that any settlement on agriculture should, as far as possible, take the form of world agreements involving some measure of market discipline. In this respect the Commission shared the attitude of the French government and it shared also the desire of the French to tie progress in the Kennedy Round with the adoption of the common agricultural policy, although it was far less dogmatic than the French Government on the need to proceed with agricultural negotiations step by step with negotiations on the industrial side. In addition, the Commission reacted favourably to overtures from the countries concerned that the Community should be prepared to give special consideration to other western European countries (generally, the members of EFTA).

These principles formed part of the recommendation which the Commission made to the Council of Ministers in December 1963 for a mandate to open the negotiations in accordance with Article 111 of the Treaty of Rome.[1] The mandate finally adopted by the Council differed little from the Commission's draft and it has even been said that the final negotiating position of the Community in 1967 was very similar to this original mandate of 1963. This might be construed as evidence that the Commission had great influence in the decision making process of the Community in this case, but it must be remembered that the draft mandate was drawn up after consideration of the different national points of view and that in any event it was only a very general document, while the main political crises which were to arise concerned relatively detailed matters. Up to the middle of 1966, moreover, the Commission was given very little discretion with which to negotiate. Progress was often halted while the Commission waited for necessary renewal or re-interpretation of its mandate from the Council of Ministers. In the earlier stages not all the member States were entirely willing to be represented by the Commission and some made direct approaches of their own to the other GATT partners.[2]

Article 111 of the Rome Treaty lays down that the Commission shall be assisted in conducting negotiations on the basis of the common customs tariff by a special Committee appointed by the Council for this purpose. This Committee, known in Community jargon as the 'Article 111 Committee', was consulted regularly by the Commission throughout the negotiations. Its role was to inform the Commission of national positions on different points and to assist it in interpreting its mandate from the Council. The Committee consists of senior civil servants from the six member countries, mainly the heads of the economic and finance ministries or their deputies. For most working purposes, however, the Committee is split up into sub-committees of more junior officials and experts which meet on a regular basis. The Committee is not empowered to take any formal, binding decisions, which can be taken only by the Council of Ministers (after discussion in the Committee of

[1] Article 111, 2 of the Treaty of Rome states: 'The Commission presents to the Council recommendations with a view to tariff negotiations with third countries on the common customs tariff. The Council authorises the Commission to open the negotiations. The Commission conducts these negotiations in consultation with a special Committee appointed by the Council to assist it in this task, and in the framework of directives which the Council may address to it'.

[2] See the report in *Agence Europe Presse*, May 8, 1964.

Permanent Representatives). There is some evidence that up to the end of 1966 little power was delegated to this Article 111 Committee and little advantage was taken of its existence to give the Commission wider discretion in negotiating on behalf of the Community.

The European Parliament is not given any official part in negotiations under Article 111 and, since international negotiations of this type are in any event generally conducted in secret, the role of the Parliament was necessarily limited. The External Trade Committee of the Parliament did, however, report on the Commission's original mandate in December 1963 (approving its main principles) and from March 1964 onwards followed the negotiations closely. The Commission negotiators, as well as a number of officials concerned with preparing the Commission's policy in Brussels, appeared before the Committee in secret session. In January 1964 the Parliament debated the External Trade Committee's report on the Commission's mandate and was addressed by M. Jean Rey, the member of the Commission chiefly responsible for the conduct of the negotiations. M. Rey stressed the need for secrecy in the course of the negotiations and pointed out that it would be impossible to hold public debates before the Parliament in the course of them, a point which the Parliament accepted and which the External Trade Committee had already mentioned itself.[1] The Kennedy Round was often a subject of general speeches during the annual *colloques* of the Community institutions and during debates on the Commission's general reports.

There were, however, few full debates in the course of the negotiations and the subject raised no Questions to members of the Commission. In May 1965 the Parliament's Agricultural Committee was authorized to conduct an inquiry into the Commission's mandate for the agricultural side of the negotiations. The Committee reported in June 1966 and three resolutions were passed, mainly in support of the Commission's policy, following a full-scale debate.[2] The plan for a world cereals agreement was the subject of another debate in November 1966, and then in March 1967 the Parliament debated and passed two resolutions on the final stage of the negotiations.[3]

[1] *Parlement Européen: Débats*, 20–24 January 1964, and Doc. 119 (63–4).
[2] *ibid.*, June 27–July 1, 1966, and Doc. 89 (66–7).
[3] *ibid.*

179

During the preparatory stage of the negotiations the Commission was concerned with formulating a general policy on the Community's approach to the negotiations and was concerned, within the Community as well as in Geneva, with the difficult question of finding a common position on disparities. The first major task which the Commission faced after the official opening of the negotiations was, as we have seen, the production of a Community exceptions list. The Commission's own aim here was to fit the exceptions requested by member States into the pattern of an overall industrial policy for the Community. This was no small endeavour given that the Community did not possess an industrial policy, or even at this time any common economic policy to speak of.[1]

In conjunction with national officials and experts a list of eighteen criteria was drawn up (based on such variables as trade flows between the United States and the Community, the size of undertakings in different industries, and so on) against which different 'candidates' for exception were tested. Lists of potential exceptions had been received for this purpose from representatives of industry in the six countries towards the end of May. These representatives were approached through their organizations in Brussels at a Community level and the Commission refused, in accordance with its general policy for consultation with interest groups, to approach them on a national basis.[2] Formal consultation with national officials and experts through the Article 111 Committee came only after the industrialists' own draft exceptions were received. The Commission maintained close contact with the representatives of industry (through their associations in Brussels) during the whole period of preparing the exceptions list and continued to do so throughout the whole negotiations.

Work on the Community exceptions list continued up to the final date for deposition of lists in Geneva, on November 16, 1964. After receiving the views of the representatives and the Article 111 Committee the Commission drew up a draft list which it then submitted to the Article 111 Committee again, and together these bodies tried to reduce its length according to the eighteen criteria already mentioned. Finally a revised list was submitted to the

[1] See further below pp. 301–7.
[2] See Lindberg op. cit., p. 71. The approach took the form of a questionnaire sent out to individual trade associations through the Community-level secretariats.

Committee of Permanent Representatives for approval by the Council of Ministers. In the course of these months the Commission worked according to two immediate objectives, both tied to its ultimate goals of making the negotiations succeed while preserving internal unity within the Community. First, it had to keep the Community's exceptions list down to a reasonable size (so as not to prompt reprisals from the Community's partners in GATT), while at the same time taking account of demands from within the Community for future industrial development. Secondly, the US negotiators in Geneva were insisting that progress on the industrial side of the Kennedy Round should not get out of step with agreement on measures to liberalize trade in agriculture. Thus, before the Community would be able to make any progress with negotiating its exceptions, it would have to reach internal agreement on its own common agricultural policy, or else risk losing the Community's aims on the agricultural side of the negotiations.

At the same time, of course, the Commission hoped to use the industrial advantages to be gained from the Kennedy Round as a bait to those members of the Community who were proving reluctant to make progress with the common agricultural policy. In this latter respect the Commission's position was the same as that of the French Government and it has been suggested that this kind of alliance with the French has always been an important tactic on the part of the Commission for achieving Community objectives. The French are encouraged to feel that the only way their own national objectives can be achieved is by accepting some form of Community solution.[1] Retrospectively, it seems that this is what happened in the summer and autumn of 1964. At first the French Government showed general dissatisfaction with the way the Community exceptions list was being prepared and at one stage was said to be insisting on submitting a separate list of its own. It was being widely predicted in the early autumn that, owing to the pressure of industrial interests in various parts of the Community (particularly in Italy), the Commission was going to submit an extremely long exceptions list which would threaten to undermine the spirit of the negotiations or, worse still perhaps, that it would fail altogether to present its list in time.[2] The Council of Ministers

[1] See Lindberg, *op. cit.*, p. 280.
[2] See, for example, *The Economist*, October 31, 1964, p. 522

181

discussed the Kennedy Round at almost every meeting throughout the summer and autumn months and finally sat up until 7.30 a.m. on the morning of November 16 to agree in a 'marathon' session to a Community exceptions list which was widely regarded as being much shorter than anyone had dared to hope and which constituted only 10 per cent of the Community's total imports. As the Commission itself commented later:

'The Community's list was reduced to a bare minimum; the exceptions it contains are . . . not simply an aggregate of the requests made by the individual member States but compare fairly closely with the list, based on Community considerations, which the Commission originally drew up after consulting the relevant trade circles and government departments.'[1]

The Commission's first immediate objective had been attained, but only, it must be pointed out, by a mixture of improvisation, good luck and its own determination and negotiating skill. First of all, a formula was found for presenting the exceptions list in such a way as to take into account the anxieties of some governments and producers, while leaving the final total of exceptions dependent upon the future course of the negotiations in GATT—a typical Community tactic of postponing (but not cancelling) difficult decisions. This was the formula (already mentioned) for dividing the list into three parts: 'full', 'partial', and 'conditional' exceptions. Secondly, the French representatives in the Community, much to everyone's surprise, dropped all threats to present a separate national list. This action was no doubt chiefly motivated by the realization that, once a Community exceptions list was deposited at Geneva, the only remaining obstacle from the Community's point of view to progress of the Kennedy Round would be German resistance to deciding on a common cereals price, upon which rested the whole future of the Community's common agricultural policy.[2] Finally, the US negotiators had in the last resort dropped their insistence that a decision on the ground rules for agriculture should be made at the same time as the exceptions lists were deposited, and had agreed instead to a settlement on a revised timetable for dealing with the agricultural side of the negotiations.

[1] *Eighth General Report on the Activities of the Communities*, 1966, EEC Commission, Sec. 275.
[2] See Camps, *European Unification in the Sixties*, p. 21.

In other words, the Commission had failed in its second immediate objective and the Community had no proposals to make for progressing with the agricultural sector of the negotiations. In fact, the Commission had had enormous difficulty in trying to get the member States to agree to enough of the common agricultural policy to enable the Community to agree a position on the Kennedy Round, and during the summer of 1964 had drawn on virtually all of the sanctions available to it without success. On June 1st and 2nd the Council of Ministers had yet again postponed their decision on the common cereals price and on June 4th President Hallstein had written to the heads of Government of the six countries warning them of the likely consequences of failure to agree this matter for progress in the Kennedy Round. At the same time M. Rey published an article in a leading Belgian newspaper pointing out the danger facing the Community and saying that failure to show a united front in the Kennedy Round might put back the Community's efforts towards further integration disastrously.[1] The Council again failed to take the necessary decisions for proceeding with the agricultural side of the Kennedy Round at its next round of meetings between July 28th and 30th. Eventually, when work resumed in Geneva in the autumn, the Commission was pressing the Council to agree to proceed with discussion of tariff items in the agricultural side of the negotiations (which was what really interested the Americans) and to leave aside until later that of commodity agreements (on cereals, for example). This met with strong French opposition and led to further bitter attacks on the Commission's conduct of the negotiations.[2] Thus, while the Commission was able to reach one of its immediate objectives (depositing a common exceptions list on time) it had to sacrifice another (equal progress on the agricultural side). This objective had ceased to be so important for the negotiations as a whole, however, when the Americans dropped their insistence on applying the deadline of November 16th to the agricultural sector. But it is a useful illustration of some of the weaknesses of the decision-making process in the Community. In actual fact, the Commission was still able to use the Kennedy Round as a means of getting the Germans to agree to a common cereals price and the Council of Ministers reached this decision in

---

[1] *Agence Europe*, June 4, 1964.
[2] *The Economist*, October 31, 1964, *loc. cit.*

a later 'marathon' in December 1964. Progress on the agricultural side of the Kennedy Round had, on the other hand, been seriously retarded.

Having at last settled the prior questions regarding the Community's own agricultural policy, the Commission was able to turn its attention to presenting a Community position in the agricultural sector of the Kennedy Round, in order to be ready for the new Geneva deadline of May 17, 1965. In the most important case, that of cereals, the Commission had drawn up a fairly elaborate plan for a world agreement, produced largely under the personal inspiration of M. Mansholt and to which he was individually strongly committed. As we have seen, the essence of this plan was the binding of support levels to an agreed world reference price for a period of at least three years. The main motivation behind this scheme was a desire to tie progress on the Kennedy Round directly to progress on the Community's own common agricultural policy (Commissioner Mansholt's main interest). The fundamental principles of this plan had been approved by the Council of Ministers in its first mandate to the Commission in December 1963, and the latter now argued that there was no need for the ministers to decide again. The member States thought differently, however, and the plan was discussed hotly at a series of Council meetings in April and May 1965. The French members of the Council were said to be holding out yet again against any concessions to the United States and to be insisting in particular that the Americans should be forced to accept an increase in the world price of wheat and that no guarantees should be given to the USA regarding access to the Community market for agricultural products.[1] The Germans were in no position to argue for a more flexible negotiating position, having forced their fellow members of the Community to accept a high cereals price in December.

On April 5th the Commission submitted its plan for a world cereals agreement to the Article 111 Committee for consideration before the meeting of the six ministers on April 8th. The Council eventually refused to reach any agreement, even though the Commission's plan raised nothing new in principle, on the grounds that there had been insufficient time for the national delegations to consider it and that there was lack of clarity on a number of specific

[1] *Agence Europe*, April 26, 1965.

184

points.[1] The issue was postponed until the next round of Council meetings in May. The differences between the various national positions became clearer in the course of discussions between the Commission and the Article 111 Committee, which now followed up until May 8th. At the end of this round of meetings, however, agreement was reached only on certain broad questions of principle: that the aims of the Community were to balance world supply and demand while establishing 'equitable and remunerative' prices and expanding world trade; that the world agreement should include coarse grains; that the basis of the agreement should be a fixing of support levels as originally suggested by the Commission. A number of vital questions were left unresolved: the means of dealing with surpluses and with low-income countries, the proposed level of the world reference price, and the method of calculating levels of support, as well as the whole question of guaranteed access. All that the discussions in the Article 111 Committee seem to have contributed was discussion of certain technical and detailed matters—how to define a 'surplus', how to calculate farmers' remuneration, how to classify different types of agricultural undertaking, and so on.[2] On May 13th the Council of Ministers met in what was described as a mood of 'great anxiety' to reach an agreement and for what was expected to be another 'marathon' session.[3]

The directive given to the Commission as a result of this meeting was described as being 'much more nebulous' even than the Commission's original proposal, and was said to be extremely cautiously worded: enough to give the Commission an opening negotiating position, but no more. On the question of surpluses all the national delegations had opposed the Commission's proposals and what was proposed instead was finding some agreement on aid to low-income countries in the form of grain. On the world reference price the Commission had taken up a position closer to that of the French seemingly in an attempt 'to split the difference' between the present world price and one which would be very much higher. *Agence Europe* commented that the Council had reached agreement only by not taking on the 'trickiest problems'. It was clear, however, that the Commission was willing to make some concessions on its

1 *Agence Europe*, April 9, 1965.
2 *ibid.*, April 26, 1965, May 13 and 14, 1965.
3 *ibid.*

original draft plan in return for firm acceptance of the basic principle of negotiating on the basis of support levels. It was in this way that it sought to 'upgrade the common interest'.[1] At any rate final approval of the plan would have to await a decision on the financing of the Community's common agricultural policy, which was not due to be taken until June 30th. This in itself, as is now well known, proved to be a cause of great disunity among the Six. In fact, the member States failed to reach agreement by the time agreed with the result that the French Government proceeded to boycott the Community institutions until the following February. As a result of this the negotiations in Geneva were brought virtually to a standstill. However, representatives of the Commission still attended the committees and sub-committees of GATT and technical work was carried on, particularly on such questions as disparities, exceptions lists and non-tariff barriers. It was not until business returned more or less to normal in the Community, (in March), that the Council of Ministers took up again the question of the plan for cereals.

Between 1963 and the spring of 1965 progress in the Kennedy Round had been directly related to the adoption of the Community's common agricultural policy and these two issues together tended to dominate Community politics during this time. The French (like the Commission) saw the Kennedy Round as an incentive to the Germans to agree to a common agricultural policy, which would contain a lower Community price for cereals than that which then prevailed in Germany itself and which would necessitate a substantial German cash contribution towards the cost of supporting European agriculture. Actually, it was felt that the French saw the adoption of such a policy as their sole remaining interest in the Community. In so far as this was true, the Kennedy Round was for them essentially a means to an end. By the spring of 1965, however, this order of priorities had changed somewhat, for the common cereals price had by then been agreed. The main political issue within the Community now concerned the permanent arrangements for financing the agricultural policy and how far these should be accompanied by some move towards independent Community finance with European Parliamentary control. The French and the other Five parted ways on this issue in the spring and summer of

---

[1] This can be compared with the Commission's role in a number of earlier decisions, see Lindberg, *Political Dynamics*, *op. cit.*, pp. 167–282.

1965 and eventually reached deadlock. At the same time, it is said that the Gaullist regime in France had come to the conclusion that the Community no longer served the true interests of France following signs that relations between the United States and Germany in the defence field were becoming increasingly close and intimate.

Whatever the reasons for the French decision to stop boycotting the Community in January 1966, it is clear that the Kennedy Round did not play a major part in the settlement of the 1965–66 crisis. New provisional arrangements for financing the agricultural policy were agreed and the question of institutional reforms indefinitely postponed. Moreover, the proposal for a MLF, German support for which had so worried the French in the previous year, had now been dropped. It was clear that the French still intended to ensure that the Americans did not have an easy time in the Kennedy Round, and in particular that protection for European wheat producers was ensured in the form of a higher world reference price and a self-sufficiency ratio. However, the negotiations had ceased to have real value as a bargaining counter within the Community and it was fairly clear from this time on that a French veto of the Kennedy Round was no longer a major threat. The atmosphere within the Community had now improved in contrast with the air of crisis of the previous year and the Commission's proposal for a new directive on cereals was accepted by the Council with little or no amendment.[1] The Commission deposited a revised and more detailed plan as the Community's official offer in Geneva on June 18th. This included proposals for a world reference price for wheat $2 or $3 above the existing Canadian price, for an agreement on a self-sufficiency ratio for net importers of 90 per cent, (limiting US exports to the Community), and for tying to this self-sufficiency ratio an arrangement for food aid.[2]

At the same time, the Council gave the Commission the directives it had requested to enable it to negotiate on the rest of the agricultural sector, as well as on a number of key industrial products. The Council also agreed to reduce the list of disparities which the Commission had originally drawn up. The main reason for this

[1] *Agence Europe*, April 4 and 5, 1966.
[2] See *Parlement Européen: Débats*, June 28, 1966. Speech by President of the Council of Ministers.

progress was clearly that the French were in a much more conciliatory mood than they had been in the previous year and that their attitude of almost outright obstruction to the negotiations had now been replaced by one of reserved co-operation. At this stage, however, the Community was merely defining its negotiating position in a number of key areas and the negotiations themselves were still at least a year behind schedule. By the end of the summer there was fairly general agreement on the principles of the Community's position in the main sectors and a general feeling in official circles within the Community that any gap between its own position and that of the USA was not the Community's fault.

The Commission had thus succeeded in getting the Community into a state of more or less serious preparation for the main brunt of the negotiations which was about to come. At the same time it had been able to use the Kennedy Round as a counter in the general bargaining process within the Community to reach agreement on the common agricultural policy. These objectives had been reached by means of the now conventional decision-making process of the Community, which seems to involve moving from crisis to crisis by means of a series of package deals and by agreeing to postpone awkward decisions until a time when the atmosphere might be more favourable. The Commission had clearly had to take important initiatives as well as to play an important mediating role, and this case study bears out the findings of other research that the role of the Commission depends as much on its independence and commitment as on its skill as a mediator. Clearly the Commission's role is much more than that of an administrative organization or bureaucracy. It is expected to adhere to certain values and certain goals of its own, which it defends against the different separatist, national positions. It is called upon for 'critical', incentive decision-making; it is faced with a constantly changing situation, and must innovate in order to survive; it must also be highly flexible and skilled at improvization. The Commissioners themselves act like popular leaders, addressing themselves to the European Parliament and to the public in order to defend their policies, and calling upon members of the national governments as their equals exhorting them to bear the common interest in mind.[1]

[1] See pp. 78–87 above; Lindberg, *op. cit.*, pp. 248–86; Camps, *What Kind of Europe?*, pp. 35–47

However, there is another side to the Commission's role. In many ways it is very like that of an administrative organization or bureaucracy in that the Commission's leaders only too clearly lack effective means to impose their own view of the common interest. Final decisions on general policy rest with the Council of Ministers and in this way the Commission depends on the whims of the member States. In the last resort it generally gets the Council to agree to a solution which replaces the six national policies with a Community policy administered largely by Community institutions. This is usually only after severe delays and it often costs the Commission many of its own specific objectives. Indeed, the Commission invariably seems to fall back on a rather vague, long-term sense of the common interest, according to which *some* Community decision is regarded as better then none at all. Even then, this common interest wins only because the vague and distant goals it represents are made to seem compatible with the immediate, short-term interests of the member States.

In this respect too much emphasis should not be placed on the Commission's ability to deal directly with interest groups. The fact that the Commission can approach such groups directly is clearly of vital importance. The information such groups have is not available elsewhere, and helps the Commission to develop a distinctive policy of its own. It is unlikely, however, that the support even of Community-level representatives of trade associations is of very much use as a sanction against member governments. Interest groups, as we said in an earlier chapter, tend to act within the norms set down by governments, and their rise in the modern industrialized state can be directly and functionally related to the increasingly bureaucratic emphasis of modern government.[1] Indeed, our own research revealed considerable scepticism on the part of many Commission officials concerned with the drawing up of a Community exceptions list in the Kennedy Round negotiations as to the value of interest groups as means of influencing the national governments. Invariably, it was felt, national trade associations were as divided as the member governments themselves, and, even though they were approached before the Commission consulted with government representatives, they had already been in close liaison

[1] See J. P. Nettl, *Political Mobilisation*, Faber and Faber, London 1967, pp. 331 ff.

with national government departments and the two tended to share the same position.

It is also noticeable that the whole decision-making process in the Community seems to reveal bureaucratic traits and perhaps this is a direct consequence of the lack of any really autonomous political leadership at a Community level. The Commission's dependence on the agreement of member States and its important role as mediator among them force it to rely greatly on such intermediary and preparatory bodies as the Article 111 Committee. Such devices are clearly essential to provide the Commission with technical advice, to prevent the meetings of the Council becoming completely bogged down and to enable the Commission to frame proposals which have some chance of being accepted by the member States. However, the decision-making process is in danger of becoming over-burdened with intermediary bodies which tend to create new arguments about scope and jurisdiction, and to give member States who wish to hold up ob block the decision-making process every opportunity to use procedural questions of this kind to do so. It could be that the Council of Ministers' refusal to act on 'unprepared' material in April 1965 was an example of this.

Indeed, bodies like the Article 111 Committee can often thwart the decision-making process in two quite different ways. First, they can 'sit on' material, (either at their own or at some superior body's insistence), which they themselves have no competence to decide in view of their technical and administrative composition. In other words, crucial decisions can get 'bottlenecked' in official channels and treated (or maltreated) as technical details. The Commission is thus constantly in danger of getting itself and its proposals reduced to an administrative level. On the other hand, similar effects can be obtained from a lack of delegation in that the process becomes equally jammed when ministers are forced to deal with excessive detail. This results when preparatory bodies 'pass the buck' and refuse to settle the technical issues before them claiming that these are too 'political'. These defects are both symptoms of the same condition, namely, an absence of really effective political authority at a Community level. The slow and cumbersome nature of the decision-making process in the spring of 1965 can be criticized in terms of either of these defects. Indeed, our research suggests that at various times throughout the Kennedy Round, the decision-

190

making process did not work smoothly, and was inefficient in terms of time and manpower employed. Apparently on one not uncommon occasion the economic and finance ministers of the Six even sat into the early hours thrashing out their respective national positions on the tariff on ladies' underwear—item by item! At other times, discussion in the Article 111 Committee might be completely halted due to the failure of a national delegation to prepare its own position. Clearly, it is the task of the Commission to ensure that such administrative difficulties do not hold up the progress of decision-making, and to insist that a clear distinction is maintained in practice between policy and administration. Such a task, however, calls for more authority than the Commission seems to have on these occasions. Each member State seems to retain an equal right to determine what is and what is not a question of policy and the only real sanctions are the fear of gaining the hostility of its partners or of undermining the vague, distant goals of the common interest. The Commission can only point out the dangers of continued obstruction and of having no decision at all. As we saw in a previous chapter, the ability to insist upon a clear and authoritative distinction between critical and routine decisions is a characteristic belonging essentially to a political leadership.[1]

In fact, it became increasingly clear during the late summer and autumn of 1966 that, in order to participate effectively in the key final stage of the Kennedy Round negotiations, the Community would have to find some alternative method of operating to the one just outlined. The fact that the Community succeeded in so doing made its role in the Kennedy Round one of the most celebrated events of recent years in the eyes of committed Europeans and was also one of the main reasons for the relative success of the negotiations as a whole.

THE COMMISSION AS NEGOTIATOR

By the autumn of 1966 bilateral contacts were still taking place between the main GATT partners in an attempt to settle their respective positions and to narrow down the areas of difference which remained. At its meeting on December 7th the Council of Ministers received a report from the Commission on the results of bilateral contacts made so far and particularly on the question of the

---

[1] See pp. 110–18 above.

warning lists posted by certain of the Community's opposite numbers in Geneva. This report was largely descriptive and avoided
making any firm recommendations. The Council was unable to
deal with the Commission's report at this meeting but did reach
agreement on some outstanding questions where the Commission
was still waiting to make progress in Geneva.[1] At the Council's
next meeting on December 22nd there was a major confrontation
of different national points of view on the Commission's report. The
French Foreign Minister argued that the Community should not
have an 'inferiority complex' about its offers in Geneva, since these
were perfectly satisfactory, and that the Commission should not
make any unwarranted concessions. The Germans pressed for a
much 'softer' position and stressed that they were owed the exporting
advantages to be gained from a successful conclusion of the negotiations in return for their earlier preparedness to support the Community's common agricultural policy. They also argued in favour of
making concessions to the Nordic countries, but the concessions they
suggested were not widely supported by the other delegations, who
had less to gain on this side.[2]

At the next meeting of the Council on January 12th, the French
raised the question of disparities and non-tariff barriers and suggested that any further concessions in these areas should be made
conditional upon the withdrawal of warning lists by the other
GATT partners. The Germans retaliated by arguing that the Community should continue to reduce the list of disparity reductions
demanded of the Americans, as an encouragement to the other
partners to withdraw their warning lists. At the same time they
argued, as they had at previous sessions of the Council, that the
Commission should be given a much freer hand in the negotiations.
As a result of this three-hour meeting a compromise was achieved
largely as a result of the intervention of M. Rey on behalf of the
Commission. In the end a decision was taken not to give the Commission a new general mandate (which might have raised serious
disagreements) but to regard the mandate of 1963 as still expressing
the Community's basic objectives.[3]

On this basis the Commission was instructed to go ahead with

1 *Agence Europe*, December 7, 1966.
2 *ibid.*, December 22, 1966.
3 *ibid.*, January 13, 1966.

the negotiations and use its discretion, but only on certain clearly understood conditions. The first of these was that any solution explored by the Commission's team of negotiators would be submitted to the Council for final decision and no final commitment would be undertaken until a general agreement had been reached in the negotiations as a whole. The second was that the Commission would keep the Article 111 Committee informed of its activities and would report to it regularly. Thirdly, the Commission was enjoined to respect the general mandate given to it in December 1963 along with the other directives made by the Council from time to time since then. Thus, though the functions of negotiating and formally deciding the Community's position were still separated, the Commission was given much more room for manœuvre than it had enjoyed previously.

It would not be true to say that from now on all was plain sailing. The Council found it necessary to discuss the Kennedy Round at virtually every session between January and May and division between its members was still apparent. The Commission got the Council to agree on the deadline fixed for the final agreement in Geneva of April 30th, but this eventually had to be put back to May 15th. Up to the end of April it certainly seemed as if the negotiations between the USA and the Community were going to run aground on most of the outstanding issues. However, the fact remains that the Community's negotiators were given sufficient discretion to play an effective part in the final weeks of vital, nerve-racking, all-night meetings in Geneva, juggling with key details of the different offers.

It is difficult to fix a specific date, some people say it was from November 1966 and some from the time of the Council's conditional 'free rein' of January 12th, but it is clear that in the final stage of the negotiations the Commission's team of negotiators was able to take up a position in response to the situation in Geneva rather than looking over its shoulders to what was happening in the Council of Ministers in Brussels. To many observers the Commission team seemed to be acting in a more responsible and consistent manner than some of the national delegations at Geneva, particularly that of the USA. The US negotiators not only took constant trips back and forth to Washington for renewed instructions, but the composition of the negotiating team had to be continually changed in response to changes of political winds at home.[1] At the end of the negotiations M. Faure, then the French Minister of Agriculture, was reported to have remarked that 'M. Rey is able to negotiate as if he were the representative of a single state'.[2] In addition, the atmosphere of meetings of the Council of Ministers during May was one of unanimous support, and even encouragement, for the Commission and most discussions on the Kennedy Round could be kept very short. In spite of the fact that some vital national economic interests were at stake, the Commission was able to take considerable initiatives and to make no small headway towards a final settlement. Its position in many cases was certainly more flexible than that of the United States. On a number of points the Commission's initiatives did not in the end prove acceptable to the Council of Ministers, but the Commission was still able in the last resort to produce a formula which reconciled the combined interests of the Community with the minimum demands of its opposite numbers in Geneva. Indeed, it is firmly believed in Community circles that M. Rey was personally responsible for rescuing the negotiations in the last few weeks, in that he was in a position to place a coherent final offer on the table to form the basis of the very last package settlement.

On April 25th M. Rey came back from Geneva and addressed the Committee of Permanent Representatives in Brussels who were about to prepare for the next and crucial meeting of the Council of Ministers on May 2nd and 3rd. A few days later the Commission's team of negotiators issued a communiqué in Geneva expressing their 'surprise . . . over comments on the present state of the Kennedy Round. . . . This delegation is in constant contact with the Commission and the Council and rumours of Geneva-Brussels disagreement are unfounded'. On May 2nd the Council expressed its 'unanimous support' for the Commission 'for the manner in which it has conducted the negotiations'.[3]

The Commission's team in Geneva now proceeded to take a series of important initiatives. First, they hinted that on certain

[1] It could be said in defence of the US negotiators that domestic support for the Trade Expansion Act might well have declined as a direct result of the EEC's earlier prevarication.
[2] *Opera Mundi Europe*, May 18, 1967, p. 6.
[3] *Agence Europe*, May 2, 1967.

194

conditions the Community might be willing to accept the principle of *découpage* (that is, a settlement in two parts) in the chemical sector. Secondly, they offered to reduce the Community's proposed self-sufficiency ratio for cereals. This was more than the Six (and particularly the French Government) had been initially prepared to accept and M. Rey had to telephone in the middle of the night directly to the Foreign Ministers in their respective capitals to sound them on the subject. Thirdly, concessions were offered to each of the Scandinavian countries. Finally, the Commission suggested tentatively that *ad valorem* duties on tobacco might be reduced along with import levies, if the agreement of Greece could be obtained.[1] On May 10th the Council approved practically all of these steps, in spite of certain reservations on the part of some national delegations, and in its press communiqué of May 11th reported: 'After a thorough examination of the main problems concerning the multilateral trade negotiations in Geneva the Council expressed its entire confidence in the Commission and gave it a certain number of instructions so as to conclude the negotiations.'[2]

On May 15th M. Rey had to consult Brussels by telephone in order to exceed his mandate by increasing the amount of food aid to be contributed by the Community from 3 or 3.5 (as previously agreed) to 4.5 million tons as part of the final package deal drawn up by the GATT secretariat. At the same time he went 1 per cent below the minimum set by the Council on the *ad valorem* duty on tobacco, and 15 per cent below the minimum agreed by the Council on the cigarette duty, as well as making a number of concessions on other minor, but particularly sensitive agricultural products.[3] On May 18th M. Rey received the Permanent Representatives in Brussels to explain why he had had to exceed his mandate and this meeting broke up in a spirit of unanimous congratulations to the Commission for the way it had successfully brought the negotiations to an end. The French delegation did not complain that the Commission had had to ignore their earlier insistence that the Community's contribution to food aid should be in the form of produce rather than of cash, although the Italians did ask for special con-

---

[1] *Agence Europe*, May 11, 1967.
[2] *ibid.*, May 15, 1967.
[3] *ibid.*

sideration to be given to them in future in view of the sacrifices they had had to make in a number of agricultural items.[1]

We must now ask what were the reasons for the Commission's ability to take on this successful role as a representative of the Community as a whole. First of all, it is clear that the representatives of the Commission involved had to show a considerable measure of political leadership, as well as the technical facility and negotiating skill which can normally be expected of them in any case. They had to establish certain clear priorities in conducting the negotiations and yet, at the same time, to be relatively uninhibited in shifting their ground in Geneva when this proved necessary to settle the negotiations. In this respect there was an important second condition for the Commission's success, which was the formulation of distinct Commission policies on most of the issues concerned in the negotiations. If the Commission had had to depend entirely on the member States for the positions it took up in Geneva it would have been impossible for it to take initiatives or to juggle with its detailed offers in the way it did. The fact was, however, that all the major aspects of the Community's position resulted from Commission drafts in the first instance. The different sections of the Commission concerned with advising the team of negotiators were thus particularly well-versed in that the policies at stake were their own. This was clearly of vital importance to the Commission in these final months of negotiation and is something which marked it off from an ordinary international secretariat and made it far more like one of the national governments with which it was negotiating.

However, a number of the circumstances of this case were fortuitous for the Commission and very probably extraordinary as well. First, as we have already seen, from 1966 onwards the French can have had little or nothing to gain in terms of Community policies by threatening to veto the Kennedy Round negotiations. It may even be the case that the French gambled on the hunch that if they conceded the Kennedy Round to the other five they themselves might be put in a stronger position to resist any new moves for British entry to the Community. In any event the French probably no longer had much to lose from the Kennedy Round from the beginning of 1966 onwards, having concentrated their efforts (successfully in many ways) on wrecking the alternative aspects of

[1] *Agence Europe*, Map 18, 1967.

the 'Grand Design' such as the MLF and even NATO itself. At the same time they and the Italians had in fact succeeded in getting the Commission to wrest a number of concessions from the Americans on agriculture which resulted, if anything, in a higher level of protection than had prevailed before.

Second, there was great pressure from outside to conclude the negotiations by the end of May. Any postponement beyond this date would have made it impossible to reach an agreement before the Trade Expansion Act expired. Thus, if the negotiations were to be saved at all, the Community had to give the Commission enough discretion to make headway before the spring of 1966. Again, it must be remembered that the initiative for the negotiations came from outside the Community (although the role of President Hallstein in encouraging President Kennedy's initiative must not be overlooked). It involved directly a number of political forces extraneous to the Community and this frequently enabled the Commission to present the Council of Ministers with a *pis aller*, given the need to work within the demands of third countries. It is indeed quite normal for the negotiators in an international undertaking of this type to exercise a wide measure of discretion. (The important role of the British representative in Geneva at the same time, Sir Richard Powell, has been commented upon in the same way in this country.)

Finally, perhaps, it can be said in qualifying excitement about the Commission's role in the Kennedy Round that these negotiations concerned the very matters on which the Community had so far reached agreement—namely, trade. It was in this sphere that the Treaty had been most precise and progress within the Community most advanced. On the other hand, removing barriers to trade within the Community and even agreeing on a common customs tariff are different matters from negotiating with third countries on the basis of a common position, especially according to the very advanced criteria employed in the Kennedy Round. We can say, therefore, that the Commission's role in this case was an example of the Community responding successfully to the challenge of positive integration, and that one condition of this success was the ability of the Commission itself to act in the final period of the negotiations with an element of political leadership. At the same time, the other conditions which made it possible were set largely from outside the Community.

THE ORGANIZATION OF THE COMMISSION

Following the Council's first directive to the Commission to open the Kennedy Round in December 1963, three Commissioners were named as being responsible for representing the Commission in the negotiations. They were Jean Rey, the Commissioner responsible for external relations, Sicco Mansholt, the Commissioner responsible for Agriculture, and Robert Marjolin, whose special field was Economic and Financial Affairs. The selection of these members followed logically from the subject-matter of the negotiations. In the final period of the negotiations proper M. Rey became publicly acknowledged as the chief representative of the Commission. At the same time, a full negotiating team had to be appointed consisting of a number of Commissioners and officials.

Three main sections of the Commission were most directly involved in the actual conduct of the negotiations. First, the Directorate General for External Relations (DG I) was given responsibility for co-ordinating the various elements which made up the Commission's negotiating position and welding them into a coherent, viable offer to the other GATT partners. The main brunt of this task fell upon a single Directorate, *General Affairs, Multilateral and Commercial Policy*. The head of this Directorate was made the Commission's 'Special Representative for the Trade Negotiations in GATT'. He was assisted by Division No. 2, *Relations with Customs and Trade Organizations, USA*. Secondly, the Directorate General for the Internal Market (DG III) became responsible for the Commission's policy in the industrial sector of the negotiations. It was represented officially by its Director General, but in practice this responsibility devolved upon one Directorate, Directorate D, *Industry, Crafts and Commerce*; the head of this Directorate became one of the leading figures in the negotiating team, and was assisted by his Division No. 1, *General Matters*. Finally, there was Directorate General VI, Agriculture, which was represented by its Director General assisted by a division of Directorate A, *General Affairs*. In addition, of course, other departments of the Commission were involved in preparing the Community's negotiating position, for example, DG II, Economic and Financial Affairs, and DG VIII, Overseas Development; but the three departments just named were by far the most consistently and most centrally involved. Our main purpose here is to examine how far the roles of the officials within these three sections of the Commission compared with what we know about the roles of members of other organizations, and with the roles of officials in other parts of the Commission itself.

(1) *Recruitment*

In an organization of the 'classical' bureaucratic type we would expect the selection of personnel to deal with a special question like the Kennedy Round to arise from the established allocation of functions. All relevant departments would be represented proportionately in the policy-making process and would be associated with framing a final position. We would not expect such elements as nationality, personal commitment, relevant experience, and the individual preference of superiors to supersede the formal disposition of posts and functions. In practice, the Commission's organization for dealing with the Kennedy Round departed from the 'classical' model in a number of respects.

When the Commission decided to appoint a special team of negotiators for the Kennedy Round, an initial list of members contained well over forty names and was the subject of great conflict—personal, political and national—within the Commission and outside it. The length of this list was a sort of helpless response to demands on various sides for representation on the group entrusted with this extremely prestigious and glamorous job. While the first criterion for membership was professional qualification and competence, the list was also drawn up according to a distribution between nationalities rather on the same lines as for the staff of the Commission as a whole. Eventually, of course, a distinction had to be drawn in practice between this official list and the active team of negotiators, the people who actually went regularly to Geneva, and in the end the Commission's list became a mere formality. This active delegation contained representatives from each of the three main Directorates General concerned. Each department chose its own representatives so the basic principle of selection was based on formal structures. This is not surprising, and it would be difficult to imagine any other kind of arrangement in an organization of any complexity at all (that is, one with some element of specialization). However, the selection did not follow strict hierarchical lines.

199

DG I was represented by the Director we have already mentioned, (who was made the Commission's 'Special Representative'), along with the relevant Head of Division. DG III was represented up to 1966, at least, by its Director General as was DG VI throughout the negotiations. In order to overcome this anomaly, however, and to avoid any embarrassment, it was found necessary to give the Special Representative the personal rank of Director General (grade A1). Thus, the main representation of the different departments during the final and crucial five or six months was: DG I: A1 (director with higher rank *à titre personnel*), and A3 (head of division); DG III: A2 (director) and A3 (head of division); DG VI: A1 (Director General) and A3 (head of division). In each case, however, the officials concerned enjoyed direct access to their Commissioner, and, as we shall discuss further below, in the work of the team in these final stages hierarchical and other status considerations seem not to have played a very important part.

It is important to note that the need to provide for representation of nationalities, as well as of informal 'political' groups, within the organization produces rigidities similar to the 'classical' bureaucratic traits. As we remarked in the previous chapter, such considerations as nationality might be regarded as being just as destructive of organizational flexibility and purpose as the 'classical' rules of personnel administration. Moreover, the latter are at least designed to serve organizational purposes, such as efficiency, even though in practice they may have 'dysfunctional' consequences. Internal conflict arising from national differences and other 'political' considerations is bound to make the maintenance of continuity and consistency more difficult. What is remarkable about the posting of personnel in the Commission for work on the final stages of the Kennedy Round negotiations is that neither the 'classical' bureaucratic elements, nor internal 'political' considerations seem to have been overriding.

Within each Directorate General the selection of officials for work on the Kennedy Round seems to have been a relatively pragmatic affair. Neither nationality nor the formal disposition of posts seem to have been inhibitive in the final resort. It is not clear how far it was necessary or possible to make special arrangements in all parts of the Commission for the sake of work on the Kennedy Round, but in the case of the Directorate General for External Relations there is no question that the selection of a suitable team was pursued as a deliberate policy. In particular, junior officials, whose past record fitted them for the job, were transferred to the division concerned from their existing Directorates General. The aim was to produce the right blend of expertise, experience and personality to produce an *équipe de travail* capable of handling the delicate business of co-ordinating the Commission's approach to the negotiations. Our own research suggests that this venture was completely successful. The whole atmosphere of this part of the organization (which was still more or less intact when we carried out our investigation) was most unlike that of a bureaucratic organization. There was lack of emphasis on hierarchy, ease of personal relationships, confidence in colleagues' approachability and discretion, and a clear understanding of what was expected of each member of the team without the need for formal, highly structured arrangements.

It was no easy task, however, to assemble this team, and it took at least two years to bring it together! The task consumed a lot of time of the senior officials concerned and involved conflict with those responsible for personnel administration in the Commission. In other words the successful formation of this team does not imply a lack of bureaucratic traits in the Commission—rather the reverse given the difficulties involved for those responsible. The point is, however, that in this case the attempt was finally successful.

(2) *Structure*

In the typical kind of rationally-structured administrative organization we would expect to find clear and precise delegation of authority to specialized departments and sub-departments. We would also look for evidence of bureaucratic 'dysfunction', in the form of officials tending to identify with the 'sub-goals' of their own particular department rather than with the goals of the organization as a whole. A similar effect of displacement of goals might be produced if the working environment of officials put them into close and continuing contact with specialists of their own type or with a particular kind of clientele. In general, the higher the degree of specialization of functions within an organization, the greater is the challenge to the organization's leadership to preserve its identity.[1]

[1] On the effects of functional specialization see particularly F. M. Marx in J. La Palombara, *Bureaucracy and Political Development*, Princeton, New Jersey, 1965, pp. 70-4.

G* 201

As we have already seen, the Commission as a whole had two, or even three, goals in the Kennedy Round at any one time. First, it desired to use the negotiations as a means of furthering Community policies; second, it needed to maintain unity between the Six; and third, it wished to bring the negotiations to a successful conclusion. As we have also seen, these aims are not necessarily incompatible with one another and it seems that the Commission was able to go some way to achieving a result which combined them all. However, officials concerned with the Kennedy Round certainly seemed to be conscious of this multiplicity of goals and most of them were very ready to interpret it in terms of a conflict between their own part of the organization and its 'sub-goal' and the others involved with their 'sub-goals'.

This was felt particularly with regard to the division from the Directorate General of Agriculture. The Commission's policy in the agricultural part of the negotiations, as we have already seen, was largely determined by Vice-President Mansholt's determination to find a policy which would improve the chances of getting the common agricultural policy adopted and of making it more difficult to undermine this policy once it was set up. Vice-President Mansholt himself was not greatly involved in the negotiations themselves, after his principle of *montant de soutien* became the basis of the Community's negotiating position. The Agriculture DG, however, remained firmly espoused to this principle and its role in the Kennedy Round was interpreted by officials elsewhere, as well as by those in the department itself, as being primarily a means of strengthening support for the common agricultural policy. The 'Industry' Division of DG III, being primarily concerned with the development of industry in the Community, was similarly said to be closely concerned with developing common industrial policies out of the Kennedy Round. Its desire to get support for this from industries in the six countries was said by some to have pushed it into a 'hard' line on making concessions in Geneva in the industrial sector. Meanwhile, the Division from DG I, as might be expected of a department concerned with the Community's links with the outside world, was regarded as being concerned much more with getting an operational negotiating position adopted by the Community. In this way each different section of the Commission was caricatured as having a particular line of policy.

Officials within the Agriculture Division concerned were found to identify quite strongly with their department's alleged 'sub-goal', namely, furthering the common agricultural policy. As we shall see further below, this part of the Commission (and perhaps the whole Directorate-General of Agriculture) seemed to be highly structured and administered on relatively formal lines of hierarchical control and differentiation of functions. On the other hand, when asked about their own department's role in the negotiations, officials in the 'External Relations' Division and the 'Industry' Division stressed the flexibility of their own department and its ability to strike a balance between attending to the internal requirements of the Community and presenting a viable negotiating position in Geneva. In the 'Industry' Division there were certainly cases of individual officials being strongly committed to the claims of their particular industrial sector, but these commitments were individual rather than departmental. The leaders of this part of the organization were understood to have taken a broad view of these individual commitments and to have successfully balanced them against the Community's aggregate position in the negotiations.

It was certainly suggested to us that, in certain parts of the Commission, internal disputes tended to take the form of clashes between departmental views and that the loyalties of officials throughout the hierarchy tended to be engaged by their own Directorate General and Commissioner. The vast majority of issues had to go up to the level of the Commissioners themselves where they would be debated on the basis partly of differing personal opinions and partly of national positions. Officials in DG I and DG III were convinced, however, that this kind of structural conflict was less marked in their particular cases than it was elsewhere and believed that, especially in the later stages of the negotiations, there had been sufficient flexibility and delegation to reach a satisfactory balance of interests in the final settlement. In fact, as we shall see below, in reaching internal decisions in the Kennedy Round personal attitudes and values were said to have been generally more important within the Commission than formal structures.

Another set of structural factors which might have inhibited officials from having a general view of the Commission's role in the negotiations was the intense specialization of functions necessitated both by the subject-matter of the negotiations themselves and by the

203

degree of specialization adopted in the GATT system of negotiating. These factors were strengthened by two general characteristics of the Commission's organization: the policy of recruiting officials on the basis of strict technical qualifications, and the need to work closely with national experts, often sitting on officially-recognized bodies like the Article 111 Committee. We have already referred to the way Commission officials were in almost continuous and regular contact with members of the Article 111 Committee, itself divided into specialized sub-sections for the more detailed work. It was even pointed out to us that the agenda of meetings of this Committee was normally broken up into different specialized sectors, so that when, say, the Committee finished discussing an industrial question, all the officials concerned with this subject would get up and leave and the representatives from agriculture,or whatever the next subject was, would take their places. Meanwhile, in Geneva the negotiating committees and sub-committees of GATT worked on similarly specialized lines.

(3) *Informal Organization*

Alongside the formal structure, there were four other factors influencing personal motivations and loyalties within the Commission. These were nationality, technical specialism, professional background and personal commitment. Yet each of these was affected by the formal structure in very important ways. The Commission worked closely with committees and sub-committees of national interest groups. The individual official of the Commission, especially on a complex subject like the Kennedy Round, had to work closely with clients who shared not only his nationality but also his specialism, and sometimes his profession as well (if he was a former national civil servant). At the same time, within the organization nationality, specialism and professional background each provided the basis of personal links between officials, who might or might not also be related structurally as departmental colleagues or superiors.

Naturally, contacts between officials of the same nationality tended to show an intimacy which cut across institutional borders. In the case of the Kennedy Round the Commission officials concerned, as in all parts of the organization, spoke French in their day-to-day working contacts, (although officials of the same nationality working closely together would tend to relapse into their own tongue). National contacts with outsiders could, of course, become valuable instruments for achieving subsidiary objectives of the Commission. An official of the Commission might be asked by superiors to approach personally the staff of his country's Permanent Representative to get them to stop blocking procedure on some particular point. Another might be approached by a counterpart of his own nationality on the Article 111 Committee and asked to use his influence with his own former department at home to get them to change their instructions. However, in the matter of basic loyalties and commitment to goals the organization came first and there was never any doubt about this in the vast majority of cases.

But it has to be admitted that there were exceptions to this general rule within the Commission as a whole and that these were evident in the case of the Kennedy Round too. Many of the officials we spoke to believed that certain officials in the Commission worked in closer liaison with their own national government than might be expected and that this often impaired working relationships within the Commission. There was generally much gossip within the organization from time to time about different individuals working for promotion in their home civil services. In the case of the Kennedy Round it was felt that one or two individual officials concerned may have had closer links with home than was regarded as normal and occasionally 'visitors' who were not members of the active team of negotiators came down to Geneva to 'observe' what was going on.

However, the effect of the policy of detaching national civil servants for work with the Commission was seen in this case mainly in the existence of different styles of administration. Sometimes seconded national civil servants were identified as a group by other officials for showing relatively more concern for protocol and for hierarchical relationships. Most of the officials we spoke to believed that the difference between officials who had joined the Commission permanently and those who were on leave from a national administration was no more important than this. Many felt that the idea of detached service was a good thing in that former civil servants brought valuable contacts and experience with them. On the other hand, the same people argued strongly that officials working for the Commission should be exclusive in their loyalty to it and seemed to think that some sort of career structure was essential to ensure that this was so. Certainly some of the seconded officials we spoke to seemed to regard service with the Commission primarily as an advantage to their career at home, and saw the current period of their lives as a natural stage in their career as a national civil servant.

The members of the work-team of the 'External Relations' Division seemed in many ways to bend over backwards not to appear as civil servants in the conventional sense. This was true whatever their background: indeed the head of the Division concerned was a former Dutch civil servant. It was surely relevant, however, that the team contained no other former national civil servants but was made up entirely of former members of international secretariats, former academics or research workers, and graduates whose first employment had been with the Commission. One of them went so far as to say, 'I know that I sometimes rub people up the wrong way here in the organization because I don't behave like a civil servant'. This 'informal' element was clearly of great importance for the success of the Commission's role in the Kennedy Round, which was an undertaking of great political importance. It was also important that the members of this team were able to take a general view, given the intense specialization within the other two departments chiefly concerned. Nationality or specialism may have prevented a new official from becoming acclimatized in the early periods of his service, but, 'After three to four months of service', as an experienced official put it to us, 'almost everyone here becomes a European'. This was also found to be the case in the 'Industry' Division, in spite of the intense degree of specialization found there.

The vast majority of officials dealing with the Kennedy Round (as in most other parts of the Commission) had been appointed mainly on the basis of specialist qualifications. Most of them had been working on similar subject matter previously in research institutes or universities or in their own national Civil Service. In the case of Agriculture, out of about a dozen category A officials directly involved with the Kennedy Round, the only real 'generalist' was the head of division himself, who was a member of the *Inspection des Finances*. In the 'Industry' directorate there were examples of intense specialization, almost of 'osmosis' between certain officials and the industrial sector with which they dealt. However, the officials in these departments were not as narrow-minded or sectional in their outlook as officials in these conditions are often supposed to be. There was never any question, however close the relationship between them and their counterparts on bodies like the Article 111 Committee (who might be former colleagues in a national Civil Service) that Commission officials served anything but the Commission. The effect of differences in specialism as with nationality and professional background was noticed mainly as a matter of administrative style.

The division from Agriculture consisted of just such a cross-section of officials from different backgrounds as that from External Relations, although the effects were different. The 'Agriculture' Division was readily identified by officials in other departments as being dominated by a rather technocratic style of administration—a kind of embodiment of the characteristics of the French *technicien*. In the other two departments concerned administrative style corresponded far less directly to structure and there was clearly an interplay of different styles. The distinctive style of the hierarchical superiors was felt to be very important in settling major conflicts, but these styles had not permeated down through the respective sections, as seems to have happened in Agriculture. Generally, the nature of the work-team of DG I was extremely important here in ensuring a fluid approach. It was clearly extremely important that in the key sector concerned with the conduct of the negotiations (the DG I team), bureaucratic values were deliberately underplayed. It was also significant that in the 'Industry' Division identification with some overall purpose had survived extreme functional specialization and close working contact with six different national groups.

At the same time, of course, the very nature of an undertaking like the Kennedy Round was bound to generate a certain *esprit de corps* among those concerned. For one thing, much of the work took place in Geneva rather than in Brussels, that is, away from the power-struggles and status problems which can become so dominant in the lives of officials working at headquarters. Secondly, much of the time of members of the negotiating team was spent with representatives from outside the Community altogether and this was bound to engender a certain broad-mindedness on their part compared with officials dealing entirely with internal matters.

207

(4) Decision-making
We must now ask how the interplay between formal structure and informal organization worked itself out in the actual process of decision-making in the case under study. One measure of the influence of formal organization is the extent to which conflicts are resolved 'analytically' rather than by a process of bargaining. In other words, in a flexible, adaptive, 'organic' system of decision making internal disputes will normally be settled by such means as presentation of fresh information, review of objectives, the staging of conferences to discuss and 'iron out' differences, (which generally turn out to have been misunderstandings). Most important of all, in such a system internal conflict will not usually involve the status of individual members of the organization and will not lead to power struggles. In a system which has been greatly routinized, however, the settlement of conflict tends to take the form of bargaining between different formal groups. Conflict will often concern the very goals of the organization and will, therefore, have to be pushed up to the highest levels for resolution. Here bargains will be struck on the basis of concessions exchanged between one department and another.[1]

It was clear that in the case under study conflicts invariably resulted from a divergence of goals and such differences had to be settled at a high level between Directors, Directors General and Commissioners. However, the officials concerned with the Kennedy Round believed that this tendency, (though it was a general characteristic of the Commission), was less marked in their own particular case than it was elsewhere. Indeed, in the crucial final stage of the negotiations there was said to have been a co-operative atmosphere on the active team of negotiators in Geneva and Commissioner Rey became a natural leader for all its members. Differences between 'sub-goals' had lost a lot of their importance, rather as had the differences between member States. A good example of how flexibility at official level proved important at this stage was the way the 'Industry' Division produced a compromise on the question of the American Selling Price, a compromise which proved acceptable not only to the Americans and the other GATT partners but also

---

[1] On the politics of 'organic' and 'mechanistic' systems of management see Burns and Stalker. *The Management of Innovation*, London, Tavistock Publications, 1963, pp. 126–55. See pp. 111–14 above.

to the chemicals industry in the six countries of the Community. The settlement of this question was widely felt to have been due to the personal skill, ingenuity and flexibility of the Director from this part of the Commission.

In fact, it was stressed to us that personality had played a vital part in the work of the negotiating team and that this had been more important than either status or department. We were sceptical about this for a long time. Most of the officials interviewed stressed the differences between departmental 'sub-goals' in talking of the ambivalence of the Commission's role in the negotiations. However, they found it necessary to refer repeatedly to the part played by individual personalities in explaining what had happened. Perhaps the internal 'politics' of the Commission in this case was not a struggle for power between structures or even a struggle over status but a direct confrontation of conflicting norms? Perhaps in the end a successful alliance was struck between the different actors involved? Certainly there was a lack of identification with 'sub-goals' on the part of subordinates (at least in DG I and DG III) and a general lack of correspondence between administrative style and formal structure, (except in the case of Agriculture). It was also only in the case of the Division from Agriculture that norms of policy seemed to have been Departmentalized. Decision-making generally was a process of bargaining and of 'politics', but it was a fluid, unstructured process in which individual officials at various levels were called upon for ingenuity, skill at producing formulae and, above all, a political sense.

If this hypothesis about the nature of decision-making in the Kennedy Round is true, then it would seem that the Commission might at this time have been in an important stage of transition where formal organization was only beginning to become decisive (as in Agriculture), yet where the organization was not, on the other hand, an informal body of like-minded partisans. Recruitment had not produced common outlook or purpose, even if it had been intended to do so. On the other hand, it was not aimed at preserving bureaucratic traits such as uniformity, obedience and personal detachment. There was a mixture of administrative styles, which was reflected in the way policy was made, but in the case of the Kennedy Round this mixture proved effective.

We have already remarked that most of the positions taken up by the Community in the Kennedy Round resulted from policies drawn up by the Commission. In at least three cases of great importance we found that these policies came from well down the organization, from somewhere about grades A6 and A7. It is well-known in civil services of all types that the 'best' ideas are often those which filter up from this kind of level. It is equally well-known among students of bureaucracy that very often initiatives from such levels cannot be effective owing to the stress on hierarchy in decision-making. Again, administrative organizations are not to be expected to take initiatives at all (that is, decisions which involve the development of new policies or programmes of action). In one of the three cases mentioned here, that of the world cereals agreement and the principle of *montant de soutien*, the Division concerned in DG VI was specifically asked by Commissioner Mansholt to find a means of tying the Kennedy Round to the common agricultural policy. This illustrates the importance of leadership clearly defining a goal and getting the necessary response from the administration. A second case, that of the Commission's solution to the procedural problem of disparities, resulted in response to a similar directive from above. The final one, however, that of ASP and the need to make this a key factor in the negotiations, definitely filtered up as a result of an initiative taken from below.

We asked a number of officials, who happened to have been former national civil servants, to comment on the main differences between work in a national civil service and that in the Commission. Nearly all of them stressed the absence of any 'settled policy' in the Commission. This is a very interesting illustration of how decision-making in the Commission—or at least in some parts of it—had not become subject to established programmes as is the case in most normal civil services. The one exception to this, as our preceding account may have illustrated, was the Directorate General of Agriculture, where, as we have seen, there was a tendency to produce decisions which conformed to the common agricultural policy and furthered its adoption. In the other sections concerned with the Kennedy Round, however, officials were clearly involved in *initiating* programmes.

We were struck by the extent to which officials, particularly in the 'Industry' Division, but also in DG I, stressed as desirable qualities in any civil servant the ability to have ideas and to put forward proposals on policy. When asked to choose between different characteristics which were important for the Commission's success, the same officials all stressed 'having a policy of its own' and rated this higher in importance than 'ability to appeal for support over the heads of national governments', 'negotiating flexibility', 'commitment to European integration' or even 'technical competence', (although this was usually rated a good second). They were also conscious of having some initiative in the decision-making process and some gave the prospect of this as a reason for having joined the Commission in the first place. In contrast, in the 'Agriculture' Division officials valued technical competence much more highly and described this as a key element in the Commission's success.

One impediment to the Commission in drawing up its own policies is, of course, its shortage of staff. In the case of most of the industrial sectors in the Kennedy Round, for example, there would be only one responsible official of about level A4/5 or A6/7 for each main sector, such as chemicals, textiles, mechanical goods, and so on. In contrast, at the national level, there are usually at least half a dozen or so administrative class officials, not to say whole divisions and sections, concerned with individual industries. While one effect of this shortage of numbers is clearly to force the Commission to rely overwhelmingly on the advice of national officials and experts as well as on interest groups for formulating policies, at the same time it means that the 'premature' development of settled policies is less likely. The 'departmental philosophies' common in a national civil service, while they may be developing in some aspects of the Commission's work (in Agriculture, for example), have had far more difficulty in getting established in the organization as a whole. This was clearly a factor enabling the Commission to be far more flexible in the Kennedy Round than a number of other delegations to GATT. While it was vital that the Commission had evolved a position of its own, (independent of the national governments), this position had not resulted from established programmes in the majority of cases and so was not a source of inflexibility. The policies had been mainly designed in the context of the negotiations and had not arisen out of organizational doctrine.

Thus the making of policy within the Commission for the Kennedy Round cannot be explained purely in terms of formal structures. To a large extent it involved an interaction of different norms of policy, in which the role of certain key individual Commissioners and officials was often crucial. Of the three distinct policy goals of the Commission only one could be positively identified with a single section, namely, the division from DG VI, which was firmly committed to advancing the claims of the common agricultural policy. Here strong executive leadership was seen as being crucial and officials were mainly concerned with sustained defence of a fixed departmental position. In spite of this conflicts within the Commission tended not to be played out rigidly on departmental lines in the later stages. Although many settlements had to be made at a high (Commissioner) level, this was due to the lack of 'settled' policy, not to a stress on hierarchy. In the case of Agriculture administrative style happened to favour support of the 'departmental philosophy'. Thus, while the 'classical' elements of organization found in this particular department must not be overlooked, to all intents and purposes the making of policy in the case of the Kennedy Round can be seen as a relatively loose, unstructured process of 'political' bargaining.

In so far as this meant that considerations of status were not greatly involved in policy making, it facilitated the negotiating team's work, demanding as it did a combination of flexibility and personal commitment.[1] The main problem was achieving some sort of unity out of the Commission's three main goals—a substantial liberalization of world trade, preservation of internal unity in the Community, and progress towards acceptance of common policies. These three goals were clearly closely linked, but too much emphasis on any one of them could endanger the others. In so far as weaknesses of formal structure provided outlets for divisive elements such as professionalization and nationality, this task was made more difficult. In the case of the Kennedy Round, although such elements were very noticeable and certainly affected the behaviour of some of the key participants, they did not prevent the negotiating team from achieving a flexible common position on the basis of which they were able to reach agreement with the Americans.

(5) *Roles*

This conclusion can best be explained in terms of the predominant 'role' performed by officials in the sections most closely involved in

[1] Burns and Stalker, *op. cit.*, pp. 141–4.

the final stages of the negotiations. As we have already seen, in the absence of 'classical' bureaucratic methods of organization, the Commission relied in the early years mainly on commitment to the 'European idea' as a basis of its personnel administration.[1] In practice, this means that many senior positions are held by men who joined the Commission out of commitment to the organization itself and out of devotion to preserving the union of the Six. However, it was suggested to us that the number of officials motivated in this way had been falling as a proportion of the total strength by about 5 per cent a year since 1958. If anything such officials were confined to certain high positions in the hierarchy and associated with a rather dogmatic, 'evangelical' attitude in the decision-making process. This partisan approach constituted one important normative element in the making of policy on the Kennedy Round, but it did not particularly facilitate the Commission's task.

While a certain amount of identification with a common cause was crucial in providing a basis for policy-making, it was difficult to pin it down and it could not be strictly identified with the partisan role just described. We have already referred to the importance in this undertaking of the relatively loose system of official relationships in the decision-making process and how this differed from a typical national civil service. Initiatives from below were common: authority in most parts of the relevant departments was easily and readily delegated in the key final phase of the negotiations; communications were appreciably free and open. Differences of administrative style, encouraged by this system of decision-making, were not, on the other hand, always embarrassing. One reason for this was certainly a widespread attachment to the aims of European unity. But in general this was a vague and relatively distant notion which did not provide sufficient ground for articulate decisions. Indeed, as we have seen, each of the Commission's goals could be interpreted in terms of this ideal; the problem was putting the proper emphasis on each of them. Moreover, some elements in the decision-making process clearly did not share this attachment. While many of those attached to the 'European idea' regarded themselves as specialists and were not ashamed to admit that they 'supposed they were "technocrats" in a sense', they were also very ready to identify a different kind of 'technician', which they un-

[1] See pp. 141–50 above.

213

doubtedly associated with the popular caricature of the French ENA graduate, consciously detached and rationalistic in his approach to administration. Such officials (who might be of any nationality in practice) were highly respected for their technical skill and competence, but were regarded as a distinct type and did not seem to be partners in the common culture which clearly existed among most officials. This was possibly because they lacked the sense of adventure and of a shared undertaking, which so many officials enjoyed even in senior positions. Many of these 'technicians' were, in fact, seconded national officials who looked forward to the time when they would return to their own capitals. This approach was often combined with 'excessive' consciousness of their own national backgrounds.

The decision-making process was repeatedly depicted to us as an interplay between partisan and technician styles. In the case of the negotiation of the Kennedy Round, however, a key role in the creative stage of policy and in its interpretation was played by officials at various levels of the decision-making hierarchy who fitted neither of these descriptions. Typically, they were relatively young officials, who had not seen previous experience with a national civil service and who were not even certain that they wished to regard service with the Commission as a career for life. Many of them were highly specialised, but this did not prove a serious barrier to them in communications with colleagues working in different sectors. Nationality was not important to them, nor was status. Their ideal of a Commission official was someone who should show loyalty rather than obedience to his superiors and who should not be afraid to speak out when his own views differed from those of the people above him. This type of official revelled in the loose, unstructured decision-making process of this particular undertaking. It was noticeable that none of them expressed the disappointment and frustration or the career anxieties, which, as the Personnel Committee of the Commission have repeatedly pointed out, are widespread among officials of their age and rank.

Many of them had joined the Commission during the 1960s rather than at the beginning in 1958 and were thus less imbued with the crusading spirit of partisan Europeans. This stereotype is, however, a little misleading in that most of the officials of this general type at the higher levels had naturally served through from

214

1958 to 1959, were slightly older (and in their forties), were less likely to be so strictly specialist in background or training, and were very often former national civil servants. Yet even in the case of these older officials joining the Commission had, as with their younger colleagues, appealed as a challenge rather than as an act of conviction. They also resisted the conventional picture of the anonymous, obedient, impersonal civil servant, whether in general terms or applied to themselves. They seemed to prefer the more free-wheeling, and pioneering atmosphere of their part of the Commission to other forms of public service. One of them quoted to us the remark of a former Vice-President of the USA, 'I would rather be right than be President', in replying to our question about frustrations in working for a body with such poor career prospects as the Commission. Career was not a major pre-occupation but nor for that matter was any single burning ideal—one stayed with the Commission out of personal momentum:

'I have lived in Brussels for ten years now. I go back to the Netherlands with my family once or twice a year on vacation. But my children have no particular affection for it, they have been brought up basically in Belgium.'

This blend of pragmatism and personal enthusiasm provided the basis of the common culture prevailing in this part of the organization. Many of these officials even seemed sceptical about the effectiveness of the Commission's role. They were on the whole not anxious to talk about the institutional limitations on the Commission within the Community, such as its lack of autonomy, and tended to have a moderate view of its objectives in the decision-making process. There was, however, a very pronounced spirit of *camaraderie*, and all of these officials shared a personal conviction attaching them to the aims of European unity. This did not take the form of burning commitment to the organization. The chief motivation of these officials was far more a desire to participate in a new and interesting undertaking, and to be given the opportunity to take some initiative in the policy-making process. This particular combination of attitudes may well be typical of the officials of most international organizations. The numbers of staff of such bodies are usually small in comparison with national administrations so that relations can be more intimate; commitment to the organization is likely to be less, on account of the impermanence of service;

215

decision-making must usually be relatively informal, in view of the lack of clear executive leadership and the need to accommodate a variety of administrative styles. (Indeed, a large number of the officials concerned in our case study had seen earlier experience with other international bodies.) It is a type of role which is highly suited to the conditions of international negotiations, but which would probably be far less suited to implementing 'settled' policies or even to introducing new programmes of social and economic administration.

The success of the Commission in negotiating the Kennedy Round on behalf of the Community cannot be explained by these internal organizational factors alone. The lack of determined opposition from any member government in the final stages, the fact that third countries were involved and the existence of a crucial deadline, were the major factors in enabling the Commission to take the initiative. It was clearly important, however, that the organization was sufficiently flexible and 'organic' in nature not to prevent the Commission taking full advantage of this opportunity.

CHAPTER 9

SOME CASES OF DECISION: (2)
THE FRONTIER REGION OF SOUTHERN
BELGIAN LUXEMBOURG AND
NORTHERN LORRAINE

TOWARDS A REGIONAL POLICY

The preamble to the Rome Treaty states that the member states are 'anxious to strengthen the unity of their economies and to ensure their harmonious development by reducing the differences existing between the various regions and mitigating the backwardness of the less favoured'.[1]

The Treaty sets up a European Investment Bank to provide financial assistance in the form of loans and guarantees to assist different types of project for regional development. There is also a European Social Fund which is responsible for promoting labour mobility between occupations and regions. Another potential source of financial support for regional development is FEOGA, the guidance and guarantee fund set up under the common agricultural policy with two main functions: to support prices on the agricultural market, and to help finance the structural improvement of agriculture. Finally, under Article 92 of the Treaty exceptions are made to the removal of subsidies and other restrictions to trade in the case of specific types of aid, including aids to promote the economic development of backward regions. However, there is no reference in the Treaty to regional policy as such and any developments in this direction have had to be tentative and piecemeal.

Nevertheless, the Commission has repeatedly recognized that the process of increasing competition involved in the establishment of the customs union will aggravate existing regional problems (for example, by driving out inefficient firms and by increasing the dominance of already prosperous areas).[1] From the point of view of

[1] Treaty establishing the EEC, Article 2.
[1] See *Documents de la Conférence sur les Economies Régionales,* EEC Commission, Brussels, 1961.

217

gaining political support for positive integration it will be essential to ensure that the problems of particular countries or regions do not get neglected. Moreover, since acute regional problems already exist within the member States, most of the latter already have regional policies of their own of one sort or another, and these will have to be co-ordinated on the basis of some common approach if they are not to distort the effects of free trade within the Community. Yet, in spite of increasing awareness of these problems and repeated expressions of encouragement from the Commission, little has been achieved so far in the direction of finding any common approach. This remains one of the most undeveloped and backward aspects of the Community.

From the start the Commission's policy has been not to disallow government aids for regional development.[1] Also in 1958 the Commission began to work out a programme of studying regional problems, to single out areas needing urgent attention, and to analyse the policies of member States.[2] Groups consisting of officials from the Commission and from national administrations, along with national experts, were set up on a number of special problems, in particular the comparison of national approaches to regional policy, and the production of a list of key 'problem areas'.[3] The Commission then proceeded to call a Conference on Regional Economies which took place in Brussels between December 6 and 8, 1961, and was attended by representatives from the member States. As a direct result of this Conference working groups were set up to report on three aspects of the regional problem: (a) the particular problem of peripheral and other special areas in need of development, (b) a comparison of the effectiveness of member State's policies, and (c) the problem of old industrial regions in decline. At the same time a number of special studies were undertaken by the Commission of the problems of two or three particular regions.[4]

---

[1] *First General Report on the Activities of the Community* 1958, EEC Commission, sec. 54.

[2] *Second General Report on the Activities of the Community*, 1958–59. EEC Commission, sec. 74.

[3] *Third General Report on the Activities of the Community*, 1959–60, EEC Commission, sec. 218.

[4] The areas were the frontier region of southern Belgian Luxembourg and northern Lorraine, the Eifel-Hunsruck area in Germany, and the Bari-Tarento development pole in southern Italy.

The reports of the three working groups set up after the 1961 Conference were received in 1964 and the Commission then proceeded to publish its own Memorandum on regional policy in 1965.[1] Though still not forming the basis of a common policy, this memorandum contained recommendations concerning the regional policies of member States and plans for further detailed studies by the Commission to be added to those already under way.

In other words, the Commission's role in the sector of regional development has been essentially that of a technical, advisory body, with few, if any, real powers of its own. It is able, however, to prod the European Investment Bank and the Social Fund into helping regions in particular difficulty, and has done this from time to time. No general policy for this kind of financial aid (or for that from the FEOGA) yet exists. Nor are any actual controls of development available to the Community institutions, although these are regarded as essential by some national governments (that of the UK, for example) in ensuring balanced regional development. There is little doubt that, apart from the very vagueness of the Treaty itself, the main reason for the failure to develop a common policy in this vitally important sector of positive integration is the combined hostility and disinterest of the various member States. Some of the member States, in particular Germany, have been associated with *laisser-faire* national economic policies, and have not been enthusiastic in principle for the development of a positive policy for helping regions at a Community level. On the other hand, the French Government, while having an active regional policy of its own, has put up a spirited resistance to any Community interest in this sector and regards regional policy strictly as a matter for the member States to decide.

THE REGION IN QUESTION

The region with which we are concerned in the present study consists of the southern section of the Belgian Province of Luxembourg (roughly that section south of the Ardennes Mountains) and the northern part of the French region of Lorraine. This is a 'natural' region crossed almost through the middle by the Franco–Belgian

[1] *Regional Policy in the European Community* Community Topics No. 24, 1965, Information Service of the EEC.

border. The region is 'natural' in a number of important economic respects, not to mention the fact that its inhabitants share a common language (French) and that both its parts are situated on the periphery of Belgium and France respectively.

The north of Lorraine is a relatively prosperous industrial area based practically exclusively on the iron and steel industry. This industry looks more to the north for its outlet to the sea and International trade (through the canalization of the Moselle River) rather than southwards to the rest of France. It also draws on labour from the north of the Belgian border and this latter area also possesses important natural resources, such as a potential supply of water, which could be of value to the iron and steel industry to the south.

The Belgian Province of Luxembourg is one of the most backward of the declining regions of southern Belgium. For a long time it has felt neglected by the central government and its inhabitants show all the symptoms of demoralization typical of a region which has been depressed economically for a long time without much hope of recovery. There is also an iron and steel industry on this side of the border but this has been in serious decline since the end of the war, owing largely to its restricted size. Production amounts to $\frac{1}{2}$ million tons of steel a year, and the industry provides employment for approximately 2,000 people (about $\frac{1}{5}$ of the industrial labour force in the area covered by the industry). About $\frac{1}{4}$ of the active population are employed in agriculture but this too is an unprofitable and stagnant economic activity in that the Province (especially its southern part) is situated far from the more densely populated areas of Belgium.

In spite of the fact that each of these two areas seems to be a natural complement to the other, the region is typical of many in this part of Europe in having been split by historical and political circumstance. As a result, a number of factors, apart from political separation, make economic and social co-operation between its two parts extremely difficult. Chief among these is communications which are based on national rather than economic lines (it is virtually impossible to get directly from Arlon, the chief town of Luxembourg, to Longwy about thirty miles away in Lorraine, by public transport). Customs and other transit difficulties inhibit Belgian workers from crossing the border to work in the prosperous iron and steel industry of Lorraine.

It is doubtful if any better illustration could be found of the need to assert economic rationality over national differences. Indeed, at first glance there seems to be an obvious role here for the institutions of an enterprise like the EEC. In this respect one cannot help but remember that the very initiative for the Coal and Steel Community, and thus eventually for the Economic Community as well, arose out of attempts to deal with the problems of the Saar, a similar economically 'natural' region split by a national frontier.

HISTORY OF ATTEMPTS TO SOLVE THE PROBLEM

The main actors in this history will be two Community institutions, the Commission and the Parliament; local authorities in the two provinces concerned; Belgian and French economic experts; representatives of local trade and industry in the two provinces; and—cast regrettably in the role of melodramatic villain—the two national governments concerned. We shall only deal here with local and national attempts to increase co-operation between these two areas in so far as they illustrate the role of the EEC Commission in the affair.

By the time the EEC was established in 1958 representatives of local authorities and of trade and industry in the provinces of Luxembourg and Lorraine were already engaged in negotiations aimed at increasing economic and social co-operation across the national frontier. These were particularly well-advanced in the case of two local advisory committees concerned with economic development, one representing the Belgian *arrondissement* of Arlon–Virton, the chief member of which was the *Commissaire* of the *arrondissement* himself, and the other, the *Comité du Bassin Lorraine* representing the iron and steel industry of northern Lorraine, the chief figure of which was the Comte de Maud'huy, a member of the French Economic and Social Council. These particular talks concerned the need of a new supply of water for the part of the iron and steel industry centred on the French towns of Longwy and Thionville and the possibility of finding this new supply on the Belgian side of the border.

In 1959 these local representatives decided to approach the EEC Commission to see if the latter could take some part in their undertaking and perhaps even offer some form of positive assistance. This

221

decision was no doubt influenced by the enthusiasm for the Community experiment felt by some of those participating in the local negotiations and was certainly helped by the existence of personal contacts between them and some of the officials concerned in the studies of regional problems currently being pursued by the Commission. It was in this way that the Luxembourg–Lorraine region booamo ono of the three or four special cases interesting the Commission at this time. M. Marjolin, the Commissioner concerned with regional policy as part of his general responsibility for the Directorate General of Economic and Financial Affairs, gave his personal backing to the department's interest in this special case.

At the Conference on Regional Economies sponsored by the Commission in 1961 the region was one of the special problems discussed and a paper about it was presented by the Comte de Maud'huy himself. Following the Conference, and at the Commission's initiative and expense, two parallel studies of different aspects of the region were commissioned respectively from an independent Belgian research organization, SOCOREC, (concerned mainly with the economic and social problems of the southern coal-mining area of Belgium) and from a professor of the University of Nancy. In April 1963 the main findings of these studies were discussed at a *table ronde* in Brussels organized by the Commission and chaired by Vice-President Marjolin, including altogether about fifty representatives from the region itself, from the Commission, and from other organizations involved.

The studies revealed that it would be viable economically and otherwise to supply water from a newly-constructed reservoir on the Belgian side of the border to the iron and steel industry in Lorraine. At the same time the Belgians could also offer to those on the French side valuable residential and industrial sites to help relieve the congestion of the conurbation of Longwy and to enable a diversification of industrial activity in the region. On the French side, financial resources could be made available in return to revitalize the industrial base of the Belgian part of the region and to ease the unemployment situation. The price of the water supplied should be sufficient to cover the costs of supply and at the same time to provide funds for development of the Belgian side of the border. In addition, the studies included recommendations for improving communications between the two parts of the region, co-ordinating plans for urban development, overcoming difficulties with customs, and co-operating in projects for professional training.[1]

In addition to accepting these findings, the *table ronde* concluded that there was an urgent need for new industrial development in the whole region, not only to relieve unemployment in Luxembourg, but also to diversify the industrial activities of Lorraine. To this end it was recommended that *Lordex*, a finance company functioning from Metz, should be authorized by the Belgian authorities to participate in financing investment on the Belgian side of the border. It was also recommended that the governments concerned should take immediate steps to facilitate the extension of the conurbation of Longwy over the Belgian side of the border, while the Commission undertook to do what it could to interest the national authorities concerned and to ease the difficulties of transit workers through the powers it had under the Community's social policy.[2] Finally, the European Investment Bank was urged to give specially favourable consideration to any projects designed to contribute to bringing the two parts of the region together.[3]

The Commission now decided to take a major initiative in the matter and on June 14, 1963, addressed an official Recommendation to the two member States concerned. The Recommendation was in three main parts. First, the Commission proposed that the French and Belgian Governments should seek agreement on means to give effect to the recommendations of the *table ronde* concerning water supply, and concerning urban and industrial development in the region. Secondly, it recommended that the governments should take other measures to encourage co-operation between the two parts of the region and that to this effect they should co-ordinate their own programmes of economic and social development. Finally, the Commission suggested that an *ad hoc* committee of liaison should be set up jointly by the two governments to carry out studies, to co-ordinate activities of local and national authorities, and so on. The Commission described itself as being 'ready to support action (by the governments) by every appropriate initiative in fields where

[1] Recommendation de la Commission du 14 juin 1963 au Royaume Belgique et a la République Française concernant un projet de co-opération économique sur le plan régionale entre le nord de la Lorraine et le sud de la province belge du Luxembourg, *Journal Officiel de la CEE*, 97/63, June 27, 1963.
[2] See above, p. 61.
[3] Recommendation de la Commission, *loc. cit.*

it is competent to do so'.[1] It later emerged, however, that the Commission interpreted its role as being that of an observer only and that it would act only if called upon to do so by the national governments. The appointment of the proposed *ad hoc* committee of liaison would be a matter for the member governments concerned.[2]

From this point on a series of disasters befell the undertaking. First, owing, some say, to the intervention of the Governor of the Belgian Province of Luxembourg, the authorities on the Belgian side refused to accept the terms which had been agreed so far for the supply of water from Belgium into Lorraine. From now on the Belgian position on the price of the water could not be met by those on the French side. The Governor concerned was shortly removed from his post by the Belgian Government for quite different reasons, but by the time his successor took up office it was already too late to try to salvage the negotiations. Secondly, following the Commission's *recommendation* the national authorities now intervened and attempted to take over the whole affair and to deal with it at the level of the Foreign Offices of France and Belgium. The French Government called a meeting in Paris which took place on December 9, 1963, and was attended by representatives of SOCOREC, the Province of Luxembourg, the Belgian Government, the iron and steel industry of Lorraine, and the local *préfecture* concerned. This meeting was a complete failure and the various delegates left the table with no proposals having been agreed. In the course of 1964 negotiations proceeded between officials of the two governments, with the Commission represented as an 'observer'. However, the matter remained, as one Commission official put it to us, 'bogged down in the swamps of traditional diplomacy for a long time'.

At this point an attempt was made by means of the European Parliament to break out of the deadlock which had been reached. Two particular members of the Parliament were involved, M. Vanrullen, a French Socialist Senator from the Pas-de-Calais, and M. Toubeau, a Belgian Socialist Deputy from Mons. These two deputies put down a joint written question to the Commission in December 1963 asking about the situation arising from the failure of the Paris meeting. The Commission's reply to this question was

1 Recommendation de la Commission, *loc. cit.*
2 Réponse a la Question Ecrite No. 57/64 in *Journal Officiel de la CEE*, September 26, 1963.

completely non-committal. On the issue of the price of the proposed water supply from Luxembourg to Lorraine, on which the Commission had been specifically asked to comment, it refused to express an opinion, saying that this was a matter entirely for the buyer, seller and prospective user to decide. The Commission felt that the Paris meeting had 'shown the intention of the parties to draw the necessary consequences from the situation', and stressed that the negotiations were entirely a matter for the national authorities. The Commission was, however, prepared to lend its assistance if called upon to do so.[1]

This was followed by an Oral Question from M. Toubeau delivered on the floor of the Parliament on March 23, 1964, and challenging the Commission to defend its inaction. Speaking on behalf of the other members of the Parliament who were concerned with this special problem, and with that of the economic situation along the whole Franco–Belgian border, M. Toubeau said: 'We believe in effect that the role of the EEC Commission did not terminate with the publication of a Recommendation and that on the contrary it must now see to it that the negotiations currently proceeding carry on and result in the positive solutions envisaged by the Recommendation itself.'

The Question asked how the Commission intended to bring about more co-operation between the parties concerned and how it thought it could play 'a positive and useful role'.[2]

In his speech in reply, M. Marjolin for the Commission went quite a long way to attempt to reassure the questioner. Given the Commission's basic decision to leave the matter to the national authorities, he gave a far more positive reaction than any official statement by the Commission so far. He offered some hope for the negotiations on water supply which were still taking place, and was able to say that preparatory work was being undertaken by the French and Belgian Governments prior to an opening of negotiations on the other problems of the region. He repeated the Commission's now familiar argument that it was up to these authorities to discuss economic objectives for the region and to determine the means for

[1] Réponse à la Question Ecrite No. 117, *Journal Officiel, op. cit.*, February 10, 1964.
[2] Question Orale No. 1, March 23, 1964, *Parlement Européen, Débats,* (1964) No. 70, pp. 64 ff. (Our translation).

H

reaching these, but he went so far as to say that the Commission would be willing to help '*même dans les domaines qui ne le relèvent pas de sa compétence.*' He stressed that the Commission was at the disposition of the governments concerned to help them decide on common action in the region, '*bien que ces domaines ne soient pas couverts formellement par le Traité*'. However, the Commission had no power to force them to accept its help: '*Il appartient aux gouvernements de nous inviter à participer à ces travaux, s'ils le désirent.*'[1]

This has remained the Commission's official attitude ever since, and so far only three really significant steps have been made to take positive advantage of it. The Commission was able to take steps under the Community social policy to make it easier for Belgian workers to cross the frontier and work in the iron and steel industry of Lorraine. The European Investment Bank has given assistance towards the establishment of a new paper mill in southern Luxembourg, with the full support of the Commission. Finally, in 1967 a Belgian publicly-owned refrigeration company requested the Belgian Government to apply to FEOGA for funds to support the building of a complex on the Franco-Belgian border consisting of a slaughterhouse, cold-storage unit, and a meat processing plant. There would also be French participation in this project and the idea would be, among other things, to help revitalize the agricultural industry in Luxembourg by supplying it with a new market in the industrial area in northern Lorraine. The idea arose from renewed talks between national representatives and between representatives of the two parts of the region. The latest news, however, was that the Belgian Ministry of Agriculture had withdrawn its application to FEOGA on account of a change of priorities, and its proposal for participation in the project had been dropped. Meanwhile, the possibility of supplying water from Luxembourg to Lorraine has finally been crushed as the French have now made arrangements to pump water from the River Chiers on their own side of the border. However, it is understood that some progress has been made locally towards improving transport communications between the two parts of the region.

In the spring of 1965 a new initiative was taken up, this time by the Grand Duchy of Luxembourg, a representative of which in the European Parliament asked why the Commission had not included

[1] Question Orale, *loc. cit*

his country in the Recommendation addressed to France and Belgium in 1963. Luxembourg, he said, should have been included 'in order to facilitate the harmonious economic development of the entire region washed by the Chiers and the Semois'. The Commission replied that it would be willing to include Luxembourg in any future action it took with regard to this region, and took the opportunity to note its pleasure that talks between the French and Belgian authorities had re-opened.[1] Meanwhile, the Permanent Representative of Luxembourg also made approaches to the Commission to express his State's interest in the problem. Finally, on August 5, 1967, a group of Belgian, French and Luxembourgian trade unions, known as the *Union des Groupements Professionels du Luxembourg*, wrote to the Commission asking that their area should be included in a study of the whole of the declining Walloon area and that this study should be financed by the Commission. Up to the summer of 1968 the Commission has been unable to make a definitive reply owing to its preoccupation with reorganizing its own services after the merger of 1967.

THE ROLE OF THE COMMISSION

The role of the Commission in this case was very limited indeed, and this was clearly not entirely its own responsibility. We interviewed a number of people in the various organizations with which the Commission came into contact during this affair and the general diagnosis they offered was that the Commission had simply lacked sufficient formal powers to take the problems out of their hands. The main culprits seem to have been the national authorities, whose combined incompetence, obstruction and indifference prevented a really positive result from emerging. Even so there are a number of lessons here about the institutions of the Community and, in particular, about the role of the Commission. The most obvious one is that the Commission lacks explicit authority to act in the field of regional development, and that without such explicit authority the Commission seemed to be unable in this case to lead the Community beyond the common market stage and into that of economic union. It was not enough to rely on member governments to follow up initiatives of the Commission in such circumstances. The Commission officials

[1] Question Ecrite No. 142/65 *Journal Officiel* April 17, 1965.

concerned felt unanimously that the lack of power to take direct action and the absence of a Community regional policy had been the fundamental causes of the Commission's failure to be of any real service in this individual case.

At the same time, of course, this would tend to imply something about the nature of the Commission as an institution. Failure to act effectively in the absence of clear and precise formal prescription is a typically bureaucratic characteristic, and so is a sense of being restrained within exact legal forms. Indeed, the official statements of the Commission throughout this episode (with the notable exception of M. Marjolin's reply to an Oral Question before the European Parliament) do seem to reveal a rather bureaucratic, self-conscious formalism. This may not be surprising, given, as we have seen already, that the Commission's responsibilities in this sector do not extend much beyond those of an advisory technical service. On the other hand, the Commission has been celebrated so often for putting life into otherwise uninteresting formal powers and for playing an active role far beyond that of a typical administrative service or bureaucracy, that we are bound to ask whether there were not special factors in this case, apart from the incomplete legal mandate of the Commission. We are also interested to see whether the bureaucratic nature of the Commission's role was reflected in its own organization.

The department of the Commission which was directly concerned with this case was Directorate General II, Economic and Financial Affairs. The specific section concerned was Division 2, *Regional Development*, of Directorate C of this department. This was not a case, however, which concerned more than two category A officials closely, or at most half a dozen throughout the whole episode. The Commission's Recommendation in 1963 was approved by the Commission itself by the written procedure so that it is almost certain that no Commissioner other than M. Marjolin himself took more than a formal, passing interest in the affair.

In fact, the part of the organization concerned with this case was not at all bureaucratic in character and the decisions taken cannot be explained in terms of organizational goals formally delegated to subordinates. In the first place the two officials most closely concerned were in no sense typical civil servants, nor did they behave as such. One was not even a full-time official with the Commission but a

Special Economic Adviser, being a well-known member of the University of Louvain. The other (also a French-speaking Belgian), while working full-time for the Commission, was also a reputable academic economist (being the author of a standard work on regional policy) and professor at the Free University of Brussels. Both these officials showed considerable personal interest in the affair under study and the fact that the matter was taken up by the Commission at all was due primarily to their initiative and active support. It is clear on any objective reading of the affair that there was little positive encouragement on the part of hierarchical superiors, with the exception of M. Marjolin himself. It is quite clear, indeed, that the whole issue would never have got as far as the Commission's Recommendation, if it had not been possible for the personal commitment and the individual relationships and background of these officials to have an influence in the decision-making process. The decision to raise the matter was not taken according to an existing programme set down by the hierarchy. The Commission had decided earlier to investigate particular cases of regional development and this was clearly a kind of framework for the activity of the officials concerned. However, any existing framework of policy was used as an excuse rather than as a reason for raising this issue, and in making an official Recommendation to the member States concerned the Commission was going beyond its original intention of carrying out 'studies'.[1]

However, from the point when the decision was taken (at the level of the Commissioner) to propose an official Recommendation on the question, the disadvantages of the loose, 'organic' system of organization began to reveal themselves. Exactly as in the Kennedy Round, it seems as if the Commission here was more complex than a partisan task-force, but still not completely 'bureaucratized' into a formalized, highly differentiated administrative organization. In this transitional stage, as we have already suggested, normative differences existed within the organization, sometimes as symptoms of an open-ended recruitment policy (for example, seconded national civil servants retaining close ties with home), sometimes simply as

[1] The Commission justified its action in making the Recommendation by reference to Article 2 of the Treaty (see p. 217 above), and to Article 155, which empowered it to make recommendations on matters coming within the Treaty when the Commission felt it was necessary.

differences of administrative style (such as the difference between
the ex-national civil service 'technicians' and the committed 'partisan'
Europeans). While this sort of situation leaves the organization
highly flexible, open to fairly quick adaptations, and while it increases
the importance of individual personality in decision-making, it must
also in the long run reduce the authority and effectiveness of the
Commission. This is because distinctive, coherent policies are a
necessary condition of the Commission's survival and of the transition to positive integration. Just as the loose 'organic' form of organization favours initiatives, such as the one with which we are immediately concerned, so it threatens them with resistance from within
the organization. Such resistance may simply take the form of a
style of administration, namely, bureaucratic inflexibility or red-tape
and a reluctance to improvise. It may also result from the existence
of competing norms, particularly when these are supported by
important power groups outside the organization.

Resistance to the proposal that the Commission should take some
positive role in solving the problems of the Luxembourg-Lorraine
region resulted from two different normative positions. First, there
were elements within the Commission, and particularly at the top
level of the administrative hierarchy of the department directly
concerned, which were attached to economic doctrines of a *laisser-
faire*, free trade variety and which regarded suggestions that the
Commission should take active responsibility for regional development as a dangerous form of *dirigisme*. These forces would, of course,
have been consistently sceptical of the need for a positive regional
policy. The specific decision to issue a formal Recommendation on
the Luxembourg-Lorraine issue was almost certainly taken without
their active support. Our attention was drawn actually to another
case where their advice had been rejected in favour of a similar
initiative from elsewhere.[1] On neither of these occasions, however,
were the officials responsible for the original initiative entirely
without support in the official hierarchy and this, along with the
support of their Commissioner, must explain their initial success.
A second blockage consisted of those who regarded regional
policy as a matter for national governments and not for the Com-

[1] This was the setting up of the *Comité de liaison et d'Action pour l'Industrie
du Soufre en Italie*. The Committee was set up by the Council of Ministers but it
is understood that the initiative came from the Commission.

munity at all. This view, strongly held and canvassed by the French Government, was influential in this part of the Commission by the beginning of 1964 and this was one reason why the Commission was helpless in the face of the *immobilisme* of the negotiations between national authorities on the Luxembourg-Lorraine problem. It was said that M. Marjolin's personal cabinet made representations to the French authorities and did their best to engineer some breakthrough but without success.

This scepticism about regional policy was clearly dominant in most of the official statements of the Commission in connection with the case. One might compare in this respect the language of the reply of M. Marjolin to M. Toubeau's Oral Question in the Parliament with that of the written replies to earlier questions and the Commission's other official statements, the one holding out far more hope and using a much less 'bureaucratic' imagery than the others. The Recommendation itself may have been a slightly watered-down version of an original draft supported by the original advocates of Commission action. In particular, there had originally been a move within the Commission to set up a working group of officials from the Commission and from the other authorities concerned, which would be chaired by a Commission representative and would carry out the negotiations proposed by the Commission's Recommendation. Instead, as we have seen, the Commission finally proposed an *ad hoc* committee appointed by the member States with a Commission representative as 'observer'. Most of the people we spoke to in the private institutions concerned with the case felt that the negotiations would have stood a much greater chance of success had the original suggestion of Commission *chairmanship* been accepted by the Commission.[1]

However, once the Commission had put the matter into the hands of the national authorities, the affair became completely 'bureaucratized', and this was the very word used to us by one of the leading local participants. In some respects, those who had been involved in the first place came to regret having raised the matter at a Community level at all. Before the Commission had been approached for its help, the local talks had been making some progress—but

---

[1] The *Comité de Liaison et d'Action* (see p. 230, n. 1 above) was a sort of precedent for this. In that case, however, inertia within the Commission had led those in favour of more positive action to appeal to the Council of Ministers(!).

after the Commission's recommendation they were further away from any settlement than ever!

This illustration of what should perhaps be called the political dynamics of *dis*integration challenges us to take a new look at some of the ways by which the Commission is said to 'upgrade the common interest'. In the first place, none of the sanctions normally available to the Commission was available in this particular case. The survival of the Community itself could not be clearly shown to be at stake, and there was no means of playing off the interests of one member State against another. There were no deadlines of any kind imposed either from within or without or by the Treaty, and there was no agreed policy according to which the Commission could act. The Council of Ministers never discussed the affair at all and, for all we know, never even had cognizance of it. Secondly, the Commission clearly had the support of sympathetic interest groups directly involved in the region concerned. The original initiative to raise the matter at a Community level came from them and as far as they were concerned the Commission was approached almost in preference to the national authorities. Yet the Commission could take no advantage of this and the support of these groups was no use as a sanction against the member States concerned. Finally, there was the role of the Parliament, which did its best to get the matter pursued more effectively at a Community level but proved to have no effective influence whatsoever over the member governments or even the Commission itself.

The record of this affair from the Commission's point of view seems to illustrate what can be achieved by an unstructured and open-ended decision-making process where the leadership (in the form of the Commissioner himself) is responsive to ideas from below. However, it illustrates equally well how such a leader can be hamstrung by lack of support within his own department and by lack of political resources. Could the Commission have been of any more use if it had been a different type of organization? What if there had been a common regional policy and the Commission had had a formal and specific mandate to act in situations of this kind (say, by sponsoring and chairing negotiations) or had had the power to lend financial assistance on its own initiative?

Under such circumstances as these, however, a wholly new set of criteria would be needed to judge the Commission's organization.

Loyalty to superiors and uniformity of outlook would then be the rule and, if the organization were successfully set up according to these criteria, the Commissioner concerned would have no difficulties in getting his way. On the other hand, under such conditions, the initiative which led to the raising of this particular case would never have been taken and the two officials most closely concerned would probably not have been working for the Commission. Indeed, for the case to be dealt with at all, the formal prescriptions laying down the Commission's role would have had to include such cases clearly and unmistakably. Under the circumstances therefore, it is not surprising that the Commission gave this case no priority. The case points to the sad but unavoidable conclusion that effective action at Community level in positive integration calls for a conventional style of political leadership combined with 'classical' administrative organization. The contrast between this case and the negotiation of the Kennedy Round is significant, as we shall see below.

CHAPTER 10

THE ORGANIZATION OF THE COMMISSION

The contemporary historian, with only clumsy conceptual tools at
hand and relying on superficial comparisons with the formal powers
of other existing bodies such as international secretariats and federal
governments, is unable to fit the Commission into any meaningful
classification. The Commission seems to have been assigned formal
powers and characteristics in an unprecedented way. It certainly is
the case, as we shall argue in the first section of this chapter, that the
Commission performs a variety of functions in the political system
of the Community. Roughly speaking in some aspects the Commission is expected to act as a bureaucracy and to have the essential
characteristics of an implementative, 'goal-seeking' organization,
while in others it must behave as if it constituted the political leadership of the Community, acting as an initiating, 'goal-setting' body.
We shall suggest here that the Commission has in practice attempted
to meet both these broad criteria and that its organization reflects
both political and bureaucratic characteristics. This assumption
fits with our empirical investigation of actual decisions in Chapters
Eight and Nine and is compatible with the conflict between political
and legal obligations which we found to underlie the administration
of personnel within the Commission. Our immediate purpose is to
elaborate upon this assumption by providing a *vue d'ensemble* of the
Commission's role in the Community process and of its internal
organization. We hope that this will enable us to reach some conclusion as to the conditions upon which the Commission depends
for performing its role as a political leadership.

THE FUNCTIONS OF THE COMMISSION

The Commission can be described as performing a number of functions of a substantially different nature. The first of these is that of
Initiative. This function derives from some of the Commission's
most important legal powers, particularly that to initiate Community
legislation.[1] It also has the power to make recommendations on

[1] See p. 79 above.

any matter it thinks fit within the framework of the Treaty. It is generally maintained that the Commission's practical initiatives are a key factor in providing the dynamic of the Community and serve as milestones in its development—for example, the 'Acceleration' decision of May 1960, the various major steps towards the achievement of a common agricultural policy, and the setting up of the various economic policy committees. Such initiatives have been backed up by the now familiar techniques of canvassing support among interest groups and public opinion in the member States, speeches in the European Parliament, and so on. At the same time the Commission has kept up a consistent stream of publications setting objectives for the future work of the Community and interpreting past achievements. It is important to note that our use of 'initiative' here must not be confused with the notion of discretion. The exercise of discretion is not necessarily related to the function of Initiative as treated here, which involves essentially the elaboration and formulation of new programmes of action. Officials exercise discretion even in carrying out existing programmes of action, as we shall see below. Initiation requires a degree of innovative activity which is not normally found in a bureaucracy, which is designed essentially for the execution of existing programmes.[1]

Closely allied to this function of Initiative is another best described as Normative. We have already referred to the fact that the Commission has a number of formal powers as 'guardian of the Treaty' and 'conscience of the Community'.[2] The way in which the Commission regards itself as having the right to interpret the Rome Treaty and to determine the Community interest is just as famous as its acts of initiative. This is illustrated by its role as honest broker in the Council of Ministers during the legislative process, in that the Commission will amend its proposals in order to find a majority on the Council only if the amendment is justified in the Community interest. Numerous examples of the Community's Normative function could be cited from the history of the Community so far, but one or two will suffice here, such as its condemnation of the French Government for going outside the Council of Ministers to veto British entry in 1963, its disapproval of the Franco-German Treaty, and its representation of the Community in the Kennedy

1 See pp. 82–3 above.
1 See p. 80 above.

Round negotiations. In all these cases the Commission took upon itself the duty of laying down the Community interest, rather as a national government interprets the public interest. The Commission has not been afraid to invoke this right against the Council of Ministers. For example, in 1964 the Council of Ministers rejected a proposal of the Commission for a new Community quota for goods transport by road and produced instead its own draft for an alternative system. The Commission thundered in its Annual Report that it 'could not see its way to accepting this solution', which diverged 'appreciably from the Commission's initial proposal, which was more in keeping with the Community spirit'.[1]

This Normative function is quite different from the regulatory function exercised by a number of public, official bodies when they interpret the meaning of statutes in individual cases. The Commission's Normative function extends to 'filling out' the provisions of the Treaty of Rome and also to having the right to react to unforeseen situations, (such as the French veto of British membership). Indeed, the Initiative and Normative functions of the Commission are interdependent and together give it the role of political leader and promoter of the Community interest. It is quite evident that without this role the Community would turn into an inter-governmental organization like OECD or the Council of Europe. It is a role, however, which may well be fully effective only under certain conditions. For example, the institution which performs it may well need to be autonomous and to derive its authority from some source which is independent, in the case of the Community, of the member states and the Council of Ministers. It must wield enough power over other actors in the system to support its initiatives by getting its own norms accepted. Again, it would almost certainly have to be capable of identifying with a particular set of values, for otherwise it would be unable to derive these norms of action in the Community. Thus, the Commission should be able to hold consistently to some body of European doctrine. Thirdly, however, such an institution must be inventive and creative, for it has to interpret values in the context of changing circumstances.

The Commission has also come to acquire an increasingly important Administrative function. We mean by this not simply the tech-

1 *Eighth General Report on the Activities of the Community*, 1965, ECC Commission, p. 267.

nical tasks of preparing for decisions, producing data, and keeping records, but also the taking of the vast number of regulatory decisions arising under the Community legislation concerning the customs union, the common policy on competition between enterprises and the common agricultural policy. At the same time, as 'guardian of the Treaty' the Commission regularly has to decide on a number of purported infringements of the Treaty.[1] These are basically mechanical activities in that they involve the implementation of existing policies and programmes. This does not exclude the exercise of discretion. For example, the making of such administrative decisions may involve deciding whether or not to enforce particular regulations on the basis of the facts of a case, applying policy to particular circumstances, or interpreting a policy which is expressed only in very general terms. Nevertheless, students of organization normally draw a fundamental distinction between this kind of reproductive decision-making according to settled policies and the taking of critical, innovative decisions needed to initiate new policies. Moreover, regulatory activity unlike the setting of norms is based on delegated authority.[2]

It may well be that the Initiative and Administrative functions each call for completely different kinds of organization. As we have seen above, recent research suggests that, in the industrial context at least, the 'mechanistic', bureaucratic type of organization, designed to produce accurate and efficient performance of routine tasks, is not suited to unstable conditions where innovation and reaction to change are at a premium[3]. Indeed, since few organizations exist in completely stable conditions, the difference is probably best expressed as a problem of management, a challenge to the organization's leaders to make special provision for innovative decision-making. This can be done by deliberately attracting resources to unprogrammed activity (for example, setting up special planning teams, or setting deadlines for the settlement of particular detailed questions which cannot be settled before decisions have been taken on wider issues of principle). However, the initiating role of an organization is under constant threat from its administrative responsibilities:

---

[1] See p. 80 above.
[2] See J. G. March and H. A. Simon, *Organizations*, New York, Wiley, 1958, pp. 177–8.
[3] See above pp. 111–13.

237

'If all the resources of an organization are busily employed in carrying out existing programs, the process of initiating new programs will be slow and halting at best. Frequently, when a new program is to be developed, a new organizational unit is created and charged with the task first of elaborating the new program and then carrying it on when it has been elaborated. This procedure provides for a spurt of innovative, program-developing activity—a spurt that automatically diminishes as the program is elaborated and the task shifts gradually from one of planning to one of execution. . . .'[1]

Finally, the Commission has a Mediative function, which arises from its duty to bring about agreement between the member States in the Council of Ministers. This is the normal function of the secretariat of an inter-governmental organization (like that of GATT, for example). Such a body tries to reconcile the proposals of different member countries, usually by drafting solutions of its own which seek to chart a middle path, or by devising formulae which compensate for the losses and gains of the various parties. The Commission often seems to be doing this in its work in the Committee of Permanent Representatives and its sub-committees and in the Council of Ministers itself, changing its own proposals in response to particular national objections. It is because of the presence of a Mediative function that the Commission involves itself in such complex and multiple contacts with representatives of member States at various stages of the decision-making process. Lindberg describes how the Commission skilfully performed such a function of mediation during the discussions on the proposed 'Acceleration' decision of 1960: '. . . a decision could not have been achieved without the Commission. The inability of the governments to agree on a precise formula forced them to delegate the task of formulation to the Commission. No-one was willing to accept the possibility of a deadlock.'[2]

The Commission also seemed to be performing this function when it was preparing a Community position before the final stages of the Kennedy Round Negotiations.[3]

In theory the Commission is meant to exercise its Mediative function in conjunction with its Initiative and Normative functions,

[1] March and Simon, *op. cit.*, pp. 186–7.
[2] L. Lindberg, *Political Dynamics of European Economic Integration*, London, OUP, 1963, p. 193.
[3] See pp. 176–90 above.

238

so that any settlement in the Council of Ministers will 'upgrade the common interest'. We have already noted that this is extremely difficult to do. Certainly, we would expect Mediative activity to be usually incompatible with Normative activity and even contradictory to it, in that the former calls for flexibility, objectivity and impartiality and the latter for commitment to certain values and even zeal in defence of them. We might assume, therefore, that the Commission is generally faced with a choice between acting as an independent, uncommitted secretariat and as a zealous band of Europeans. We might also assume that the effective performance of the Mediative function does not necessitate the exercise of a great deal of power over those between or among whom one mediates. Far more important are qualities such as impartiality and detachment and a reputation for fair-mindedness combined with negotiating skill and a full technical knowledge of the issued involved. The mediator may well be frequently called on to innovate and to invent new courses of action, although the proposals he makes may not get beyond the drafting stage without the support of at least some of the agents of his mediation. Indeed, the Initiative and Mediative functions are often combined in existing international secretariats, and this probably explains why such bodies spend much of their time in a crisis concerning the proper extent of their powers (witness the United Nations' General Secretariat's hesitation about intervening in military situations). Basically, however, the two functions are on opposite sides of the organizational spectrum. The mediator who initiates too frequently runs the risk of seeming partisan or at least of making enemies by accident. The initiator in his turn must have the backing of some legitimizing, norm-setting authority, whether this be a representative assembly, or a mass political movement, or whether the authority is in some way vested in himself (as in the case of the Commission). The mediator does not require such authority and may well find it an embarrassment, for his role depends on his unimpeachable independence and impartiality. In this sense, while the administrator lacks the creativity and inventiveness required by the mediator, there is a certain complementarity between the two. (This is, perhaps, why, although diplomats are usually civil servants, the diplomatic service of most countries is generally regarded as showing more initiative, and as being less anonymous, than the home Civil Service.)

In the decision-making process of the Community it must be a great temptation for the Commission to stick to the role of mediator and to 'split the difference' between various national positions, rather than go to the lengths of asserting a distinct Community point of view. Similarly, it is a great temptation to any organisation to administer existing programmes of activity rather than to initiate new policies. There must be a constant strain within the Commission between its Normative and Initiative functions, on the one hand, and its Mediative and Administrative ones, on the other. The dichotomy between the two different sets of functions could be described roughly as that between a political or promotive role and a bureaucratic or implementative one. The promotive role exercised by the Commission in performing its Initiative and Normative functions is usually identified within the national State of Western experience with the political leadership, say, a cabinet of ministers, which is popularly elected, or which is responsible to a representative assembly. This is the way the promotive institution acquires legitimacy and wields the necessary power for its task. The Administrative and Mediative functions, on the other hand, are in theory performed in the national context by regulatory agencies, government departments, advisory committees, or other sections of the bureaucracy, whose power is essentially based on delegated authority. Parallel to this difference in the amount of power exercised in performing different functions is a difference in type of organization. The highly structured, mechanistic type of organization associated with the performance of routine administrative tasks is not adaptable to the exercise of initiative or to the setting of norms. It may not even be suitable for the Mediative function, as we shall see.[1]

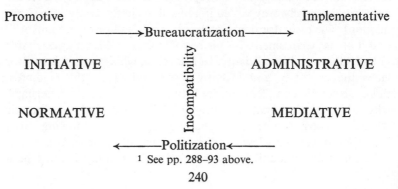

THE FUNCTIONS OF THE COMMISSION

Promotive   Implementative
————→Bureaucratization————→

INITIATIVE   ADMINISTRATIVE

NORMATIVE   MEDIATIVE

←————Politization←————
[1] See pp. 288–93 above.

240

To the student of organization the analysis presented here should be familiar enough, the only real difference between it and the cases he normally studies being that the latter are usually examples of industrial activity. The concepts of initiation and norm-setting used in the previous section to describe the Commission's functions in the Community political system are directly related to the concepts associated with institutional identity used at the 'micro' level of government agencies and business enterprises. The effective performance of promotive functions can, therefore, be considered as depending, not only on the Commission's relations with other parts of the Community, but also on its very nature as an institution. Thus, Selznick distinguishes between the term 'organization', referring to a formal system of rules and objectives—a rationalized administrative instrument—and the term 'institution', denoting 'a natural product of social needs and pressures—a responsive, adaptive organism'. The distinction is similar in many ways to that between 'mechanistic' and 'organic' systems of management as used by Burns and Stalker to distinguish between systems where formal statuses and roles are emphasised and those where management relies on an informal common culture or code of conduct.[1]

'The formal, technical system is therefore never more than a part of the living enterprise we deal with in action. The persons or groups who make it up are not content to be treated as manipulable or expendable. As human beings and not mere tools they have their own needs for self-protection and self-fulfilment—needs that may either sustain the formal system or undermine it. These human relations are a great reservoir of energy. They may be directed in constructive ways toward desired ends or they may become recalcitrant sources of frustration. One objective of sound management practice is to direct and control these internal social pressures.'[2]

The student of institutions examines organizational doctrines, which act as defences against a hostile environment; the extent to which recruitment and training foster particular common values; or internal conflict over norms based on lines of informal group loyalties (which may in turn reflect external pressures on the organization).

1 See pp. 109–15 above.
2 See P. Selznick, *Leadership in Administration*, New York, Harper and Row, 1957, p. 8.

For the rest of this chapter we shall consider the extent to which such institutional conditions exist in the case of the Commission of the EEC. Two main types of criteria will be applied to the Commission's capacity to 'institutionalize' itself into an initiating, goal-setting body. First, there are those which stress the effectiveness of the organization's leaders in setting and maintaining a mission and role. Second, there are those which stress the evolution within the organization of a social system which allows for flexibility, adaptation to change, and individual commitment. Thus the establishment of a bureaucracy (in the form of rationalized, administrative machinery geared to the attainment of fixed goals) can be distinguished from the creation of institutional identity and purpose. In the first place we need to recognize the challenge presented to the organization from its working environment.

THE EFFECTS OF 'CO-OPTATION'

The Commission's policy of 'co-opting' national officials and other representatives into the decision-making process has been widely celebrated, as we have already seen. Certainly, the development of the Committee of Permanent Representatives and the sub-committees attached to it was essential to prevent excessive delay and congestion in the Council of Ministers, the real decision-making authority. It has also provided the Commission with an opportunity to 'Europeanize' numbers of national officials.[1] However, it also presents a major challenge to the institutional identity of the Commission.

One reason for this is the extent of specialized decision-making which it entails. We have already met this phenomenon in our detailed study of the Commission's role in the Kennedy Round negotiations, where we remarked on the tendency for officials to work almost exclusively on specialized committees or sub-committees with national officials of their own particular technical discipline.[2] Such an orientation must threaten to undermine an official's ability to identify with some set of general institutional goals or purposes. Most officials with policy-making responsibilities in the Commission have such a specialized orientation. A high official in a position to have a broad perspective of the Commission's rela-

[1] See pp. 86–91 above.
[2] See pp. 203–4 above.

242

tions with the Permanent Representatives admitted to us that the vast majority of category A officials spent their working lives in specialized groups of experts. Working contact with corresponding specialists from the member governments and from interest groups was more frequent than that with colleagues in other parts of the Commission. (The only exceptions to this rule were officials in 'generalist' departments, such as the Executive Secretariat, the Legal and Information Services, Administration, and in the Commissioners' cabinets.) This contact extends to bodies like the Article 111 Committee and the Monetary Committee and to the numerous 'mixed' committees, set up as common policies have evolved, consisting of national officials and experts with Commission representation (such as the various financial and economic policy committees), as well as to the new management committees designed to assist the Commission in implementing the common agricultural policy.[1] Since about 1963 the Commission's own work has become dominated by that of these various intermediary committees of national representatives.

The Commission is represented permanently on the Committee of Permanent Representatives by its Deputy Executive Secretary (and sometimes by the Executive Secretary himself). In addition, for each point on the Committee's agenda the relevant department of the Commission is represented. The Executive Secretary reports to each meeting of the Commission on what has taken place at the previous session of the Committee of Permanent Representatives. This ensures that the Commission keeps abreast of what is happening in the Committee and that it is in a position to assert its right of initiative in the Community interest should the need arise. At the same time, however, it shows how far the Commission has to preoccupy itself with the work of the Committee. There is an obvious danger that the representatives of the Commission in day-to-day contact with the Permanent Representatives and dealing with the other intermediary bodies may lose sight of the Commission's overall purpose. Moreover it is even difficult to define this purpose in any way which is not ambivalent. The representatives of the Commission are faced with two general institutional goals which may well often conflict— namely, to defend (not to say, promote) the interests of the Community and to try to bring about agreement between the member

[1] See p. 49 above.

243

States (the Normative and Mediative functions mentioned earlier).

Thus, quite apart from the stress on specialization which it entails, the important role given to intermediary bodies between the Commission and the Council must make it extremely difficult for officials of the Commission to maintain a balance between these different goals. It is important for the independence and right of initiative of the Commission that differences between government departments in a member State should get through to its own policymakers. Yet early on in the Commission's life the Permanent Representatives insisted that all correspondence between Community institutions and national governments should go through them. In practice, however, this threat has not really materialized and in most cases the Commission has not hesitated to establish and maintain direct contacts with the national administrations, using the Permanent Representatives purely as a kind of postman[1]. As we shall see below, however, attempts have recently been made to restrain the Commission's direct contact with national administrations. In any event, formal and informal contacts between the officials of the Commission and the Permanent Representatives and their staff have become extremely numerous and a fundamental element of working life in the Community. The Executive Secretary of the Commission has admitted that, while these contacts are invaluable as channels of communication and as means by which the Commission can influence the member governments, they can, nevertheless, 'also involve the risk that a department of the Commission itself may be influenced unilaterally'. He has also denied, however, that this risk is of any real moment, and claims that 'the impartiality of the Commission's departments is nowhere doubted':

'The Commission for its part has always taken a national interest into consideration without, however, renouncing its independence and its impartiality for this reason, and its example has been understood by its staff. To this must be added the guarantees of all kinds provided by an integrated administration and a collegial Commission.'[2]

This is, we suggest, a very revealing remark and puts the emphasis quite rightly on the challenge to the Commission to maintain

---

[1] E. Noël, The Committee of Permanent Representatives, *Journal of Common Market Studies*, 1967, Vol. V, No. 3, pp. 219–51.

[2] *ibid.*

institutional identity and purpose. We shall examine below the effectiveness of the 'guarantees' mentioned here.

One means by which the Commission seeks to establish direct relations with national administrations, of course, is involving national officials in its working groups on legislative proposals before these get to the Permanent Representatives or the Council of Ministers. Representatives of interest groups and other national specialists are also called on in great numbers at this stage. These *ad hoc* or permanent working groups serve four main purposes: first, they compensate for lack of numbers and lack of expertise in the Commission's own ranks; second, they enable the Commission to base its proposals on first hand knowledge of national positions; third, like the intermediary committees between Commission and Council they provide an opportunity to 'convert' national officials and representatives of interest groups to European measures before their governments are committed; and, finally, they are yet another means of saving the time of the Council by trying to reach agreement on the technical aspects of proposed measures at an early stage.[1] Senior officials of the Commission firmly believe that these groups are a vital means of preserving the Commission's initiative in the decision-making process. It is certainly the case that these groups could have an important persuasive, as well as conciliatory, function. Be that as it may, they must present very much the same challenge to the Commission's organization as the intermediary committees and Permanent Representatives. They must share responsibility for the intensely specialized, compartmentalized pattern of the working lives of Commission officials and for the intensity of contact between the latter and national representatives (many of whom will be former colleagues of some of the Commission officials concerned).[2] The second of these challenges is less serious in the case of the working groups in that the latter are assembled at the Commission's initiative and on the Commission's own terms. However, in psychological terms the challenge must still be there.

This policy of 'co-optation' in all its various forms intensifies a problem to which we gave particular attention in our case study of

[1] See pp. 86–91 above.
[2] For example, one working group on 'Obstacles to free trade resulting from provisions of a technical nature' is divided into twelve sub-groups, each of which is in turn sub-divided into several sub-sub-groups.

the Kennedy Round negotiations, namely, the need to distinguish in practice between questions of policy and questions of administration, between critical and routine decisions. Within the Commission it is customary to name these different types of decision, 'political' and 'technical', respectively. It is well known that such terms as these are strictly relative and can be understood only in given situations. Some general and wide-ranging decisions are not critical for the future of an organization while some detailed and technically specialized ones are.[1] In order to draw an operational distinction between policy and administration, the organization (or its leaders) must have a clear and firm awareness of its ultimate purposes. The leaders must refuse to allow decisions to become programmed or routinized when they are likely to be subject to changing technology or shifting evaluations.[2] The distinction is also a question of efficiency: decisions which can be satisfactorily 'programmed' should be delegated to administrators so as to leave the higher, directing levels free to make critical, policy decisions. The congestion and overloading of the decision-making process in the Community, along with the occasional desire of some national government or other to slow down progress towards unification by whatever means available, may well lead to a number of decisions becoming routinized and treated at the level of national and Commission officials acting on instructions, when they are really so critical as to require settlement at ministerial or Commissioner level.

Indeed, while the 'Points A' procedure, by which some decisions are virtually taken by the Committee of Permanent Representatives, has proved to be a valuable part of the decision-making process, there are dangers in too rigid a separation between 'political' and 'technical' questions.[3] Two senior officials of the Commission have pointed out that, if used too systematically in a particular sector, it might eventually block progress there.[4] Indeed, this is a general danger of delegating decisions to intermediary, mixed committees of officials, which seems to have been the main strategy employed

[1] See D. Coombes, *The Member of Parliament and the Administration*, London, George Allen & Unwin, 1966, pp. 31–4, 153–4.

[2] See P. Selznick, *Leadership in Administration*, *op. cit.*, pp. 74–82.

[3] On this procedure, see p. 87 above.

[4] *Quelques aspects des rapports et de la collaboration entre le Conseil et la Commission*, Communication by E. Noël and H. Etienne, Information Service of the European Communities, (undated), p. 15.

to overcome congestion in the process of decision-making. The degree to which each government is willing to delegate tasks to representatives on committees of this kind is bound to vary in practice. This raises the prospect of interminable arguments about agenda and procedure. Moreover, there must be a danger that such committees will function on the basis of the instructions of the national representatives with the minimum amount of delegated authority. This threatens to lead, not only to a pre-occupation with procedure and protocol, but also to delays and misunderstandings because questions are being treated at the wrong level.

PROBLEMS OF LEADERSHIP

This challenge from the Commission's environment would be interpreted by many students of organization primarily as a challenge to its leadership. In this sense the latter could be described as being responsible for setting the mission of the institution and creating an organization which was adequate to fulfil it. In practical terms, this responsibility falls on the members of the Commission themselves, and takes the form of a challenge to their ability to behave like ministers or political leaders rather than as civil servants or bureaucrats.

Indeed, as we have already seen, contrary to a widespread misconception the members of the Commission are not faceless officials. While the term 'eurocrat' has been applied to them just as readily as to the officials of the Commission, a distinction should be made between the members of the Commission and their staff. In a great number of respects the formal relationship between the Commissioners and their departments is very similar to that between ministers and civil servants in a national government. We have already made this clear when dealing with the administration of personnel in the Commission.[1] Furthermore, the Commissioners are also like executive leaders in that they are expected to identify completely with the institution and there is provision for a kind of collective responsibility. Great stress is placed in official descriptions of the Commission's organization on its collegial nature.

Indeed, this is referred to in the very first article of the Commission's Rules of Procedure (*Règlement Intérieure*): the official regula-

[1] See pp. 122–4 above.

tions laying down the main principles of the formal organization of the Commission.[1] While it is the President of the Commission who lays down the draft agenda for each meeting, any other member may ask to have an item added to it or to have any point on it put back until a later meeting. The final agenda is fixed by the Commission as a whole in full session (the quorum for a meeting of the Commission of the EEC before the merger of the executives was five). The draft agenda and all related documents must have been communicated previously to each member according to fixed intervals of time. Any member may veto discussion of a question not included in the agenda or of one where the associated documents have not been distributed within the time provided. The minutes of each meeting of the Commission have to be approved in draft form at the next meeting. This strict collegiality is not undermined by the 'written procedure', in that any member of the Commission may request that an issue being treated by this procedure should be considered orally at the next full session of the Commission. As we have seen, each member of the Commission is given special responsibility for a particular sector or sectors of the Commission's work and before the merger it was normal for each Commissioner to be responsible for one Directorate General. Under these circumstances the department concerned 'received its instructions from' the responsible Commissioner.[2] The Rules of Procedure, however, made it clear that this was not intended to conflict with the collegial nature of the Commission and that the administrative services constituted 'a single administration'.[3] (It was mainly in order to embody this principle in some way that specialized groups of Commissioners were formed for each main sector of the Commission's responsibilities.) At the same time, the Rules of Procedure laid down that the administrative services should work 'in the closest possible co-operation'. All parts of the services concerned with a particular question should be consulted before a proposal was submitted to the Commission, and along with any such proposal the department concerned should present the Commission with the dissenting views of other departments.[4]

[1] Règlement Intérieure de la Commission, *Journal Officiel des Communautés Européennes*, No. 17, (1963), January 31, 1963, pp. 181–5.
[2] *ibid.*, Article 13.
[3] *ibid.*, Article 17.
[4] *ibid.*, Articles 21 and 22.

In spite of these elaborate statutory provisions, we are bound to question whether the administrative services of the Commission were as united in practice as was intended. As we have already seen in the case of the Commission's attempts to form a 'European Civil Service', the legal framework of organization is invariably overlain, or even extinguished, by political factors or by designs of expediency.[1] In view of the challenge to the Commission's institutional unity represented by the decision-making process of the Community, and in view of the fundamental difficulties of forming a multi-national organisation, it is most unlikely that the embodiment of principles in an internal statute will be sufficient.

In fact, the Commission did go further than this and attempted to institutionalize its collegiality in the form of an Executive Secretariat. This body has a very similar role to that of the Cabinet Secretariat in Britain and acts as guardian of the collegial nature of the Commission. Largely on account of the devotion and single-mindedness of the first Executive Secretary (and the only one so far), M. Emile Noël, this body has played a key role in the development of the Community. Its main functions are set out in Article 16 of the Rules of Procedure as to assist the President of the Commission in preparing for the Commission's meetings, in conducting the written procedure, and in ensuring that the decisions of the Commission are followed up as required ('s'assurer . . . la régularité de l'exécution des délibérations de la Commission'). In order to perform these functions the Executive Secretary must see that all the necessary and proper documents are produced at meetings and also 'check' ('s'informer') that the Commission's decisions are being carried out. In addition, he is responsible for the publication of the Journal Officiel, where all the official acts of the Commission must appear, and for the Commission's working relations with other Community institutions. The importance of the post is underlined by the fact that the Executive Secretary must countersign the minutes of Commission meetings as well as all acts adopted by the Commission. The Executive Secretary and his deputy attend the meetings of the Commission, unless the latter expressly decides otherwise.[2]

The Executive Secretariat is clearly in a key position, being the only body (other than the Commission itself) which is responsible

[1] See pp. 122–40 above.
[2] Règlement Intérieure, op. cit., Article 9.

for taking a view of the organization as a whole. The Executive Secretary and his staff are permanently involved at the nerve centre of the organization. However, in view of its responsibilities for linking the past with the future and for maintaining cohesion between different parts of the organization in the present, it might be expected that the Executive Secretariat would need to be essentially bureaucratic in outlook and behaviour. Certainly its junior staff are mainly young lawyers who see their task as the rather precise and mechanical (if, nevertheless, vitally important), one of ensuring consistency and regularity in the work of the Commission. However, the Executive Secretary himself and his senior assistants are regarded as being highly skilled at organizational 'politics'. The Commission's rise to institutional maturity is widely-regarded as owing much to M. Noël's own personal contribution.[1]

The main task of a corps of this type is to convince the various individual sectors of the organization to accept the official (that is, the Commission's) interpretation of the common interest. From our study of the Commission's organization so far, there would seem to be far more real normative conflict inside its policy-making cadres than in a typical bureaucracy. In face of such conflict the Secretariat's position must often seem to be extremely conservative and cautious. For, when there are conflicting views as to what is settled policy, a body like the Secretariat must often resort to established formulae and precedents in an attempt to ensure consistency. The only alternative for it would be to take sides in a dispute, which would prove fatal for its influence and for its proper function of co-ordination. At the same time, we might well question whether this bureaucratic style of co-ordination is altogether adequate under the circumstances.

One vital aspect of the work of the Executive Secretariat is that it acts as a direct link between the Commission itself and the outside world, in particular, the Committee of Permanent Representatives and its offshoots. This gives it the responsibility, not only to ensure that the Commission takes every opportunity to maintain its own prerogatives on these committees, but also to keep the Commission within the bounds of what is possible in view of the positions of the national delegations. In this respect too, the Secretariat is sometimes viewed as taking a narrow and conservative position in conflicts

[1] See, for example, R. Lemaignen, *L'Europe au Berceau*, Paris, Plon, 1963, pp. 69–70.

with other parts of the organization. However, the Secretariat would not be doing its duty if it did not warn the Commission against hostile reactions from outside to particular lines of policy and if it did not seek to remind the Commission of agreements already entered into and commitments previously made. It is obvious that anybody entrusted with overseeing the execution of programmes and with preserving continuity must seem conservative in outlook. By the same token, the Secretariat can have only limited effectiveness in 'chasing up' individual Commissioners and their departments when these have failed to measure up to the objectives set by the Commission as a whole. It is certainly part of the Secretariat's task to maintain a timetable for the performance of settled programmes and to see to it that the Commission carries out a regular review of all its various activities. Here too, however, its role is strictly bureaucratic—it cannot compensate for the absence of interest or of action on the part of the Commission itself.

We have dwelt on the role of the Executive Secretariat to stress that the existence of this body can be no substitute for political leadership from the Commission itself. We do not wish to suggest that the Secretariat has gone out of its way to have a bureaucratic or conservative influence on the organization, for we have no evidence that this has been the case. Indeed what evidence exists seems to point in the opposite direction and the members of the Secretariat seem to have done their best to give a positive interpretation to the objectives and opinions of the Commission. The key question, however, is how far the Commission itself is equipped to provide its individual members and its administrative services with clear decisions and directives out of the diverse and sometimes conflicting elements which make up the organization.

It is clear that in some respects the Commissioners are most unlike political leaders or the ministerial heads of government of a nation state. First of all, the members of the Commission are not elected by any popular majority with any mandate to govern, nor are they responsible to any directly elected representative assembly. They are not even the acknowledged leaders of some ideologically based and bureaucratically organized mass party similar to that which governs the states of eastern Europe and the Soviet Union. They owe their positions to the member governments and, except in the case of the President and Vice-Presidents, their appointments are not usually discussed by the six governments together. Their authority is thus strikingly bureaucratic (in the strict 'classical' sense of the term), in that it rests basically on legal devices such as the oath of allegiance and the relevant provisions in the Treaty of Rome.[1]

The Commissioners also differ from most national executive leaders in that they are not bound together by membership of the same political party or by adherence to the same mandate. Since each Commissioner is approved in practice by his own country's government it cannot truly be said that they are collectively responsible for their tenure of office. Indeed no one has yet found a satisfactory explanation of what holds them together. Perhaps this is a question which never occurred to the founders of the Community, or perhaps it was that they simply saw the Commission as a body with power which was essentially delegative and derived from the Treaty— as the name 'Commission' might suggest. Certainly the Commission has not been manned by figures of great political importance. Of the fourteen men who had served on it at one time or another up to the merger, only five had had experience as fully fledged national ministers, while President Hallstein had been a Secretary of State in the Federal German Foreign Office, and Commissioner Caron an Italian junior minister and deputy. The remaining seven had all been civil servants, academics, or 'technicians' (although one or two of these had served in their country's parliament).[2]

[1] See pp. 122–3 above.
[2] The fourteen Commissioners are listed below with notes of their previous occupations before joining the Commission. Taken from S. Holt, *The Common Market*, London, Hamish Hamilton, 1968, pp. 41–2:

W. Hallstein, Professor of Law, diplomat, State Secretary for Foreign Affairs.
S. Mansholt, Minister of Agriculture and Fisheries.
R. Marjolin, Secretary-General, OEEC . . . Assistant to Jean Monnet.
G. Petrilli, Specialist in economics, finance and social insurance.
L. Levi-Sandri, Administrator, professor, municipal councillor.
G. Caron, Industrialist, senator, junior minister.
H.v.d.Groeben, Civil servant . . . Spaak Committee.
R. Lemaignen, Businessman, Dep. Chairman of International Relations Committee of CNPF.
P. Malvestiti, Deputy . . . Under-Secretary in various ministries.
C. di Paliano, Asst. Secretary-General, OEEC . . . Asst. Secretary-General, NATO
M. Rasquin, Minister of Economic Affairs, ECSC Council of Ministers.
J. Rey, Minister of Economic Affairs, ECSC Council of Ministers.
H. Rochereau, Senator, Minister of Agriculture.
L. Schaus, Diplomat, Minister of Economic Affairs and Army, Permanent representative to EEC.

The only thing which the members of the Commission had in common—at least in the first four or five years—was the fact that they were all considered 'good Europeans'.[1] This was certainly what President Hallstein himself believed and he did his best to cultivate it into a recognizable common political identity. Certainly, all the members of the Commission in the early years had previously been involved in some way with the foundation of the Community—some of them very closely indeed. Right up to the time of the merger, the Commission was still regarded by some close observers as a relatively intimate and cohesive body. The Commission usually met regularly once a week (all day Wednesday) in what seem to have been conditions at least as intimate as those of the British Cabinet. With the exception of Mr von der Groeben, all the members could and did express themselves easily in French, so that there was little need for interpreters. Meetings could be attended by a few well-chosen officials—the Executive Secretary or his Deputy, the Official Spokesman, often an expert or two from a department, occasionally the member of a cabinet—but there were no serried ranks of officials as are common in high-level international executives. Votes were rarely necessary and the proceedings were usually informal and congenial.[2] At the same time, individual Commissioners have done their best to make up for their isolation from political forces by taking full advantage of the European Parliament and the Economic and Social Committee, of their own Information Service and access to the mass media, and of their independence and right to speak freely, to publicize and identify with the views and policies of the Commission and to attempt to mobilize support for European measures. Many of the members of the Commission under Hallstein's Presidency established themselves as the equals of the ministers of the member States, receiving deputations from third countries, representing the Commission on visits abroad, and above all, appealing informally, though regularly, over the heads of the Permanent Representatives to the member governments themselves. For example, President Hallstein himself repeatedly made visits to Bonn for this purpose. Moreover, in addition to maintaining a

[1] The political complexion of the first Commission in 1958 was roughly as follows: Socialist or Social Democrat, 3; Christian Democrat, 3; Liberal and French *Indépendant*, 2; unknown, 1.
[2] See R. Mayne, *The Institutions of the European Community*, PEP/Chatham House, 1968, pp. 30–31.

timetable for the regular consideration of projects being undertaken in various parts of the organization, the Commission has regularly held great 'debates of orientation' with a view to preserving a sense of general direction and purpose in spite of the intensely specialized and diffuse day-to-day work of the organization. The results of these debates are published in general memoranda and circulated.

Thus, from one point of view the Commissioners could be seen as a kind of united party leadership, disagreeing among themselves only over tactics and competing only to champion the common cause. Service of such a body would most probably be based on a shared loyalty rather than on bureaucratic motives such as a desire for personal security or status. Our research has already suggested that the Commission's organization was based on such principles to a large extent in the early years and probably still is, though to a much lesser extent. It is widely felt that the Commissioners themselves have now become less and less united on key issues. For example, Mrs Camps describes how the French veto of British membership brought disunity within the Commission to the surface:

'Although the tactics employed by General de Gaulle were universally deplored, it was clear enough that while sympathies were entirely with the British in some quarters of the Commission, in others there was thinly disguised relief that the task of 'digesting' the British had, at least, been deferred. For the first time, Community officials, at all levels, were aware of their own and each other's nationality. The crisis of confidence was very real, not only among the six Governments but in the most Community-minded of all the Community institutions as well.'[1]

The same author also confirms that the Commission was divided over the decision to link the questions of *ressources propres* and of increasing the powers of the European Parliament with proposals on financing the common agricultural policy in the spring of 1965.[2] In these conditions the preservation of collegiality has come to involve reconciling different norms by a process of internal politics. It has certainly been confirmed to us that on the Commission itself conflicts have tended increasingly to be settled by bargaining between different positions sometimes on national lines. In this way

[1] M. Camps, *What Kind of Europe?*, London, OUP, 1964, pp. 3–4.
[2] M. Camps, *European Unification in the Sixties*, London, OUP, 1968, p. 47.

some Commissioners have acquired a representative function towards the organization and the sessions of the Commission itself have become an arena in which decisions are legitimised by a process of confrontation of different norms of policy.

In view of this it is perhaps not surprising that on the whole the role of the Commissioners' personal cabinets is more important than that of the Executive Secretariat in exercising co-ordination and control. At the start of the Commission's life President Hallstein wished to keep the membership of personal cabinets as small as possible and was generally anxious to keep the number of people admitted to full sessions of the Commission itself as low as possible.[1] This supports our hypothesis that in the beginning the Commission was seen by its members essentially as an intimate, partisan type of body. The Commissioners were entitled to appoint cabinets under Article 15 of the Rules of Procedure, but were limited to two members for each cabinet. It proved possible in practice, however, to overcome this limitation by filling a cabinet with officials formally attached to the Directorate General for which the Commissioner was responsible. The importance of the cabinets has grown along with the increasingly representative nature of the Commission itself.

The main function of the cabinet is to fill the gulf which very often exists between its Commissioner and the Directorate General for which he is responsible, given that the latter will be appointed according to the fixed distribution between nationalities and that it may well be infiltrated by hostile or, at least, unfamiliar 'parties'. In fact, some cabinets have concentrated on this task more than others and some Commissioners have acquired the reputation of 'living in' their cabinets. The heads of cabinet regularly meet together to prepare for meetings of the full Commission and since the merger this meeting has been given official recognition. A second important function of the cabinet is to maintain links with the government of the Commissioner's own home country. Again, some cabinets have done this much more than others, while some may not have regarded it as their proper function at all. The importance of such a role is obvious, however, as some Commissioners come more and more to represent national points of view. Closely linked with it is a third function, namely, to keep an eye on the distribution of posts

1 See Lemaignen, *op. cit.*, pp. 49–50.

255

in the administrative services of the Commission with a view to preserving the quota of the cabinet's own nationality and selecting candidates for posts reserved for that nationality. We have already seen how most higher appointments, and even some lower ones, practically always go up to the Commission itself for settlement.[1] It is widely felt that the cabinets exercise great influence over appointments and that this gives them considerable power in the decision-making process. It also makes them unpopular with many officials in the departments. It is clear that such a function of maintaining numbers of one's own 'party' in the ranks is extremely important in a loose, open-ended organization such as the Commission has acquired in the course of time. In this sense, the cabinet's role in appointments is likely to enhance the inventiveness and creativity of the Commission, in that they are more likely than a formalised department of personnel administration to advance the careers of bright young officials and even to bring suitable people in from outside. The cabinets themselves serve as means of bringing up young 'high-fliers' and, indeed, most of the cream of the Commission's younger staff can be found in the cabinets themselves.

Not all of the cabinets stress these 'representative' functions. Mr Mansholt's cabinet for example has concentrated overwhelmingly, not on running the Directorate General of Agriculture, but on keeping their Commissioner informed of activities elsewhere in the Commission and of advising him on matters outside agriculture. It is worth noting that a major reason why this was possible was that Mr Mansholt had no difficulty in communicating with his Directorate General, the key members of which were handpicked by him from the beginning.[1] This expresses the spirit of the more partisan, loyalist type of organization of the early years: the cabinet's main function seems to be preserving collegiality by acting as the Commissioner's eyes and ears in other parts of the organization. For this purpose the members of Mr Mansholt's cabinet each specialized on a different aspect of the Commission's responsibilities. The cabinet of Mr von der Groeben has recently developed on similar lines.

1 See pp. 157–60 above.
2 See L. N. Lindberg, Decision Making and Integration in the European Communities, *International Organisation*, Vol. XIX, No. 1, Winter 1965, pp. 62–63.

It was from this collegial point of view, no doubt, that cabinets were first instituted, but, as we have seen, with the increasingly representative nature of the Commissioners themselves, their functions tend to have broadened considerably. Among the Directorates General themselves it has been increasingly felt that the cabinets have tried to interpose themselves between the Commissioners and the rest of the organization, and that the cabinets (as predominantly national enclaves identifying with their Commissioner rather than with the organization as a whole) might threaten the institutional identity of the Commission. Even the cabinets, therefore, are no substitute for unified political leadership to provide an overall mission and purpose for the organization.

BUREAUCRATIZATION

We may now recognise added significance in our earlier discussion of the Commission's attempts to found a European Civil Service. In the beginning recruitment and administration of personnel did not need to be a major preoccupation of the Commission. Officials were selected from lists drawn up by individual Commissioners largely on the basis of personal acquaintance and known commitment to the European cause. This is the main way in which the loyalist, partisan Europeans came into the organization from national administrations, from universities and business, but mainly from other European and international organizations. Very soon, however, the organization entered a condition we shall refer to as 'porous'. The increasing demands for skilled, experienced specialists led to the recruitment of seconded national civil servants, many of whom had no intention of making service with the Commission a career, or even anything more than a useful interlude in their national careers. At the same time, the making of individual appointments (even in categories B and C), became a question of internal politics, as some Commissioners inside, and some national governments outside, began to take a keen interest in their representation in the ranks of the Commission. The 'classical' career civil service, based on impartiality and impersonality and with highly-structured arrangements for personnel administration, could not be established in spite of the existence of a legal basis for it. We remarked that this was probably quite in keeping with the nature of the Commission at this time and fostered the necessary flexibility and inventiveness in decision-making.[1]

The loose, open-ended system of organization was related to the Commission's Mediative function as well as to the representative nature of its leadership. For one thing, in an organization where the leaders tend to support different normative approaches there will be a tendency to drive decisions up to the representative level, a tendency which can lead to serious inefficiencies by overloading the directing body (in this case the Commission itself). This threat can be counteracted by underplaying formal hierarchical relationships and allowing 'parties' to form within the organization, linking lower with higher levels and even linking section with section horizontally. This allows conflicts to be played out at lower levels. We found evidence of this type of porous organization in our case studies of the Kennedy Round and Regional Policy.[2] We also found generally that recruitment and personnel management have allowed for effective infiltration and for the formation of cross-departmental loyalties. But we suggest that even this type of organization must be only temporary or at least confined to certain sectors, particularly in a body in the Commission's position. On the one hand, the transitional porous organization fosters creativity and inventiveness which is suited to the Commission's initiative function, while it also seems to provide for flexibility and responsiveness which suits the Mediative function (and was found to be most suitable for the Commission's role in the Kennedy Round). On the other hand, it is bound to threaten institutional identity and purpose by multiplying values and loyalties within the organization. At least it might bog the organization down in interminable internal frontier disputes and 'party' squabbles. Indeed there is evidence that this has increasingly come to be the case, with more and more issues needing to be voted on by Commissioners and an increasingly dominant role being played by the cabinets. Above all, it conflicts with the Commission's Administrative function in that the implementation and defence of Community policies calls for organizational characteristics such as consistency and uniformity.

In face of this, and in the absence of inspired leadership from above or of underlying common values, decisions will tend to be

1 See pp. 163–4, 214–16 above.
2 See pp. 198–216, 227–33 above.

based on rigid formulae and precedents, and bureaucratic symptoms of 'retreatism' and 'ritual' will appear.[1] The porous organization resorts eventually to strict regulation of appointments and promotions to ensure impartiality and equilibrium between different competing groups, rigid definitions of powers and jurisdiction, and other bureaucratic means of preserving equilibrium and consistency. Delegation becomes increasingly difficult in practice because of the lack of confidence in subordinates who might be members of other 'parties'. Conversely, initiative is deadened by mistrust of superiors. As a cumulative result of these tendencies, the directing part of the institution becomes preoccupied with internal administrative problems, such as the allocation of functions, regulations concerning administration of personnel, and so on. The vicious circle of bureaucracy now sets in.[2] Many of these tendencies were reported to us by officials of the Commission, and we found some evidence of them in our study of personnel administration.[3]

It was clear to us that by the time of the merger such a bureaucratic vicious circle had begun to set in, and was beginning to affect the whole of the organization. The Hallstein Commission, influenced greatly by the 'charisma' of the President himself, was initially able to establish a relatively united, committed partisan organization, ideally suited to the Commission's promotive functions. It is clear that out of the nine Commissioners, two at least (and possibly more) exercised the kind of strong political leadership which such an institution requires. These were the President himself and Vice-President Mansholt, who were as it happens the best known Commissioners in the six countries (the latter in particular has warranted the description, 'Euro-minister'[4]). This kind of 'charismatic' leadership was clearly of supreme importance in getting the early initiatives taken, and must go a long way to explain the Commission's success in getting a common agricultural policy adopted. However, research in other fields has led students of organization to infer that such leadership is problematic in the long run in an organizational context, in that the 'charisma' does not survive the leader himself and his followers. We might add the suggestion

[1] See M. Crozier, *The Bureaucratic Phenomenon*, London, Tavistock Publications, 1964, pp. 175–208.
[2] See p. 109 above.
[3] See pp. 150–65 above.
[4] Lindberg, Decision Making and Integration, *op cit.*, p. 63.

that even where the leader remains, his very success must lead to a routinization of his 'charisma' so that after the exciting innovative stage when the policy is being championed and adopted there comes the more mundane and mechanical process of defending the policy and implementing it. (Thus, perhaps, our discovery of bureaucratic traits in the Directorate General of Agriculture in the Kennedy Round negotiations.) Moreover, as we have seen, such leadership is constantly threatened by the demands of the Commission's Mediative function and lacks the external sources of support to build itself up into a truly political leadership.

Far more relevant in the open-ended, porous conditions which increasingly came to characterize the Commission from about 1963 onwards was the existence of the common culture belonging to the younger, free-wheeling, less partisan type of officials, with their highly sensitive political antennae, whom we found to be so important in the case of the Kennedy Round.[1] Our research suggests that this common culture is not an evangelical kind of organization commitment, which might prove inflexible and doctrinaire, so much as a sense of shared adventure, common loyalty to the European idea, and common interest, which cuts across nationality, professional specialism and status.

Thus, in spite of the diffusion of decision-making into numbers of specialized cadres as necessitated by the process of decision-making in the Community, and in spite of the increasing difficulties of providing clear political leadership from above, the Commission has retained some identity as an institution. Commission officials still enjoyed regular face-to-face contact with their colleagues, in spite of having to work closely with national representatives. The size of the EEC Commission is partly instrumental in this (even in the whole of category A there are not more than a thousand officials). The atmosphere of the organization is far more that of the senior common room of an English red-brick university than that of a government department or public agency. The common culture is based less on a sense of exclusiveness, of membership of a closed *élite*, or of a shared ideology, than on the sharing of certain common characteristics. Most of the younger officials are professionals of one sort or another; few are committed to careers as civil servants; most find the enterprise in which the Commission is involved an

[1] See pp. 212–16 above.

inviting task and are keen to identify themselves as Europeans. It is well known that language has not been a real difficulty in social intercourse within the Commission—the vast majority of officials at every level finding it possible and natural to converse in French. Most of the officials (below the very top levels) lunch together in the self-service cafeteria on the top floor of the Commission building in the *Joyeuse Entrée*. A less routine lunch (and often dinner) can be taken in the small Italian restaurants situated in the side streets around the building. The main social distinction here has become a functional rather than cultural one—between Pinnocchio's, say, where no conversation is private, where the food and drink are cheap and the service informal (a venue for exchange of ideas), and Perry's Grill where the atmosphere is executive and formal, the prices inflated, and the tables arranged for discreet interviews (a venue for organizational politics).

However, this element seems bound to give way now to bureaucracy. First, as the leadership becomes more representative of outside interests, hierarchy must be stressed more and more, as we have already suggested. In any event, the common culture is constantly being threatened by recruitment of nationalistic and technically minded officials and as a reaction to this rigidities develop in an attempt to 'cure' the organization of its flexibility and openness. Finally, of course, the porous organization is unsuited to the performance of the Administrative function and no doubt it will be increasingly 'bureaucratized' as the organization acquires more tasks of this type.

It must also be remembered that the Commission's Normative function, which is absolutely vital in the process of unification, requires it to take a definite stand on the future direction of the Community and to adhere to some set of principles or doctrines which will enable it to evaluate different proposals and actions in the common interest. The porous type of organization must pose as a constant threat to the Commission's ability to do this. The common culture on which such an organization must be based is far more like the partisan authority which was prevalent in the early years than the loose, flexible, adaptive, 'coalition' arrangement which has developed. In view of this, and in an attempt to re-create the more reliable kind of organizational unity, we must expect more and more resort to bureaucratic forms of authority. This trend might be

261

lessened considerably if the Commissioners themselves were party leaders representing some identifiable electoral majority. Yet the authority of the Commissioners is itself primarily bureaucratic, as we have seen. Thus, even committed Europeans favour increasing bureaucratization.

This probably explains the growing concern of the Personnel Committee for guarantees concerning career prospects, pensions and other conditions. The increasing conflict concerning personnel administration signifies a collapse of the common spirit and a loss of confidence, which must be closely related to this trend. Paradoxically enough the Personnel Committee has been motivated above all by a desire to *foster* a common culture, to create a 'European Civil Service'. Yet its demands for greater regularity and impersonality in appointments and career management signify in fact the lack of such a common code and the transition from a partisan, loyalist body to a bureaucratic, mechanistic one. Thus, the establishment of a 'classical' civil service may well have become the only means of achieving the level of conformity required. Yet, paradoxically, this kind of conformity must in all probability drive out the common culture we have been describing.

Of course, it is not unusual to find some conflict between line and staff sections in any organization. Most civil servants have complaints about the 'little grey men' in the Establishments divisions.[1] Preoccupation with such conflicts, however, which seems to be very significant even at the level of the Commission itself, is a symptom of a highly mechanistic, predominantly administrative, body. Moreover, this increasing preoccupation with administrative problems in the Commission has developed alongside a general tendency towards reliance on formal rules and prescriptions and on hierarchical commands in the decision-making process.

Thus in many parts of the Commission we found officials who insisted that no progress with ideas or suggestions was now possible without the support of one's Commissioner. Very often leadership from the Commissioner—or rather the lack of it—was the explana-

[1] Some commentators on drafts of this book felt that we had slightly overestimated the importance of such 'normal' impatience with personnel administrators and with 'red tape' by taking it as serious evidence of bureaucratization. However, none of these commentators had had recent experience of working in the Commission and they might have tended themselves to underestimate the strength of the present preoccupation with administrative details.

tion given for failure. Contrasting with the self-confidence, commitment and common loyalty, but co-existing with it there seems now to be a growing sense of frustration, of lack of initiative, and of a feeling of insecurity. This is evidence of more than a failure of leadership, or of effective co-ordination and control from above. It is a type of loss of institutional identity just as deleterious to the organization's goals as the existence of competing parties within it. The resulting *malaise* seems to be a recent sickness spreading through the Commission—the men of initiative and personal commitment have become frustrated by an organization rapidly turning into a place for obedience, detachment and impersonality.

To summarize: the partisan organization of the early Europeans cannot altogether survive the pressures of the early Commission's environment and the requirements of the Mediative function. However, the more open-ended (what we have called 'porous') organization which emerges as being better adapted to these conditions threatens to break the Commission up into separate conflicting parties and to destroy institutional identity and purpose. But this type of organization can be beneficial if the institution is held together meanwhile by a common code of behaviour arising from a common culture—in this instance, a vague sense of being 'European', a feeling of shared adventure, and a sharing of occupational background (young specialist professionals). The dilemma is, however, that, while the porous organization requires a common culture, the latter seems unable to survive in porous conditions. It is threatened by the infiltration of nationally oriented careerists, by bureaucratic 'dysfunctions', and by the changing tasks of the organization. The features of a 'classical' career service are no substitute for such a spontaneous culture in creating institutional identity. On the contrary they must be expected to engender rigidity, ritualism, and remoteness, and to usher in a mechanistic system of decision-making. In other words, for a time the organization seems able to overcome any hostility in its environment, partly be being adaptive, but partly also by being socially cohesive. But beyond a certain point further adaptation to the environment will undermine social cohesion, and the organization's leaders will resort to bureaucracy as an apparent defence. While certainly not being entirely disintegrative (we have seen that it played a crucial role in the Kennedy

Round negotiations), the porous organization threatens to be strictly transitional in nature.

The only alternative to decisive, clear-cut and united political leadership on the part of the Commission seems to be bureaucracy. It seems that organizational factors alone are no guarantee that the Commission can play a political and promotive role in the Community. In the next chapter we shall attempt to assess the external conditions upon which such political leadership depends, and try to estimate its chances of survival. For the rest of the present chapter we shall examine a recent event which seems to offer some confirmation of our hypothesis regarding the increasing bureaucratization of the Commission. This is the merger of the three Community Executives which began in the summer of 1967 and was to bring about some major changes in the organization of the Commission.

THE MERGER OF THE EXECUTIVES 1967-68

The merger of the Executives of the three Communities (the two Commissions of the EEC and of Euratom, and the High Authority of the ECSC) took place officially on July 6, 1967, and was followed by a reorganization of the three sets of administrative services into a single institution—'The Commission of the European Communities' —which was still not fully completed a year following the date when the merger officially took place. This event was of supreme psychological importance for the Commission and its officials and was in the forefront of their life and work for a good deal of the time during which this study was carried out. It is essential, therefore, to make some mention of the main effects of the merger, even though it is still too early to trace its full administrative—or even political —consequences. At the same time, it has brought about some important changes in the structure of the Commission.

The most striking change and the one with probably the most drastic effects is the increase in the size of the membership of the Commission from nine to fourteen. This is only a provisional measure and according to the Merger Treaty the number is meant to revert to nine after three years. However, the enlargement was a direct result of pressure to increase the representativeness of the Commission by making it possible to include, for example, a Flemish

264

as well as a Walloon Belgian, and a Roman Catholic as well as a Protestant Dutchman. The overall effect must be to make the maintenance of collegiality more difficult than ever without resort to bureaucratic devices, without making the institution increasingly conservative, and without considerably slowing down the decision-making process. It will also increase the importance of the Commissioners' cabinets in keeping Commissioners in touch with what their colleagues, and (more important) their colleagues' departments, are doing, and in ensuring that each Commissioner 'represents' his particular 'constituency' to the latter's satisfaction. Indeed, the Meeting of the heads of cabinets to prepare for Commission Meetings has now been given official status in the Rules of Procedure.

The most important immediate effect of this enlargement of the Commission is a psychological one. In so far as the Commission of the EEC had already become increasingly representative (as opposed to partisan) in its outlook and method of working, and in so far as this was having the effect of bureaucratizing the Commission the open recognition of a need to make the new single Commission *more* representative must have a dramatic effect on the common culture of the institution and must encourage even further the formation of different 'parties' in the decision-making process. Of equal psychological importance is the departure of some very crucial old faces from the EEC Commission, in particular that of President Hallstein. The new President, M. Rey, is regarded as being a less 'charismatic' figure than his predecessor of the EEC Commission and is expected to play the 'backseat' role of chairman and broker rather than the active one of promoter and instigator. Moreover, the member governments have agreed that henceforth the tenure of the Presidency shall rotate every two years, so that all the major countries shall have a better chance of being represented. All these things signify what is clearly a major development in the nature of the directing body of the institution, a development away from a partisan body to a representative one. As we have seen such a development was for various reasons already taking place in the EEC Commission and thus the new changes seem destined to engender a general retreat from political leadership.

Another point of great interest for our main study is that the administrative process of carrying out the merger preoccupied almost the whole organization and brought progress in many parts to an absolute standstill for some months. Naturally, some discomfort and inconvenience, and some distraction from normal duties, was inevitable at such a time. The merger was intended to be the opportunity for a rationalization of the administrative services of the three Executives and this is never an easy thing for an organization statfed with professional employees (with virtual security of tenure) to achieve. At the same time, the seat of the new Commission is in Brussels and this will involve the gradual transfer of former ECSC officials from Luxembourg, with all the domestic and other problems associated with it. But the extent of preoccupation with this administrative upheaval seems to have been quite extraordinary. In the first place, a body which was as allegedly partisan and co-operative in nature as the original High Authority in 1951 or the EEC Commission in 1958 should have taken such a thing in its stride. Officials who serve primarily out of commitment to the organization (like the partisan Europeans of the early years) should overlook such personal discomfort as being less important than the moral duty of serving the cause. Those who enjoy the unpredictability and informality of work in a porous, open-ended organization should exult in the opportunity for renewal brought about by the destruction of existing statuses and structures. On the contrary, however, the Commission has hardly ever had worse problems with its staff, and morale was at an all-time low during the merger. This suggests that the time of the partisan band of committed Europeans is near an end. Even that of the open-ended, organic system, based on a common culture, may be threatened. The Commission now begins to appear like any typical administrative organization, where security, conformity, and predictability are the most treasured values.

One reason why the reorganization did not meet with co-operation from the staff side was the widespread feeling that the Commission was not autonomous in carrying it out. The criteria of the rationalization were very largely set by the Council of Ministers. Experience had led the officials of the Commission to react defensively against the administrative proposals of their ultimate paymasters, the member States. It is even possible that the powers-that-be in the Commission deliberately dragged out the process of reorganization in the hopes that the Council would soften its demands regarding reductions in numbers of staff. Eventually, in fact, the provisional cuts turned out to be relatively small by comparison with the Council's original demand of an across-the-board 20 per cent off the total of the three executives. According to the draft budget approved by the Council in January 1968 category A is reduced by 86 officials, category B by 40, and categories C and D by 84. The blow was softened by getting the Council to accept the argument that many functions of the Commission had been seriously neglected up to now owing to staff shortages, and that the reorganization should be an opportunity to redress the balance in this respect. Thus the secretaries, clerical staff, and executive assistants of categories B and C, already in short supply, were easily re-employed.

The main problem was in category A, particularly at the most senior levels, where the number of officials at A1 (equivalent to Director General) was eventually reduced by 25 per cent from 36 to 27. For political reasons, it proved incredibly difficult to weed out the organization at this level. We have already seen that the appointment of a Director General is a matter of supreme political importance, engaging the loyalties and energies not only of the Commission itself but also of the member governments, and sometimes taking months and months of negotiation. Just imagine what it must be like to make one of these precious creatures redundant! The rationalization became, therefore, a bitter political wrangle within the new single Commission. As one close observer has commented:

'Between July and December the Commission itself—which includes the former Minister of Agriculture of the Netherlands, the former Minister of Economic Affairs of Belgium, the ex-secretary General of NATO, one of the most brilliant professors of economics in France—spent the equivalent of two whole weeks of all-day sessions, including Sundays, discussing case by case the appointment of a hundred or so officials, haggling with each other in a way reminiscent of the slave market.'[1]

Apart from this, the Commission was bitterly criticized by its officials for the way the other aspects of the reorganization were managed. The principle source of grievance here was the delay in announcing the size and disposition of the new organization and in deciding how to treat redundant officials. It was, moreover,

[1] J. Lambert, Une Commission Qui Sombre?, *Agenor: European Review*, Brussels, No. 5, 1968, p. 57. (Our translation.)

strongly believed that, when a new permanent statute finally came into effect, it would abandon the principle of a career service and replace it with that of secondment of national officials. A new provisional Statute of Service did not come into force until March 4, 1968, even though there were to be hardly any changes of substance from the old Statute of the EEC and Euratom. By October 1967 the Commission had still only decided on measures to compensate redundant officials of grades A1, 2 and 3. One problem was that, if it produced too generous a scheme for indemnifying officials at grades lower than this, it might lose its most talented and most highly prized younger officials in grades A4, 5, 6 and 7. Even so the Commission and the officials responsible for personnel administration roused much antagonism for the way the whole procedure was carried out. The Personnel Committee refused to attend meetings called by the Commission to discuss the draft of a new Statute, on the grounds that the real issues would be decided not by those formally responsible within the Commission, but by political organs like the Commissioners' cabinets. No doubt the important point about the merger, therefore, was that personnel management proved to be necessary, not that the personnel managers of the Commission were incompetent.

The effect on the services themselves of poor relations between management and staff and of the unbelievable delays in drawing up new structures and posts was considerable. A provisional list of new Directors General was drawn up in July of 1967, but the officials so named could not yet take up their posts officially and the services thus rearranged were unable to continue where they had left off in the previous June. The definitive list of Directors General did not become official until January 1968 (even though there was only one change from the earlier July list, due to an official having since left the Commission voluntarily). This list had to be drawn up according to strict consideration of nationality and politics. A distribution between nationalities among the 24 Directors General actually heading services had been agreed at six each for France, Germany, Italy and Benelux. The appointment of heads of division was not confirmed until March 1968 when the new organigram was finally established. The paralysing effect of this uncertainty and delay is described by a writer in *Le Monde* in January 1968:

'The *malaise* is spreading and intensifying as the decisions drag on and on, and as the heavy machinery meanwhile seizes up bit by bit for the want of new initiatives. The new directors general *designated* by the single Commission in the month of July have still not been appointed five months later. There is no doubt that some of them, assured of receiving confirmation of their posts, continue to run their departments as if nothing had happened. On the other hand, former incumbents who are about to leave are not taking any new initiatives. So the paralysis is overcoming the lower echelons in the hierarchy. There is no more ringing of telephones or tapping of typewriters. Only tongues are active.'[1]

The reorganization which has now resulted is itself nothing to celebrate. In place of the twenty-five Directorates General and three joint services of the two Commissions and the High Authority there are now twenty Directorates General and two services. In addition to these, the new Commission has taken over intact from the old Euratom Commission two special services (the Supply Agency) and Office of Security) and one from the High Authority (Security Control). (On the other hand, there is now one Executive Secretariat —renamed 'General Secretariat'—and one Spokesman's Group.) This really represents an expansion in organizational units due partly to a failure or inability to merge a number of departments from Euratom and the High Authority with the former nine Directorates General of the EEC Commission. It is no doubt partly due also to the sheer difficulty of getting rid of Directors General. In these respects the merger has actually been postponed or perhaps abandoned altogether. Finally, it was felt desirable to give greater attention to certain activities of the Communities by taking them out of existing Directorates General and setting them up on their own.

In addition to the special services mentioned above, two other departments from Euratom ('Dissemination of Information' and the Joint Research Centre) and one from the High Authority (Credits and Investments) were retained as individual Directorates General. Five former EEC Directorates General were also retained (though with important additions in some cases from similar departments in the other two executives): these are External Affairs, Agriculture, Transport, Social Affairs, and Aid for Development (formerly 'Overseas Development'). However, part of the old External Rela-

---

[1] A. Murcier, La Commission à l'Heure de la Fusion, *Le Monde*, January 18, 1968, p. 18. (Our translation; italics in original.)

tions Directorate General of the EEC Commission has been split off to form a new Directorate General, External Trade. In the EEC Commission there were three Directorates General concerned generally with economic affairs, and trade and industry within the Community; these have now grown into no less than *six* new Directorates General. Perhaps most striking of all, there are now *three* Directorates General concerned with budgetary and administrative questions whereas there was only one in the EEC Commission before (the old DG IX)! In addition to the reasons already given for this relative expansion, it has been suggested that the Commission also bore in mind that the increase in departmental units would increase the number of senior officials concerned with a general area and thus lessen the chances of the latter being dominated by one particular nationality or group. It seems, therefore, that the representative principle is now the official basis of the Commission's formal organization.

One immediate disadvantage can be seen to flow from the new allocation of functions (apart from the sheer number of units) from the point of view of the single Commission's ability to act as a dynamic, initiating body. It is now no longer possible for each Commissioner to be responsible for one particular Directorate General comprising some identifiable general sector of activity. Some Commissioners now take responsibility for two or even more Directorates General and services. Responsibility for some general sectors is now split up between different Commissioners (no doubt on the representative principle): for example, there is now a distinction between external *trade* (under M. Deniau) and external *relations* (under Signor Martino), and between regional policy (Mr von der Groeben) and economic and financial affairs (M. Barre). In order to ensure 'internal co-ordination and co-operation between the Commission members and the Directorates General concerned' seven specialized groups of Commissioners have been formed each with a chairman and one or two deputy chairmen. The chairmen and deputy chairmen are not, however, always the Commissioners directly responsible for the activity with which the group is concerned. No doubt the formation of these groups will be expected to change according to political and other developments. In any event it seems that not only the spirit and personality, but also the general structure, of the Hallstein Commission has now been undermined.

ADMINISTRATIVE SERVICES OF THE COMMISSION OF THE
EUROPEAN COMMUNITIES, AUGUST 1968

	Name of service	Previous name in EEC Commission or previous location
	General Secretariat of the Commission	Executive Secretariat
	Legal Service	(joint service)
	Spokesman's Group	No change
	Statistical Office	Statistical Service (joint service)
DG I	External Relations	No change
DG II	Economic and financial affairs	No change
SG III	Industrial Affairs	No change
DG IV	Competition	No change
DG V	Social Affairs	No change
DG VI	Agriculture	No change
DG VII	Transport	No change
DG VIII	Aid for Development	Overseas Aid
DG IX	Personnel and Administration	Administration
DG X	Press and information	(joint service)
DG XI	External Trade	*
DG XII	General Research and Technology	*
DG XIII	Dissemination of Information	(Euratom)
DG XIV	Internal Market and Harmonization of Legislation	Internal Market
DG XV	Joint Research Centre	(Euratom)
DG XVI	Regional Policy	*
DG XVII	Energy	*
DG XVIII	Credits and Investments	(ECSC)
DG XVIX	Budgets	(Euratom) (ECSC)
DG XX	Financial Control	*
	Supply Agency	(Euratom)
	Security Control	(ECSC)
	Security Office	(Euratom)

*New service.

271

CHAPTER 11

THE COMMISSION AS A
BUREAUCRACY

In this chapter we shall describe how the Commission's Mediative and Administrative functions rather than its Initiative and Normative functions must now come to characterize it as an institution. In addition, we shall remark how it is a strongly held view among some leading participants in the Community that the Commission should confine itself to those former functions, leaving the latter to the member governments. A number of students of the Community currently believe that the balance has certainly shifted towards this bureaucratic view of the Commission's role. Indeed, the political system of the Community, originally regarded as a vital means of dynamic integration, is now much more often critized as a cumbersome and inefficient diplomatic procedure.

This 'decline' of the Commission is generally acknowledged within the Community, but the explanation which has been generally (and enthusiastically) given is the hostility of the Gaullist regime in France. It is certainly the case that this regime has effectively resisted attempts by the Commission and other member States to expand the role of Community institutions and to allow the Community to develop in accordance with its original objectives. The main apologists of the Community Method predicted that, as soon as the Gaullist regime disappeared, things would return to 'normal' and the Commission would once again assert itself as a political leadership, promoting unification by exercising its Initiative and Normative functions.

There is something basically unconvincing about this thesis, however, in that—like the 'Lindberg thesis' considered above—it pays little attention to the role of institutions. It is certainly realistic in treating the role of the member governments as a key variable in the process of unification. But is it justified in assuming that it was only the antagonism of the contemporary French government which prevented the Commission from acting as a political leadership? As

272

we have already seen, from the point of view of the Commission's internal organization the existence of a strong Gaullist 'Opposition' did no more than contribute to bureaucratization. The organization was forced to adapt to conditions in which different interests and norms demanded representation in its own decision-making *cadres*. Even without General de Gaulle, will there be such consensus on the aims and methods of European unity as to restore the organization to its partisan origins without firm political leadership from the Commissioners themselves? We have already seen that the threats to the common culture of the Commission's organization arise mainly from the nature of the Community decision-making process and the Commission's Mediative function within it. We shall take this argument further below. Certainly, in the absence of clear leadership from the Commissioners, it is difficult to see what could be the basis of collective, normative decisions by the Commission. Yet without such decisions, the Commission could hardly be regarded as an institution providing political leadership. The need for internal political leadership is underlined by the growing Administrative function of the Commission, which invites a mechanistic, routinized style of organization. This is another question we examine further below.

It is evident that the Commissioners can act as political leaders in relation to the Commission's own organization only if they can act as political leaders of the Community itself. From the point of view of those who blame everything on the Gaullist enemy the political legitimacy of the Community must come from the member governments. For they argue that, as long as the national governments are favourable to further integration and are prepared to support the Commission's Initiative and Normative functions (as they surely will now that de Gaulle has left the political scene), then the Commission can be expected to play a fully political, promotive role. In other words, what is envisaged here is not a federal system at all, in which there is an autonomous, legitimized central authority, but a system of inter-governmental co-operation in which a 'supra-national' bureaucracy acts on behalf of the member States and depends for its political authority on the latter's support. In such a system, the national governments and not the Commissioners exercise real power. While the Commissioners may seem to exercise functions of the Initiative and Normative type in this system, in

273

actual fact they must be acting within norms already established by the national governments and can initiate only after having ascertained that the member governments will give their support. This explains the nature of the present decision-making process of the Community, which consists essentially of an interaction between the Commission and other bureaucratic representatives of the member governments. Whatever the *behaviour* of individual Commissioners, they are performing the function of bureaucrats in relation to the political system of the Community. Their authority is strictly delegative and derived; their purpose is the implementation of a consensus reached by the member governments acting together under the mediative agency of the Commission.

This system has certain advantages. It avoids a head-on challenge to the sovereignty of the member States. It leaves to one side the extraordinarily difficult question of how the Commissioners could be legitimized directly, assuming they were to become the political leaders of the Community. In view of the discredit into which the conventional parliamentary and electoral methods of legitimizing political authority have fallen, this is no small blessing. These are advantages, however, only in so far as inter-governmental co-operation can provide the necessary, united political leadership. Even if Gaullism is to be regarded as an historical accident, can such an assumption about the potential consensus of the national governments be made? More important, can this form of Community 'government', even though supported by a supranational bureaucracy like the Commission, prove adequate to the function of initiating and upholding an economic union—indeed, a political union—of the countries of western Europe. Let us stress again that the Commissioners in this system can be regarded only as performing a bureaucratic function in relation to the member governments. The Commission's organization under such circumstances must be perpetually threatened by the 'dysfunctions' known to result from a delegative, impartial and hierarchically-structured organization.[1] Unless there is some form of independent, central, political leadership for the Commission the latter cannot be relied upon to take its own initiatives or to lay down its own norms. Only the member governments can do that on its behalf.

We have moved ahead of our theme, for it is in the concluding

[1] See pp. 116–17 above.

part of this book that we intend to take up the question of what kind of 'government' the Community requires, and on what type of legitimation this government might possibly be based. We have yet to show more explicitly that the Commission's role in the present political system of the Community is that of a bureaucracy rather than that of a political leadership. We have already dealt with the Commission's Mediative and Administrative functions at some length and what follows will be in the manner of a summary and conclusion. First, however, in the manner of an illustration rather than an explanation of the Commission's bureaucratic role, we shall describe the Commission's impotence in face of the hostile attitude of General de Gaulle.

> . . . .
> *'I', said the sparrow,*
> *'With my bow and arrow*
> *I killed Cock Robin.'*

It was impossible to mix in Community circles in the last few years without becoming considerably exposed to what might be called the 'homicidal' thesis of the Community's development. It would be a mistake, however, to suppose that the Gaullist regime in France has simply wrecked what could otherwise have continued to be a going concern. A full interpretation of recent events must take account of the underlying weaknesses in the institutional system of the Community such as those to which we have just referred. However, the French government of General de Gaulle clearly made a major contribution to preventing the Commission from acting as a political leadership.

In the first place, the Gaullist regime clearly believed that the Commission should confine itself to bureaucratic functions (and here it has been supported by other voices in the member countries). Two particularly important statements of the French view were made just after the French boycott of Community institution had begun in July 1965, the first being General de Gaulle's press conference on September 9, 1965, and the second M. Couve de Murville's speech before the National Assembly on October 20, 1965. From these utterances it is possible to draw up a kind of Gaullist manifesto on the role of Community institutions and, in particular, on that of the Commission. According to this view, the Commission's function is essentially Mediative: to put forward objective proposals and to attempt to find a compromise between the different national points of view.[1] It had already been clear for some time that General de Gaulle viewed the Commissioners as 'mere technicians', useful for the long-term interests of France, but performing a limited advisory role to which they should be confined.[2] The French regime has repeatedly objected to the way the Commission attempts to exercise functions of the Initiative and Normative type.

An attempt to put a stop once and for all to the Commission's role as promoter was contained in the 'Decalogue' proposals which were designed to act as a basis for an agreement to end the 1965-66 boycott. These proposals maintained, for example, not only that the Commission should consult the member governments before agreeing on proposals to the Council of Ministers (which in practice it did already), but also that it should refrain from informing the Parliament of the content of its proposals before officially submitting them to the Council, and should not publish them in the *Journal Officiel* (or elsewhere) on its own initiative. The 'Decalogue' also claimed that the Commission had too often presented proposals which were excessively broad in scope and that undue discretion had been delegated to the Commission as a result. It proposed that the Six should scrutinize draft Regulations more closely in future in order to avoid giving the Commission too much power and should then retain the right to review the tasks thus delegated. The right of the Commission to represent the Community in international organizations like GATT was also attacked, as well as its privilege of receiving diplomatic missions to the Community. The proposals also sought to restrain the Commission's information policy and to prevent the Commissioners themselves from speaking so freely in public. Finally, the Commission was criticized for making its Directives to the member governments far too narrow in scope, giving the latter too little discretion in achieving the objectives laid down.[3]

For the government of a key member State to take this restrictive attitude towards the role of the Commission must clearly have repercussions on the whole decision-making process, and it did undoubt-

[1] M. Camps, *European Unification in the Sixties*, London, Oxford University Press, 1967, pp. 81-6, 89.
[2] L. Lindberg, *The Political Dynamics of European Economic Integration*, London, Oxford University Press, 1963, p. 289.
[3] Camps, *op. cit.*, pp. 104-9.

edly affect for some time the attitude of French representatives in the Committee of Permanent Representatives and in the Council. Even before the boycott of the Community, however, the French regime had insisted on pursuing a firmly independent attitude in Community affairs. By deliberately conceiving and championing a distinctly French policy General de Gaulle has provoked disunity within the Community and even within the Commission itself. The first real evidence of this French 'independence' was the first veto of British membership in 1963. This was announced, significantly enough, not within the institutional framework of the Council of Ministers, but at a press conference in Paris. The methods by which the veto was applied were later criticized by the President of the Commission, who also openly rebutted General de Gaulle's claim that the negotiations with the UK were unlikely to succeed. The second main French 'declaration of independence' was General de Gaulle's rejection of the Commission's proposals for financing the common agricultural policy in the spring of 1965, leading subsequently to the French boycott of Community institutions. Mrs Camps suggests that the French attitude towards the Community had hardened irrevocably some months before the spring of 1965 and General de Gaulle had then finally decided that the future destiny of France could no longer be served by co-operating with the 'technocrats' of Brussels.

Indeed, up to this point the Commission had not come out into full and open opposition to French policy (even over the veto). It has been suggested that one factor which led to the Commission's decision to put forward its 1965 package proposal was the strong feeling of some Commissioners that the apparent identity of interest between the Commission and the French regime was proving embarrassing for the former and that a stronger line should be taken in order to rally support among the Five. At the same time, it was felt necessary to ensure that the French did not get what they wanted out of the common agricultural policy without making concessions on strengthening the role of Community institutions.[1] It is thus significant that the French concentrated their attack on the way the Commission's proposal was presented—on the way institutional progress was tied with 'purely agricultural' questions, and on the way the content of the proposal was revealed to the European

[1] Camps, *op. cit.*, p. 47.

Parliament before being considered by the Council of Ministers. The essence of the initiative was the linking of progress towards the 'single market stage' in agriculture with the granting of independent financial resources to the Community and increasing the powers of the European Parliament and the Commission over the Community budget. The Commission and the Five regarded these three proposals as inseparable and the Commission later tried to justify its inclusion of institutional reforms as follows:

'The Commission considered that such a large budget arising from independent Community revenues raised the question of parliamentary control over the use of these funds, and therefore felt impelled to propose that the budgetary powers of the European Parliament be strengthened. It also felt obliged to take into consideration the similar views expressed by several members of the Council.'[1]

The French representatives on the Council, however, strongly objected to tying the first part of the proposal with the second two, and when the deadline for agreement on means of financing the common agricultural policy was reached on June 30th with no decision having been made, the French Foreign Minister, who at that time was the chairman of the Council, brought the meeting to an end. Forthwith the French government withdrew its representation from the Council for seven months, during which time it was prepared to transact only routine business. The Commission continued to function as best it could and the Five continued to meet for the conduct of business even though no major decisions on further progress with the Community could be made.

Eventually, in January 1966, owing partly to the hostility to General de Gaulle's European policy expressed in the French elections of the previous November, the French agreed to take up their part in the Community again on certain conditions. At an 'extraordinary session' of the Council of Ministers in Luxembourg a document was drawn up on certain aspects of the future working of Community institutions and on a timetable for future decisions. The document on the working of the institutions (known as the 'Heptalogue'), laid down a hypothetical basis for future consultations between the Commission and the Council on their working relations

[1] Ninth General Report on the Activities of the Community, 1966, Commission of the EEC, Brussels, Sec. 3.

with one another, according to Article 162 of the Treaty.[1] However, the terms of the document simply represented an 'agreement to disagree' and no such consultation has yet taken place. Nevertheless, it does serve to illustrate the extent of Gaullist opposition to the promotive role of the Commission. As we have already seen, the document sought to formalize the existing practice whereby majority voting did not take place on the Council on any 'matter of vital national interest'. As for the relations between the Commission and the Council, the agreement also sought to formalize the existing procedure whereby the Commission 'before adopting any particularly important proposal' took up 'the appropriate contacts with the governments of the member States, through the Permanent Representatives, without this procedure compromising the right of initiative which the Commission derives from the Treaty'. Another point of the agreement which simply repeated what was already normal Community practice was that:

'Proposals and any other official acts which the Commission submits to the Council are not to be made public until the recipients have had formal notice of them and are in possession of the texts.'

Furthermore, the agreement stressed that, whereas these and the other proposals it contained were 'to be adopted by joint agreement, on the basis of Article 162 of the EEC Treaty', this should avoid 'compromising the respective competences and powers of the two Institutions'. It made no mention of French demands that the Commissioners' freedom of speech should be restricted. Instead of demanding that the Commission's proposals should not be published in the *Journal Officiel*, it simply called for a clear distinction to be made there between those acts of the Commission which had binding force and those which had not. The other proposals were all greatly watered-down versions of French demands in the 'Decalogue' while some of the latter did not receive any mention at all. The most important proposals concerned the information policy of the Commission and control of the Community budget, but the operational meaning of these was, (perhaps intentionally), far from clear:

'Co-operation between the Council and the Commission on the

[1] Article 162, paragraph 1, of the Treaty of Rome states that: 'The Council and the Commission shall institute joint consultations and shall arrange by a common agreement the means for their collaboration.'

Community's information policy . . . will be strengthened in such a way that the programme of the Joint Information Service will be drawn up and carried out in accordance with procedures which are to be decided upon at a later date, and which may include the establishment of an *ad hoc* body.

'Within the framework of the financial regulations relating to the drawing up and execution of the Communities' budgets, the Council and the Commission will decide on means for more effective control over the commitment and expenditure of Community funds.'[1]

Since the end of the boycott and the Luxembourg Agreement the Community has continued to make progress in some sectors; for example the Kennedy Round negotiations were brought to a successful conclusion in May 1967 and agreement was reached on a common system of value-added taxation in the same year. The merger of the executives of the Communities took place as agreed on July 1, 1967. Although the French found it necessary to have recourse to escape clauses of the Treaty in a number of instances following the internal political and economic crisis in France in May 1968, the establishment of a common market in industrial and most agricultural products was achieved two years ahead of schedule on July 1, 1968. In spite of this, the Gaullist regime continued to impose its independent will in the Community wherever its crucial interests seemed to be at stake, with the effect of so far seriously blocking real progress in any new direction.

First of all, the French carried out an act of vengeance against President Hallstein by showing such strong opposition to his continuation as President of the Commission after the expiry of his term in 1968 that he resigned from office as from the date of the merger. Secondly, owing to French obstruction regarding the provision of finance, the Euratom programme for the third stage had to be indefinitely postponed. Finally, of course, General de Gaulle vetoed British membership for the second time and, in the same way as before, at a press conference in Paris. This was in spite of a report by the Commission recommending that the British

1 The full terms of the Luxembourg Agreement are set out in the Ninth General Report on the Activities of the Community, *op. cit.*, Secs. 13–15. See also Camps, *op. cit.* pp. 111–15; and R. Mayne, *The Institutions of the European Community*, London, PEP/Chatham House, 1968, pp. 46–8.

application (along with those of Denmark, Norway and Iceland) should form the basis of negotiation for full membership.[1] The British application still rested with the Council on Ministers and a number of attempts were made by the Five to get it taken up. However, the regime of de Gaulle clearly refused to countenance any progress on this question and the result was more or less continuing deadlock in the Community from November of 1967 right through to the autumn of 1968, when the Community gave signs of beginning to return to normal business with the publication of a new 'Mansholt plan' for agriculture and the revival of the 'Maréchal committee' on science and technology.[2]

It could well be that without the hostility of General de Gaulle the Community might now have been expanded to include more members, including Great Britain, that the Commission might have been granted financial resources of its own, and that the role of the European Parliament in budgetary matters might have been significantly increased. It might even be supposed that with a different regime in France the Community might have developed in yet other ways by now, such as adopting a system of direct elections to the Parliament and entrusting the Commission with more autonomous powers of decision-making. It is evident that French opposition to initiatives taken by the Commission, by other member governments, and by actors from outside the Community has resulted in stalling the Community's development in certain crucial directions. It is also clear that the official French attitude has helped to worsen the atmosphere within the Community and to make the various weaknesses of the decision-making process more damaging than they might have been otherwise. However, the main reason for this is that political leadership at a Community level can only be effective with the support of the national governments. General de Gaulle recognized this and took full advantage of it to assert an independent French policy. His tactics made effective inter-governmental co-operation on European measures impossible. But this is no justification for the exaggerations of the importance of French opposition which have been made by many apologists of the Community

[1] Opinion on the Applications for Membership received from the United Kingdom, Ireland, Denmark and Norway, Commission of the European Communities, Brussels, September 29, 1967, COM (67) 750.

[2] Bulletin of the European Communities, No. 1. 1969 Supplement, and March 1969, pp. 50–1.

Method. There is no case for treating the Gaullist regime as a scapegoat for the underlying institutional weaknesses of the Community.

In the first place, as we have seen, the Commission itself was divided over such questions as prospective British membership in 1963 and the initiative of spring 1965. Indeed, enlarging the Community would have created a number of problems for the institutions and may well have threatened the degree of unity which already existed within the Community.[1] It would have strengthened the case against a system of inter-governmental co-operation, in that the Commission's Mediative function would have become enormously more difficult in a Community of ten or more members. The administration of the Treaty on such questions as safeguards and infringements would also have become considerably more complicated. These factors would have made it urgent to move towards a more federal type of political system necessitating a major abandonment of sovereignty by the member States. The criticisms we have made of the role of the Commission would apply all the more strongly in a larger Community. It must also be stressed that the Community must soon move to the stage of agreeing common economic and social policies, and in the field of positive integration political leadership at a Community level will become all the more crucial, as we shall see below.

On the other hand, would not institutional reforms in the direction of greater 'supranationality' have been more credible in the absence of the Gaullist regime? What if the Commission now controlled its own financial resources and was accountable to the Parliament in this respect? What if the Parliament was directly elected in each of the six countries? It is clearly almost impossible to say whether or not the Community would have achieved these major advances towards a federal system if the French Government had been more co-operative. There must be a possibility that other voices of national opposition might have been raised. Moreover, we have not been struck in our research by any anxiety on the part of Commission officials to see the powers of the European Parliament increased. If anything, there is scepticism within the Community as to the value of the conventional forms of Parliamentary government, a scepticism

[1] See A. Etzioni, *Political Unification*, New York, Holt, Rinehart and Winston, 1965, p. 237.

engendered by experience of the French Fourth Republic and of other cases of *'immobiliste'* coalition government. It is enough to say here that there is great uncertainty about the consequences of directly electing the European Parliament or giving it greater power to control the activities of the Commission. The main source of such uncertainty is the lack of any existing political structures designed to mobilize support for a European Executive based on Parliamentary votes. The present Community Method by-passes real political activity altogether, concentrating on the role of interest groups, national governments, and civil servants. Leaving aside French resistance to institutional changes within the present Community, the whole question of how a Community government might be legitimized has yet to be approached. We shall attempt some discussion of this question in the concluding part of this book.

The obstruction of the Gaullist regime in France cannot be invoked, therefore, to cover up the inadequacies of a system based essentially on inter-governmental co-operation with the assistance of a 'supranational' bureaucracy. This system depends on the ability of the member governments to take a common stand on major issues and to allow the Commission to act as a political leadership. What was significant about the Luxembourg Agreement of 1966 was not only Gaullist opposition as expressed in the terms of the Agreement, but also the fact that it was the Five governments who largely achieved the compromise and not the Commission.[1] In any event, the Agreement itself is not likely to induce major changes in the working of the institutions.[2] Not only is the present political system of the Community extremely inefficient, as we are about to see, but it is also in danger of being ineffective as the main executive organ of the Community becomes increasingly concerned with bureaucratic functions. The reasons for this constitute gaps in our account which we must now fill. This will involve first of all taking up from our earlier account of the decision-making process of the Community in Chapter Four the discussion of the Commission's main strategy of *engrenage*, of involving the member governments and their representatives in the making of Community decisions. The illustrations provided in our two detailed case studies will also serve to support the main argument.

1 Camps, *op. cit.*, p. 124.
2 Mayne, *op. cit.*, p. 50.

THE COMMISSION AS MEDIATOR

The decision-making process of the Community consists of a series of predominantly bureaucratic procedures. The initiative for legislative action is entrusted to the Commission, which, as we have seen, is structured as much like an administrative organization as an organ of political leadership. The key to the process, the system of *engrenage*, consists of involving national civil servants in Community decision-making rather than mobilizing popular support. In addition to these fairly obvious bureaucratic traits, this type of collective decision-making rests on a set of procedures which are highly characteristic of decision-making in bureaucracies.

One essential procedure is the tying together of decisions on different aspects of policy so that they are taken simultaneously as part of a 'package deal'. This procedure has been rigorously followed up to now, and most of the major achievements of the Community owe something to it. For example, progress towards the common market in industrial goods was tied to agreement on a common agricultural policy and, as we have seen, progress in the Kennedy Round negotiations was linked with agreement on Community price levels in agricultural products. However, whereas this procedure may have a progressive effect in some circumstances, it may also have a regressive effect in others. Thus, progress in sectors where common policies are easy to conceive may be made to depend on concessions to national interests in other sectors, where integration may be much more difficult. Moreover, the principle assumes that further integration must appeal equally to different national and special interests, and this is bound to impose a major restriction on policy-makers, who will be tempted to make decisions according to the 'lowest common denominator'. This produces a situation in economic and social policies where 'the tail wags the dog'. Citizens within the Community find themselves faced with a choice between a national policy, which is at least positive, flexible and based on a coherent philosophy, and a Community one, which is negative, inflexible, and based on a compromise between the best (or the worst?) in each of the national policies. This principle of the 'package deal' informs most aspects of the work of the Community. For example, it is observed by the Permanent Representatives when they draw up the agenda for meetings of the Council of Ministers.

In order to avoid facing the inherently political issues involved in the timing of decisions, they have recourse to a previously agreed basis of timing and to a rule of 'parallel consideration':

'In short, one could say that in each meeting of the general Council a certain equilibrium is maintained between business relating to External Relations and that concerning the internal development of the Community. Such a system leads quite naturally to the making of "package deals", whether by deliberate intention, or by ensuring in point of fact that certain decisions are taken simultaneously.'

In the view of the senior officials of the Commission who wrote these words, this has proved to be a positive and successful formula in the past, but it is not ideally suited to solving the multiple problems which will arise in an economic union.[1]

Secondly, there is the tactic of settling disputes by agreeing to postpone decisions in the hope that a more favourable time will be found in the future. Again, this has often proved to be a successful means of preventing a willingness to compromise from evaporating owing to failure to agree on 'details'. In a number of contexts the use of this tactic seems to have led to remarkable progress towards the achievement of common policies. Its success can, however, be somewhat misleading. Indeed, it is a common impression on the part of outside observers that one never really knows what stage the Community has reached. Students and journalists are constantly having to ask 'Has "x" been done yet or has it only been agreed to be done?' Most often the answer seems to be that 'x' has been agreed to be agreed to be done! The postponement of decisions, as Mrs Camps has illustrated, is a vital source of dynamic when there is a feeling of common interest in the ends to be achieved.[2] On the other hand, the French boycott of 1965–66 arose out of a proposal, the framework and timing of which had been agreed in advance. This technique of making decisions 'academic', by setting a future deadline for them and establishing the necessary machinery, is a poor substitute for real political leadership and authority.

Both the principle of the 'package deal' and the tactic of postponing awkward decisions form part of the Commission's central

[1] *Quelques aspects des rapports et de la collaboration entre le Conseil et la Commission . . .*, Communication by E. Noël and H. Etienne, Information Service of the European Communities (undated), pp. 10–11 (our translation).
[2] Camps, *op. cit.*, p. 25.

strategy, which is the deliberate engineering of regular crises. Much of the life and work of the Commission is now geared to the famous 'Community cycle', according to which major decisions tend to be taken all together in great marathon sessions of the Council of Ministers in December of each year, and then again, but to a lesser extent, at the end of June and early July. There is little doubt, as Mrs Campo has said, that this procedure leads to a confusion of crisis with progress.[1] It is significant, in this respect, that bureaucracies are commonly said to react to major challenges and to the need to adapt to change by manufacturing crisis. Deciding key issues by means of engineered crisis necessitates, as indeed in many ways it results from, a considerable degree of centralization in decision-making. Crisis is attractive, therefore, when agreement becomes all-important and when, the less the numbers of people involved and the more intimate and private their association with each other, the greater are the chances of success. In a crisis the very survival of the undertaking and of the values it represents can be shown to rest on the shoulders of a few key men. In the quasi-military conditions thus created, however, bureaucratic characteristics such as discipline and impersonality are at a premium for those in the lower ranks. Crozier suggests that change through crisis is particularly typical of the French bureaucratic model, where political instability has often made it impossible to reach positive decisions by an open, popular process of consultation and deliberation. By these essential qualities crisis engenders a bureaucratic style of decision-making and stresses hierarchical relationships and the remoteness and impersonality of leaders.[2]

The feature of the decision-making process which has been remarked upon most by insiders in the Community, and one which has taxed the ingenuity of many of those directly involved, is naturally enough that it is an extremely *inefficient* means of taking collective decisions. The work of the Council of Ministers has threatened for some time now to become impossibly congested. It is, of course, almost impossible to quantify such a thing, but one is bound to suspect that the output of Community decisions is far

[1] *European Unification*, pp. 34–5. See also Lindberg, Integration as a Source of Stress on the European Community System, *International Organisation*, Vol. XX, No. 2, pp. 233–6.
[2] See above, pp. 187–9; M. Crozier, *The Bureaucratic Phenomenon*, London, Tavistock Publications, 1963, p. 197.

less than is warranted by the amount of time and energy put into them. Two considerations are uppermost here: first, the growth of Community legislation, with its concomitant of more delegated rule-making powers; and second, the development of the Community into more complex and more controversial fields of economic and social policy. Before the merger of the Executives the EEC Commission was sending about 200–250 communications to the Council each year (half of them formal proposals). The Council was taking about 150 official acts a year. Apparently, in 1966, out of about 150 proposals currently being examined by the Council, 43 were more than a year old, 25 more than two years old, and 8 more than three years old.[1] If the 1965–66 boycott and other factors are taken into account, this may not seem too great a delay. However, what is probably more important than the proposals actually sent before the Council are those which the Commission might have put up but did not, either because it realized of its own accord that the Council would be unable to give a decision, or because it was already so occupied with existing problems of congestion that it did not get round to framing them.

In this respect, it must be remembered that, whereas the Committee of Permanent Representatives has been invaluable in easing the problem (particularly with the help of the 'Points A procedure' explained earlier), the Council itself must make the final decision in all cases. This places an enormous responsibility on the foreign, economic and other ministers of the six countries, for whom service on the Council is, of course, only one aspect of their official lives, the most important one being running their departments at home. The existence of the written procedure for taking decisions does not seem to have helped significantly in this respect.[2] Thus, seen as a whole, a system which places the onus of final decision in all but the most detailed and technical cases on a body like the Council is highly inefficient in terms of time and manpower.

The main remedy for this up to now has been to entrust more and more of the preparation of decisions to intermediary, mixed committees like the Committee of Permanent Representatives, and like the Medium-term Economic Policy Committee and its counterparts. In many respects, however, this cure is worse than the disease.

[1] *Quelques aspects des rapports . . . , op cit.*, p. 2.
[2] *ibid.*, p. 16.

As we have already seen, it tends to bureaucratize the decision-making process even further by raising arguments about delegation and jurisdiction and by threatening to destroy the institutional identity of the Commission. Furthermore, if it is to work, it must place more and more responsibility on civil servants relative to other actors in government, not only at a Community level, but also in the national political systems as well. Such a development in key aspects of government can hardly be a satisfactory solution for the people of the member countries.

An alternative solution, and one which might do something to de-bureaucratize the decision-making process generally, might be to extend the practice of qualified majority voting on the Council of Ministers. According to the Treaty, qualified majority voting should become the rule for most questions, even those of major political importance, after the end of the Transitional Period. So far, however, it has applied to numerous decisions of a more technical and detailed nature, and it seems on the evidence of those cases where it has been necessary so far that it is a procedure which greatly facilitates the taking of decisions. In circumstances where a decision could be taken by a majority and where the proposal of the Commission (as it usually does) takes up a position which is more or less in between the positions of the member States, officials of the Commission have suggested that that member State will lose less which moves first towards a position in the centre and which thus avoids isolating itself or being forced into accepting a majority decision. Moreover, it is sometimes the case that a particular member State will, for internal political reasons, find it far easier to accept a majority decision than a unanimous one. If in practice majority votes have not often proved to be necessary, this has usually been because the Commission was willing to adjust its own proposal and because the member States were willing to rally to a common position at the last minute.

The whole procedure of reaching agreement is greatly eased and speeded up by this device.[1] However, as far as major political questions are concerned, majority voting is most unlikely to be applied even after the Transitional Period. This is not only because the Luxembourg Agreement ending the French boycott of 1965–66 suggested an 'understanding' not to use it where 'vital interests'

[1] *Quelques aspects des rapports . . ., op. cit.*, pp. 16–17.

288

were involved, but also because it has only ever been applied to such questions on the rarest of occasions. However, there is much scope for applying the procedure to the more technical and detailed questions (witness, for example, the willingness of the French since 1966 to allow themselves to be outvoted on budgetary matters). Even so, the procedure of majority voting does little to relieve the Commission of its role as mediator, for its value in terms of the efficiency of decision-making seems to depend on the ability of the Commission to take a middle course and to act as 'honest broker'.

Indeed, it would seem that the real problem in the Community, as well as the root cause of the delays and congestion in the legis-lative process, is the lack of a real political authority at a Community level. If the power to make decisions rested, not with the member governments or their representatives, but with a directly-legitimized federal institution, the whole situation would clearly be different. Any system of decision-making based essentially on mediation be-tween national governments must give rise to similarly slow, cumber-some and inefficient procedures. The more important the issues with which the Community is concerned and the wider the scope of integration becomes, the more serious this can be expected to be.

The most popular reform among Europeans would be to streng-then the powers of the Commission by delegating more and more decisions to it rather than to intermediary committees consisting of national officials. However, it is easy to see why this would be completely unrealistic at the present time. It would, indeed, be quite undesirable in that the Commission does not at present con-stitute anything more than a 'supranational' bureaucracy. On what basis could the national governments surrender the interests of their people in certain vital social and economic matters to such a body? The Commission can be given more formal powers only when it comes to represent the people of the member countries more fully. Indeed, it is easy to predict what would happen if the Administrative function of the Commission were increased at the present time. It would no doubt immediately set up working groups of national officials and representatives of interest groups to assist it in making the necessary decisions. These representatives would themselves in most cases be unable to give their advice without first consulting

K 289

their own governments and the situation would be virtually back where it started. The Commission's Mediative function is not so much an outcome of the Commission's lack of formal powers; it is built into the political system of the Community.

THE COMMISSION'S ADMINISTRATIVE FUNCTION

It seems inevitable however that in the long run the Commission will be increasingly entrusted with the implementative, regulatory tasks, which we have lumped together and called the Administrative function. If the Community is to continue to develop in the direction of adopting common policies, then this will be the only alternative to increasing congestion and overloading of the Council of Ministers. If the Commission is to perform these delegated tasks adequately, however, it will have to adopt an increasingly hierarchical and mechanistic type of organization. The alternative would be further co-optation, which as we have seen does not really help at all. Even at the present time the establishment of a common market in industrial products, and now in agriculture as well, threatens to overwhelm the Commission because of the sheer number of acts required to apply Community legislation to individual cases. These acts take the form usually of official Decisions addressed to a government, a firm, or an individual. From January 1958 to July 1962 no more than 200 such individual Decisions had to be taken by the Commission, most of them relating to the granting or refusal of tariff quotas by member governments. In the agricultural sector alone, however, about 100 decisions have been taken every month since July 1, 1962, when the rules governing the implementation of the common market for agriculture came into force. At the same time, the Commission is responsible for ruling on alleged breaches of the Treaty or of other forms of Community legislation. Up to now most of these have arisen from mistaken interpretations but the increase in quantity of Community legislation is bound to lead to at least a proportionate increase in the number of such cases.[1]

In spite of recent attempts to delegate some of the formal decision-

[1] E. Noël, *How the European Economic Community's Institutions Work*, Community Topics No. 11, Information Service of the European Communities, Brussels, August 1963, pp. 3–4.

making power arising under Community Regulations to particular Commissioners, or even to particular officials of the Commission, the sessions of the Commission itself are becoming increasingly congested with administrative material of this type.[1] Most of the senior officials we spoke to who had some first hand experience of the proceedings of the Commission itself (such as members of cabinets and of the Executive Secretariat) regarded this as a major problem. Clearly, the more the Commissioners themselves are occupied with such questions, the less time and energy they will have for leadership and innovation.

Apart from this, a porous organization, such as we have noticed in parts of the Commission, in which different styles of administration and different normative approaches compete for domination, is most unsuited to the performance of delegated tasks of a regulatory nature. It is suited to the Commission's Mediative function in that it helps to ensure that the organization is sufficiently flexible and impartial to react to different national positions. This is why we would predict that the Commission's main reaction to a greater Administrative function now would most probably be to co-opt national officials and restore its role as mediator. If really effective delegation is to take place, however, then clear, detailed legislative prescriptions will have to be provided by the governments, leaving as little room for argument within the Commission itself as possible. After all, on what authority could the Commission claim the right to interpret such measures at the present time?

The only alternative to the Mediative function of the Commission, in the absence of real political leadership at a Community level, seems to be an increasing Administrative function. Indeed, the acquisition of duties of an implementative, regulatory nature could be said to follow naturally from the inefficiencies associated with the process of *engrenage*, just as a mechanistic and routine type of

[1] An example of the type of delegation mentioned can be found in the case of export subsidies for fatstock, cereals, pork meat, eggs, and poultry, which have to be fixed according to rapid changes in the markets for these products. Unless the Commission as a whole decides otherwise, these subsidies can now be fixed or modified by the Vice-President of the Commission, Mr Mansholt, acting alone in the name of the Commission, or, if he is prevented from exercising this responsibility, by the Director General for Agriculture. If the latter official is indisposed the power can be exercised by junior officials. (See *Décision de la Commission des Communautés Européennes*, July 5, 1967, 67/424/CEE, Journal Officiel des Communautés Européennes, No. 146, (1967), pp. 12–13.)

organization was said to follow as a natural reaction to the disunity and uncertainty of the porous type of organization. While this development represents a certain kind of progress, in that it implies that agreement has already been reached on certain common policies, it does ironically enough augur poorly for the future. This is basically because the body entrusted with the Administrative function, the Commission, is also at present the sole source of real dynamic towards further integration. There is plenty of evidence from other fields to suggest that a bureaucratic organization is of strictly limited value in sponsoring and maintaining political or economic development. This is particularly so where such development calls for inventiveness and change, and where existing structures have proved unwilling or inadequate. This is a point which has emerged very clearly from recent studies of developing societies, but in key respects the Community is in a parallel situation. In the Community, too, dynamic political and economic integration could be said to rely on the development of new institutions of political leadership.

'Bureaucracies are caught up in their experience as engineers of the administrative process. Theirs is the task of operating governmental machinery in the day-to-day accomplishment of public purposes. Not surprisingly, the directing cadre cannot readily slip out of character. It is rarely seen on the barricades or in revolutionary conclaves.'[1]

The lesson of this is that the problem lies not in the Commission's lack of formal powers of decision but in the absence of real political leadership at a Community level. Indeed, the more formal the powers that are delegated to the Commission, the more vital will become the need for such leadership and the greater will be the demands upon it, given the need to provide bureaucracy with a mission and purpose. While it may compensate in certain respects, the process of *engrenage*, of co-opting national officials into the decision-making process, is itself no substitute for political leadership. The results of work of other students of bureaucracy suggest that it would be pointless to rely on the bureaucracy itself to produce the necessary initiatives and to provide the normative support for political leadership of the Community. Bureaucracy is essentially conservative, derivative and impartial. That the Commissioners are subject to increasing pres-

[1] J. La Palombara, Notes, Queries and Dilemmas, *Bureaucracy and Political Development*, Princeton, New Jersey, Princeton University Press, 1963, p. 77.

sures to adopt such a role is unquestionable.[1] In the conclusions to this book we examine some possible means by which they might be able to avoid it.

[1] See the incredible correspondence reported in Le Rôle Politique des Commissaires, *Agenor—European Review*, No. 8, 1968, pp. 65–6. The French Foreign Minister, Michel Debré, wrote to the President of the Commission, M. Rey, complaining about a 'political' speech attacking French policy towards the Community given by Vice-President Mansholt. M. Rey replied dissociating the other members of the Commission from M. Mansholt's remarks and defending the impartiality of the Commission:

'J'aurais peut-être pu ajouter que M. Mansholt est une personnalité politique dynamique et batailleuse, et que si nous avons bénéficié, dans la construction européenne, de ce dynamisme, il faut peut-être en supporter avec patience quelques inconvenients.'

PART FOUR

CONCLUSIONS

CHAPTER 12

POLITICAL LEADERSHIP AND POLITICAL UNION

Since the beginning of 1963 commentators have increasingly adopted a pessimistic and sceptical tone when writing about the European Communities and the future prospects of European unity. Certainly, the customs union of the EEC has been achieved ahead of schedule, along with a number of other policy measures designed to prevent economic discrimination between people of the six countries. It is also true that it has still not proved necessary for any member State to have such recourse to the escape clauses in the Treaty of Rome as to undermine the fundamental objectives of the common market. The new disillusionment is the result, not of failure to carry out the specific objectives regarding non-discrimination as laid down in the Treaty of Rome, but rather of the lack of any real sign of growing political union between the six countries. Indeed, the degree of political cohesion has been so small that it has proved impossible as yet to develop the Community into an economic union, although many economists regard this as an essential concomitant to the freeing of trade.

THE WEAKNESSES OF THE COMMUNITY METHOD

Far from the establishment of the Community proving a source of ever closer political union between the six countries, as we have seen, international events between 1962 and 1969 were marked by increasing dissension between France and her five partners. For some time there was optimism that the deeper political differences between the Six on such questions as enlarging the Community and relations with the USA would not seriously affect progress towards further economic integration. Such optimism is no longer possible today. Indeed, not only are the foreign and defence policies of the member States as far apart as ever they were before the Community was set up, but it seems that failure to co-operate in other fields (such as monetary policy, science and technology, and economic strategy) has made it difficult to consolidate the progress already made towards a customs union of the Six. Meanwhile, institutional objectives such as increasing the powers of Community as opposed to national institutions seem very distant. Even the modest institutional developments envisaged in the Treaty of Rome, such as giving the Community its own financial resources and directly electing the European Parliament, have been indefinitely postponed.

It can now be seen quite clearly that the 'spillover' concept, according to which integration in one sector (in practice, the economic) is meant to extend almost automatically to other, related sectors, is an inadequate explanation of the process of unification in the case of post-war Europe. The scope of European integration, it seems, can be extended only by the agency of some political initiative and support. Moreover, in an effective economic union government decisions have to be based on certain fundamentals of social and economic policy and there have to be common institutions capable of defining the ends to be achieved to the satisfaction of all the key actors involved. These facts were not ignored by the 'functionalists', the Europeans who believed in a 'gradualist' approach to unity and who inspired the founding of all three Communities. Indeed, the necessary political impulsion was allegedly provided for in the shape of common institutions like the Commissions and the High Authority, the Council of Ministers, the Parliament, the Court of Justice and the Economic and Social Committee. Monnet himself presided over the High Authority up to 1955 and from that date led the Action Committee for the United States of Europe, a pressure group designed to provide support and ideas for the development of the Communities from the leading non-communist political parties and trade unions of Europe. Moreover, the Treaty of Rome provided for the evolution of common economic and social policies by the member States and gave the Community institutions a very free rein to produce initiatives in directions beyond the common market stage.

Our main conclusion is that the chief weakness of the Community Method is the failure to take sufficient account of the need for political leadership independent of the national governments at a Community level. While its motives were both sincere and intelligent, the 'gradualist' strategy has proved to be unrealistic in certain key respects. What it provided in practice was a 'supranational' bureaucracy (the Commission), a court of arbitration in matters arising under the Treaty (the Court of Justice), certain consultative and hortatory representative bodies (the Parliament and the Economic and Social Committee), and machinery for inter-governmental co-operation (the Council of Ministers). The really important part of this institutional system is the dialogue between the Commission and the Council of Ministers, by means of which all the major decisions at a Community level are made, including particularly the Community laws which determine the future scope and level of integration. Yet the Commission on its own cannot approve such decisions: on every major issue the final authority to make Community decisions rests with the ministers of member States' governments sitting in the Council and these men are responsible only to their own national governments and Parliaments. The governments also appoint the members of the Commission, provide its financial resources, and approve the Community budget. The 'supranational' element is confined to a body whose constitutional relationship to the national governments is parallel to that of a bureaucracy to the executive leadership of a state. Most of its formal powers are delegated and its members are appointed by the national governments, who also authorize its legislative proposals.

It is clear, however, that the Europeans who conceived this system went beyond purely constitutional analysis and, basing their hypothesis on a fairly reasonable reading of the actual working of political institutions in modern western democracies, believed that the system would in practice provide political impulsion and authority to support further integration. The key to their reasoning was the Commission. This was not in their minds a bureaucratic body at all, at least not in the functional sense of a body concerned with the administrative function of the political system, implementing defined enactments and providing technical advice. The Commission is expected to perform two vital functions of political leadership, what we have called above the Initiative function (inventing and

296

'selling' means of extending the scope and level of integration) together with the Normative function (legitimizing measures by its uniquely European character and defining the common interest). Constitutional means are provided to enable it to make a reality of these functions; for example, its unique right to initiate Community legislation (including the provision that its proposals can only be amended by the Council unanimously), the 'independence' of its members, and so on. It is also intended that similar constitutional means will be added as time goes on, in the form of giving the Commission its own financial resources and delegating to it more formal powers to make final decisions. These developments, however, had to depend on the success with which the Commission performed its role as political leader by convincing the member States that such measures were desirable. It is also conceivable that in time a more conventional political system might emerge, in that the Treaty of Rome contains provision for directly electing the European Parliament at some later date. It may be, therefore, that in time the Commission will lose most of its bureaucratic features by becoming fully responsible to the Parliament just like the executive branch of any typical federal government. This development, too, however, depends on the success of the original interpretation of the Commission's role as that of a political leadership.

This notion of a constitutional bureaucracy exercising political functions is, as we have remarked, not entirely unreasonable in view of the experience of government in the states of western Europe. As we pointed out in an earlier chapter, there may even be a case against using the term 'bureaucracy' to refer to the part of the state defined in the constitution as being responsible for the administration of executive decisions and for 'servicing' the state.[1] This part of the constitution is in theory recognizable as the civil service or as various government agencies, known collectively as the 'Administrative State'. Yet, it is now well known that the 'Administrative State' invariably does far more than simply 'administer', in the narrow sense of this term. Certain public officials wield considerable political authority as economic planners or even simply as the managers of government departments when ministerial leadership is weak or unstable. It is even said that permanent officials are sometimes more competent and better equipped than demo-

[1] See pp. 102–4 above.

cratically elected politicians for taking responsibility for certain political undertakings, (such as gaining the support of industrialists and workers for a national economic plan).[1] Indeed, in the experience of some western European countries (now members of the Communities) Parliamentary government has become greatly discredited following years of 'immobilisme'. Government by party leaders has sometimes become associated with government by patronage, in which the short-term interests of various groups have been satisfied at the expense of the long-term interests of the general public. In such countries, it is very often permanent, salaried public officials who are credited with major social and economic advances rather than the more conventional politicians elected as Parliamentary deputies.[2]

Our previous analysis of the concept of 'bureaucracy' also warned, however, that it was important to distinguish between using the term in a *constitutional* sense to refer simply to the 'Administrative State' and using it in a *functional* sense to mean the people and institutions actually engaged in the administrative function of the political system. The latter may or may not be the constitutionally accredited civil service or Administration. However, those organizations which are engaged in the administrative function wield authority which is delegated and are designed ideally for the most efficient implementation of the tasks assigned to them. Such organizations must be essentially conservative, mechanistic, and impartial in their outlook and procedure. They cannot be called on to take initiatives, to evaluate or to hold convictions. It is the exercise of the administrative function which identifies the bureaucracy in the sense we have used the term and in the sense sociologists have used it to analyse organizations at the 'micro' level of the business firm and government agency.

The main purpose of our detailed empirical study of the role of the Commission of the EEC has been to illustrate that the Commission is bound to become a bureaucracy in this functional sense, whatever its constitutional powers may be and whatever the founders of the Community might have envisaged. What we have suggested

[1] See pp. 326–34 below.
[2] See, for example, P. Lalumière, *L'inspection des Finances*, Paris, PUF, 1959; B. Chapman, *The Profession of Government*, London, George Allen & Unwin 1959, pp. 273–96, etc.

is that, in order to provide political leadership of the Community, it needed itself to be led by men who were legitimate political leaders of the Community. The matter is not nearly as simple as this in practice, of course, and we shall summarise the essential qualifications to this view of the Commission's role in later parts of this chapter. In effect, the Commission of President Hallstein (and, we have reason to believe, the High Authority of Jean Monnet) at least in the first three or so years of its existence was clearly not a bureaucracy. But we shall suggest below that the special nature of its organization at this time was determined by conditions which cannot be expected to reappear. At the same time, of course, it is not possible to make a categorical classification of the Commission as one type of body or another. In practice, its role and its organization are constantly evolving in response to environmental changes and in depicting it we see that one institutional type overlaps with another at any one time. But at certain phases one type dominates the others and since we can discern clearly enough on what conditions each type depends, then it is possible to make some general remarks about the role of the institution as a whole, now and in the future. In general, therefore, we would conclude that the Commission has come to perform predominantly the role of a bureaucracy and that its organization has evolved accordingly. In view of this, and in view of what is already known about the nature of bureaucracy at the level of single organizations in various sectors of society, we can conclude that political leadership at a Community level is more than ever essential to provide the Commission with a sense of purpose and to endow it with an organization which can provide inventiveness and innovation.

The case for establishing a European political leadership, which is independent of the member governments and is legitimized by some viable political process such as a Community-wide election, is based on three conclusions regarding the present Communities. As we tried to show in previous chapters, political authority now rests overwhelmingly with the member governments and this is insufficient guarantee that the necessary political leadership to support further integration will be available. The experience of Gaullist hostility to the Community is evidence of this. Although the other member States have mainly succeeded in preventing General de Gaulle from wrecking the Community it was always extremely diffi-

cult to make any real progress without his support. Nor was the
Commission ever in a position effectively to counter the Gaullist
challenge.

It is unlikely that Monnet and the 'functionalists' were so naïve as
to discount the key role given to the national governments in the
Community Method. They did not reckon, however, for a phenomenon such as the French Fifth Republic. Perhaps they should not be
criticized for this lack of premonition: they were certainly not alone
in their ignorance of the future. Indeed, perhaps the coming to power
of General de Gaulle was an accident and does not affect the basic
reasoning of the 'functionalists' that the leading politicians and
representatives of interest groups in western Europe were coming to
see the inevitability of ever closer union between the countries of
western Europe. We cannot provide a full discussion of these
hypothetical questions here for they take us far beyond our main
theme. Nevertheless, whatever the full implications of Gaullism for
the future of France and Europe, and whatever the view of Monnet
and his supporters when the Community was founded[1], it is clear
that many Europeans underestimated the reluctance of the national
governments to lend their support to European measures.

For example, there is too much emphasis on bureaucratic methods
of decision-making in the application of the Community Method.
Thus, 'co-opting' national civil servants and the representatives of
interest groups into the decision-making process and even con-
verting them to technical measures, such as the common agricultural
policy and the system of value-added taxation (TVA), is no guarantee
that their governments will become more European or will be more
likely to act in concert in future. At the very least, such dependence
on bureaucratic means reveals an extreme scepticism regarding the
conventional political processes, such as general elections and
Parliamentary votes. It implies great confidence in the absence of
ideology and in the 'consensus view' of modern democratic politics.
It is a position that very probably Monnet himself did not share and
it is true to say that other 'functionalist' Europeans saw the limita-

[1] Little has been written about the motives and ideas of the early leaders of
the European movement after the war and it would be most useful to know
more about the exact intentions and expectations of Monnet and his followers.
We have been advised by sources close to Monnet that he was, in fact, quite
aware of the need to provide continual political impulses to support the process of
integration.

tions of the process of *engrenage*.[1] It is also the case, of course, that the decision-making process of the Community, based as it is primarily on inter-governmental co-operation, is extremely inefficient, as we have shown above.[2] It may well be that the only way to prevent the system from seizing up altogether will be to delegate more powers to the Commission, but this, as we have seen, increases the need for effective Community political leadership in that it will further disable the Commission from performing a promotive role.[3]

However, while it is the argument most readily appreciated up to now in view of the recent Gaullist threat, the possibility of disunity and obstruction among the member governments is by no means the only reason why some independent, legitimate Community political authority is essential. A second reason is the need for measures of positive integration to consolidate the common market and to take advantage of the removal of barriers to trade. This kind of integration is of a different quality from the negative integration with which the Community has been mainly concerned so far. For its effective achievement the bureaucratic method of decision-making may well be quite inadequate.

Finally, as the bulk of this book has been designed to illustrate, the organization of the Commission cannot be depended upon to provide the Initiative and Normative functions so essential for further unification, unless legitimized political leaders are provided to give it direction and purpose. This argument rests to some extent on what is already known about the nature of bureaucratic organizations, but our own studies of the role of the Commission have shown its application to the present case.

THE DISILLUSIONMENT OF THE ECONOMISTS

The Community has been heralded as a unique and striking achievement in economic integration. Certainly, in view of the economic and other divisions among the six countries prevailing before the

---

[1] See, for example, R. Lemaignen, *L'Europe au Berceau*, Paris, Plon, 1963, p. 91 : '*Le fait est qu'au sein des grandes administrations, l'on rencontre des fonctionnaires profondément dévoués à la construction européenne, mais que les collectivités administratives prises en bloc se montrent rarement animées par le même sentiment.*' What a marvellous (accidental) rebuttal of the behaviouralist case!

[2] See pp. 284–90 above.

[3] See pp. 290–3 above.

second world war, the establishment of an industrial customs union only twenty-three years after it seems remarkable. On the other hand, modern trends in economic theory and even the wider objectives of the founders of the Community themselves call for more than the establishment of conditions of free trade in industrial goods between the six member countries. By these more sophisticated, but nevertheless currently widely accepted, standards, progress has been far less encouraging. In order to glean the full benefits of free trade, if not in order to overcome the severe problems of adjustment which it creates, economists expected the Community to develop common economic strategies for dealing with such eventualities as balance-of-payments difficulties on the part of individual member states or severe regional disequilibria. At the level of national governments instruments have now been evolved in most western European countries for managing economic activity so as to increase the general standard of living of the people and to lessen severe inequalities of distribution. Thus, the removal of barriers to trade (which in itself may deprive the national governments of some of the means of managing their own economies) is a totally inadequate form of integration and may even be harmful on its own. The founders of the Community went some way to recognize this in that the Treaty of Rome contains provisions for the evolution of common economic and social policies. Yet in many respects these provisions are only vague and indefinite and it is now very much open to question whether the decision-making machinery which was provided to give them greater clarity and definition can prove adequate to the task.

Apart from the customs union, the main achievement of the Community has been an agricultural common market. It is important to note, however, that this was achieved largely for reasons of *realpolitik*, in that the French made it an essential condition of remaining in the Community.

'Economically, the European Community was for France a bargain in which a risk was taken for French industry in exchange for a great and certain gain for French agriculture.'[1]

The Community policy now adopted has proved increasingly unpopular outside the farming community. The positive aspect of

[1] John Pinder, Positive and Negative Integration, *The World Today*, Vol. 24, No. 3, March, 1968, p. 100.

the policy (the modernization and restructuring of European farming) has yet to get off the ground. The Community system of marketing which has been established depends primarily on the fixing of agricultural price levels by the Council of Ministers, itself a process of regular hard bargaining and political give-and-take. Indeed, the fixing of common prices for cereals for 1968 necessitated one of the longest marathon sessions ever held in the Council, lasting from October 25 to 27, 1967.[1] In another sector where the Treaty laid down the achievement of a common policy as a specific objective, namely Transport, progress has been notoriously slow owing to the highly protective attitudes of most member governments. While agreement was finally reached on the first stage of a common policy, this was possible only by a departure from the normal Community Method, the member States having drawn up their own agreement.[2] Experience in sectors such as these does not augur well for the future prospects of positive integration:

'The experience of the Community is . . . that with respect to managed markets a common policy that is at all effective has been formed and applied only where there was a political motive powerful enough to over-ride the very tough national interests that exist in these sectors; and even where, as in agriculture, an effective common policy has been formed, it has tended to be based on the sum of the member countries' protectionisms rather than on a rational conception of the welfare of the Community as a whole.'[3]

The adoption of a common customs tariff towards third countries led at first to expectations that the six countries would soon reach common trading policies with the rest of the world, a step which would take them a long way towards evolving a common foreign policy as well. As we have already seen, however, the opposite has been the case and lack of agreement on foreign policy has been an impediment to co-operation in the question of trade with third countries. The negotiation of the Kennedy Round as one unit was clearly a major achievement in positive integration but, as we saw in our detailed study of this undertaking, the Community's unanimity was achieved only as the result of a hard-won bargain in which

1 See T. Parfitt, The EEC's Common Agricultural Policy, *The World Today*, Vol. 24, No. 1, January, 1968, pp. 37–40.
2 See p. 237 above.
3 Pinder, *op. cit.*, p. 102.

German industrial gains were offered in return for German support for a Community agricultural policy which was largely favourable to France. In negotiations in UNCTAD, for example, the Community has proved a far less cohesive or dynamic concern, and it is still a long way from realizing a common policy on trading with Eastern European countries.

In sectors where the Treaty of Rome is not specific about the achievement of common policies, little more has been achieved than organized co-operation between the member governments under Commission 'sponsorship'. The measures of April 1964 to set up joint committees in the economic and financial sphere have clearly done much to increase contact between member States on these problems, but only at an inter-governmental level. Observers still question the Community's ability to react collectively and effectively to serious economic difficulties on the part of one member State, or even in the Community as a whole. Mrs Camps suggests, for example, that the Community's 'fumbling' in responding to the Italian balance-of-payments crisis of 1964 contrasted with the 'speedy response' of the United States and other international sources.[1] John Pinder has pointed out that in order to deal with such eventualities the Community must establish common policies of a positive sort in a number of key fields.[2] In few of the respects he mentions, however, has positive integration been approached with much measure of success. In the social field, for example, as the Commissioner responsible has himself pointed out, the Community's existing powers need to be extended to cover unemployment and retraining in general. It seems, however, that in this sector progress has been restrained by the Treaty and the reluctance of the member governments to delegate the necessary powers to the Commission.[3] We have already had a close look at the difficulties the Community has experienced with developing a common policy for aiding underdeveloped or otherwise problematic regions, difficulties which arise largely from the lack of specific powers given to Community institutions in the Treaty.[4] In the field of fiscal policy the Community has

[1] M. Camps, *European Unification of the Sixties*, London, OUP, 1967, pp. 11–12.
[2] Pinder, *op. cit.*, pp. 104–9.
[3] L. Levi-Sandri, *Social Policy in the Common Market*, Community Topics No. 20, 1966, Information Service of the European Communities, Brussels.
[4] See pp. 217–27 above.

recently congratulated itself on achieving the first major step towards a harmonization of turnover taxes. However,

'If one looks for the principle which has guided the discussions and decisions on fiscal harmonization within the Community, it is simply the principle which underlies the economic side of the Treaty of Rome and subsequent directives of the Community institutions, the principle of fair competition. Nothing must be done to distort the conditions of competition in favour of one country as against another, one firm against another. Hence the insistence on conformity of tax structures, and equalization of tax rates or burdens'.[1] Little or no thinking seems to have been applied to the possibility of using taxation policy as a positive weapon of Community economic strategy. Thus fiscal powers could be used by Community institutions for purposes such as regional development, industrial policy, unemployment assistance, social policy, aid to developing countries overseas, as well as for conducting an active monetary and fiscal policy within the Community.[2]

So far we have considered the necessity of economic and political union from the point of view of the internal stability and consolidation of the common market. Equally pressing, and in many ways more dramatic, is the need to respond to external threat. The Community has not evolved in a vacuum. It has been only too evident that the welfare of individual member States has been only partly involved in the functioning of the Communities. To a very large extent that welfare is still dependent upon factors presently outside the range and scope of Community affairs. Thus the economic policies of the countries of western Europe have recently had to cope with the effects of a world monetary crisis, yet in reacting to this crisis the Community has largely failed to act as a single unit. Yet many people now argue that the greatest external threat to all the countries of western Europe is the challenge of economic 'colonization' by the United States.

The psychological importance of this particular challenge is signified by the remarkable success of M. Jean-Jacques Servan-Schreiber's book *Le Défi Américain*, published in 1967, and rapidly becoming a 'classic' in all the countries of the Community as well

---

[1] D. Dosser and S. Han, *Taxes in the* EEC *and Britain*, London, PEP Chatham House, January, 1968, p. 42.
[2] Pinder, *op. cit.*, pp. 106–8.

as in western Europe as a whole.[1] The theme of the book is familiar enough—that the main advantages of the establishment of a common market in western Europe have accrued to American investors. This is because the largest and most successful establishments now functioning in Europe on a Community basis tend to be American-owned. At present there seems to be no effective European competition to the managerial expertise, capital backing, or technological inventiveness of these American firms. M. Servan-Schreiber argues—and many Europeans agree with him—that this is a cause for great alarm in that industrial colonization on this scale, and particularly in the science-based industries, is bound to undermine the sense of identity of those colonized, as well as their ability to control their own destiny.

In order to respond effectively to the American Challenge six courses of action are prescribed. The first of these is the establishment of great European industrial combines, gigantic in their managerial outlook and not just in their physical size, to compete with their American counterparts. Second, one of the most telling features of the American Challenge is the ability of American companies to corner the European market for products with a high research and technological content, thus blocking up the outlets for Europe's own resources of inventiveness and creativity. If there is to be any future for an independent European economy, European technological resources must be developed by the launching of European technical projects. Third, and most important from the point of view of the future of Community institutions, these two steps can be achieved only by the establishment of a minimum amount of federal power capable of promoting and backing Community enterprises. The other three prescriptions of M. Servan-Schreiber concern reforming and revitalising various key aspects of European economic and social affairs: changing the relationship between state, universities and industry; expanding adult education; and releasing latent skills and energies by reorganizing social structure.[2]

According to M. Servan-Schreiber the present Communities have failed to meet this challenge. His diagnosis points to very similar conclusions to our own. In other words, he sees the crucial failure as being the lack of a common economic strategy. In his view, over

[1] J. J. Servan-Schreiber, *Le Défi Américain*, Paris, Denoel, 1967.
[2] *ibid.*, pp. 171–80.

the last few years, far from consolidating itself, Community Europe has been in a process of debilitation. The centre of gravity in all the key sectors of industrial development and economic strategy is shifting from the Community institutions in Brussels and Luxembourg to the member governments: '*la Communauté se défait*'. The response which the Community should be making to the American Challenge is to develop a concerted policy on European science, technology and industry. Yet the scale of public intervention which such a policy usually involves—in, for example, the United States—cannot be managed effectively at a national level: national planning has reached its limits. This calls in the first place for a Community budgetary policy, which in any event is a prerequisite if business enterprises are to amalgamate on a Community-wide basis. Institutionally, it calls for a '*minimum fédéral*', namely Community organizations with autonomous power in the relevant sectors (a major step towards which would be the abandonment of the practice of unanimous voting on all major Community decisions) and with their own financial resources. Ultimately this must mean a transfer of legitimacy to a European federal authority based in some way on universal suffrage:

'The technocrats, however technically qualified they may be, will never have the necessary authority to make one superior interest prevail over particular interests. In order to assert the necessary will to succeed there must be elected leaders who will mobilize opinion and appeal to the reserves of vitality in the European people over the heads of conservative *élites*.'[1]

THE ROLE OF POLITICAL INSTITUTIONS

It has been a central theme of this book that the Community venture cannot succeed unless it is regarded as an essentially political undertaking. Subsidiary to this has been a related theme bearing the warning, increasingly resonant among economists and commentators of all kinds in recent years, that real political unification is not an automatic consequence of agreeing to take certain economic decisions in common. There can be a very real obstacle to unification in the authority and self-consciousness of the governments of nation

[1] J. J. Servan-Schreiber, *Le Défi Américain*, p. 195.

POLITICS AND BUREAUCRACY

states. Yet this authority and self-consciousness cannot be under-mined simply by a process of paying off tangible short-term interest in exchange for vague long-term commitments, of buying *ad hoc* decisions on immediate economic issues by agreeing to postpone confrontation of one's ultimate goals. Similarly, government officials and the representatives of interest groups do not represent the power of governments. Bureaucratic activity in the Communities may have been re-oriented in many important respects on to a European axis, but this means little or nothing in terms of real political support. Power in all essentials still rests in the national capitals of Europe. It may have to be channelled through Brussels more than before—but this means little to national political leaders who are in the long run aware that their power does not depend on decisions taken by this means.

According to the 'Functionalist' view of integration, however, it was a sufficient beginning in the attempt to unite Europe politically to establish a magnet for economic interests. Thus political mobil-ization within the Community was entrusted primarily to the Com-mission, which would be expected to gradually increase its own power and scope in economic matters at the expense of the national govern-ments and by this means act as a magnet for political forces in the six countries. In time, when the latter were oriented towards the common economic centre of the Community, the European Parlia-ment would be directly elected and gradually no doubt the Com-mission would derive its support from this body to which it would become increasingly responsible.

Although it lacked some of the essential features of the government of a nation-state (including even a source of popular support or independent means of raising finance), the Commission was expected to perform functions normally associated with the political leaders of a state—initiating policies for the common good and setting and preserving norms of action. The leaders of the Commission were appointed not elected, most of their actual powers were to be delega-ted not intrinsic, and superficially it looked more like an ordinary international secretariat whose job was to mediate between the claims of national governments and to administer certain common services. However, the Hallstein Commission seems to have per-formed the promotive role expected of it by developing an *esprit-de-corps* and by behaving like a committed band of partisans, fighting

308

for the European cause. As we have seen, there are still definite traces of such elements in the Commission's organization. However, given the distribution of functions and roles in the institutional system of the Community, and given that the final power of decision rested with the national governments, the Commission had, on the one hand, to perform a Mediative function, and, on the other, to acquire administrative tasks of implementing Community legislation. Yet the pursuit of these courses of action demanded a different kind of organization from the partisan type, with the result that, in the first instance the Commissioners themselves became increasingly representative of extraneous interests, and eventually the administrative services were infiltrated by means of a loose, open-ended recruitment policy. This evolution into what we have chosen to call a porous type of organization immediately triggered off a defensive reaction on the part of the Commission in the form of the growth of bureaucratic rules and methods of working. In any event, an organization based on such representative principles is bound to fall prey to rigidities of one sort or another (for example, the need to maintain equilibrium between nationalities in the deployment of posts). Finally, these automatic pressures towards bureaucracy must now be intensified by the growing number of tasks accruing to the Commission of a regulatory, implementative character, calling as they do for a mechanistic system of management suited for the making of routine decisions.

The 'Hallstein' approach was remarkably effective and a number of successes can be attributed to it—the foundation of the Community in the early years in spite of an unfavourable international situation[1], the achievement of an industrial customs union, agreement on a common policy for competition between enterprises, the establishment of an agricultural common market.[2] Of vital importance was the creation of an organizational common culture based mainly on a sense of shared adventure and common commitment to European unity and supported by a relatively loose and open-ended system of personnel administration. This common culture seems to have lasted even after the partisan phase of the Commission had passed and beyond the early years of pioneering, purposive commit-

[1] See L. Lindberg, *The Political Dynamics of European Economic Integration*, London, OUP, 1963, pp. 167–205.
[2] *ibid.*, pp. 219–82.

ment to getting the Community off the ground. The organization came to rely increasingly on seconded national officials rather than on specially selected partisan Europeans and, at the same time, it was becoming far more difficult to maintain unity within the organization without forming 'coalitions' based on different styles of administration and different norms. Nevertheless, the survival of a common culture served to hold this porous organization together and supported such ventures as the Commission's successful negotiation of the Kennedy Round on behalf of the whole Community.[1]

The same approach was also responsible for a number of initiatives which failed to come off, but which, nevertheless, met the criterion of providing political impulsion and which, in conditions of consensus among the national governments, might have resulted in striking advances towards European unity. In this category one must mention the Commission's reactions to the Gaullist veto of British membership in 1963 and 1964, and the famous proposals for financing the common agricultutural policy in the spring of 1965.

If, then, the Commission was initially successful, and if its later failures can largely be explained by severe dissension among the member States which many observers believe to have been a temporary phenomenon lasting only for the tenure of office of President de Gaulle, why are we so sceptical about the present institutional arrangements of the Community? The answer is partly, as we have said, that one cannot depend on the national governments for political leadership of the right kind. Partly, again, the answer is that the Community has not so far made significant steps towards positive integration and, even without Gaullism, such steps are qualitatively different from the achievement of negative integration, involving as they do evaluative decisions of major social and economic importance. Finally, the answer is concerned with the nature of organizations and our conviction that the organization of the Commission must increasingly perform bureaucratic functions, which will disable it from behaving as a partisan body and will eventually change it from its present porous condition.

This part of our argument tends to prejudge another, in that it implies that there was insufficient consensus among the member States to support the partisan Commission. The organization which President Hallstein led in the first few years of the Community, and

[1] See above pp. 198–226.

which left its mark on the institution for many years afterwards, is best typified by making an analogy with a political party or highly organized pressure group rather than with an administrative organization. This organization was held together largely by common loyalty and understanding—there was little demand for mechanical rules and regulations and little stress on hierarchical lines of command and on departmental prerogatives. The values esteemed in this organization were energy, enthusiasm and creativeness. Yet to be effective its initiatives and its authority depended upon the willingness of the member governments to allow themselves to be committed to measures designed in the long run to lead to European integration. The tactics by which this was achieved are significant. In general, the governments were led to accept European measures because of the short-term, selfish advantages they could get from them.[1] This procedure often involved, as we have seen, tortuous bargaining on matters of incredible detail. The main strategy of the Commission was to work through national officials and interest groups and to get the national governments into a position where they had to agree to a Community solution or else have no solution at all.

There is, however, an inherent contradiction in the role of the Commission in this procedure. We have already remarked on this and it is what has led so many observers to puzzle over what sort of political system the Community represents and to describe the system as *sui generis*. On the one hand, the Commission must be European—or as we have now come to call it, partisan. On the other, the fact that Community legislation can be legitimized only by the national governments requires it to be independent, to perform the function of impartial mediator among the various national positions. Of course, in situations where the national governments were so at one over the social and economic questions involved in the Community that the attitude of one coincided with that of all the others, the role of mediator would be very simple, not to say hardly necessary at all except as a purely secretarial, clerical function. However, such situations are most unlikely to occur, even in the absence of General de Gaulle and his supporters. Consensus on short-term goals can

[1] This is the interpretation we derive from Lindberg's analysis of the Community Method, see Lindberg, *op. cit.*, pp. 284–6.

certainly be engineered; even General de Gaulle could be convinced that France's interests would be served by an agricultural common market (on certain terms) and that a common system of corporate taxation should be adopted throughout the Community. But engineering such a consensus places the Commission into the position of a bureaucracy, by demanding of it a Mediative function requiring impartiality, and resting on delegated authority. The partisan commitment of the early Hallstein Commission was based on organizational principles which were basically unsuited to the role the institution was performing. Ironically enough, its very successes were probably the result of a role which was incompatible with the values the organization held so highly. Its initiatives which failed did so because the Commission had proved too partisan and insufficiently impartial for the member governments. So in time the Commission's leadership and its organization adapted to necessity, by becoming more and more representative. This was the only realistic course for practical men to take—any other action would have grossly overestimated the ability of national governments and socio-economic interests to achieve consensus. Our main point about the bureaucratization of the Commission is that this porous organization is essentially transitional, in that we predict that an automatic, built-in resistance to its open-ended nature is bound to arise. This resistance will result (indeed, has already resulted) in mechanistic devices of personnel administration. At the same time, the present decision-making process of the Community is so inefficient, in that the mediative agency of the Commission can achieve only a limited amount of agreement in a certain amount of time, that more and more decisions will have to be delegated to the Commission. This has already begun to happen in the case of policy on competition, agriculture, and so on. These decisions will be of a programmed, routinized variety—though naturally there will be differences of degree—in that it will have been the member governments and not the Commission itself which will have approved the legislation under which the powers are delegated.

Of course, if President Hallstein, along with Vice-Presidents Mansholt and Marjolin and all the other partisan Commissioners, had been able to stand for election, or to gain direct legitimation in the six countries in some other way, their partisan style of leadership would have made considerable sense. This may sound an excessively

312

vague qualification, for we know little enough about processes of legitimation, about the nature of political leadership, and about the way executive leadership should be exercised over bureaucracies. It is a vitally important qualification, however, for, at least, it points us in the right direction so that we know what problems we have to solve in order to build an institutional system capable of promoting European unity. We shall only touch on the subject here. This qualification also places the onus of proof regarding the likelihood of consensus of the member governments on those who argue the 'functionalist' case. It must be remembered that the amount of consensus required is not just a preparedness to agree to some vague, long-term goal such as European unity (which might well be possible after de Gaulle), but sufficient consensus to provide active leadership for the officials and representatives who must make the short-term decisions necessary to make this long-term goal a reality. The governments of national states spend a major proportion of their time drawing on resources of legitimacy acquired from electorates, or parliamentary majorities, or referenda, or party machines, in trying to reconcile the demands of competing groups within their countries with a view to promoting the national interest. How much more difficult it must be for an institution whose leaders are appointed by six different national governments from whom practically all its powers are derived to do the same thing at an international level.

In actual fact, attention has been paid increasingly to finding some means of injecting new political impetus into the process of unifying Europe. A full analysis of the different ideas and schemes which have been put forward would take us beyond the scope of this book, but we shall now present an outline of one or two of the more interesting ideas for institutional development which have been circulating in European circles in the last few years, that is, before the resignation of General de Gaulle.[1] What is important is that two kinds of distinction could be drawn between the different approaches. The first is between proposals which regard the existing Communities with their existing institutional framework as an essential starting

[1] For the account which follows we have drawn extensively on the papers and discussions at a series of seminars and conferences organized by the Federal Trust for Education and Research in the course of 1967 and 1968. Since the proceedings of these sessions were confidential we cannot give detailed references.

point for future development and those which think in terms of a completely new initiative, probably with a new treaty or set of treaties between the European powers.

The first and more conservative approach, working through the existing Community system, would seek to proceed by inter-governmental negotiations between the Six to merge the three existing Communities and to expand their scope and depth. It also assumes a widening of their membership to include at least the four countries whose applications are presently before the Council of Ministers (namely, Britain, Denmark, Ireland and Norway). However, it was argued against this that immediate development of the existing Communities was out of the question even as far ahead as 1972, in view of the hostile attitude of the Gaullist regime in France, and in view of the unwillingness of the Federal German Government to take any real initiative which might be interpreted as hostile to France. As for initiative from outside the Communities, there was nothing much more the British Government could now do, having already tried to enter the Communities twice and having failed on both occasions. At the same time, as we have already seen, economists and others who supported European integration on technical grounds had begun to lose faith in the existing Communities, even to the extent of regarding the kind of integration they represented as being unfavourable in economic terms. Similarly, it was argued that many of the conditions which determined the nature of the original Communities had changed: the need for independence of the USA was now much more widely felt; the fact that the 'spillover' concept had yet to prove itself in practice had reduced the attractiveness of 'functional' integration in principle; attention had anyway shifted from the subject matter of 'functional' integration (coal and steel and industrial free trade) to other sectors such as monetary policy, research and technology, economic strategy, and even defence. There was also evidence of a possible revival of the 'radical' approach to unification of the earlier federalists (such as Spinelli), according to which political unification could only be based on a conscious and decisive transfer of sovereignty to popularly-elected federal institutions.[1] From this point of view the main hope was some sort of governmental initiative from outside the Six for a new Community in

[1] See pp. 19–22 above.

314

some new sector or sectors (for example, monetary policy, technology and defence) with a new treaty containing explicit provision for an eventual transfer of legitimate authority to a federal government. In answer to the charge of lack of realism these 'radicals' replied that their approach was no less realistic than that of the 'conservatives' who would work through the existing Community system, given the semi-permanent stalemate which that system seemed to have entered. Indeed, the 'radicals' could claim to have taken the more realistic approach to the role of national governments in their strategy. In the case of either approach, some national initiative was essential. Yet while the modern gradualists had to rely for this on the present members of the Communities and had to overcome the seemingly permanent French veto, the 'radicals' were in a position to call for the support of the British Government and their plans did not depend on the support of General de Gaulle: (French support of the proposed new Community would have been highly desirable for obvious reasons, but would not at first have been essential). At the same time, the new Community need not include the subject matter which was reserved to the existing Communities, for there were, as we have already said, a number of other sectors where a strong case for integration could be made out.

A second important distinction is between those who envisage a federated Europe with institutions along the lines of the present Communities and those who seek to establish some entirely new federal system. In the case of those who take the existing institutional framework as their starting point, the European Parliament is seen as the key instrument for mobilizing political support for a future federal authority. The Parliament, it is hoped, will eventually be directly elected by universal adult suffrage in each of the member countries, and will acquire control over the budgetary powers of the Community (the Commission having by this time acquired its own financial resources). Following these steps, it is said, the constitution of the Community should be further amended so as to make the Commission fully responsible to the Parliament. Here full responsibility means, not only the possibility of a vote of censure forcing the Commission to resign *en bloc*, but also the right of the Parliament (rather than the member states) to appoint the Commission. Eventually, the Parliament might acquire the power to approve all Community legislation introduced by the Commission, the

Council of Ministers being reduced to the status of a kind of second chamber or senate with only limited powers of delay and obstruction.

In other words, the system of institutions envisaged would be more or less that regarded as conventional in the countries of western Europe, and known roughly as Parliamentary Government. It is for this very reason that the scheme has been criticized. For one thing, it is partly because the national political systems have been found wanting in various ways that many people have turned their attention to creating a new federal Europe. More particularly, it is realized that over large areas of continental Europe Parliamentary institutions have become discredited in the public mind and associated with unstable and ineffective government. Thus in France a definite move seems to have been made away from Parliamentary government to a unique kind of presidential system. It is feared that the centrifugal, fissiparous tendencies of the national political parties would reappear at a federal level and make orderly progress towards a united Europe impossible. This is quite apart from doubts about the likelihood of federal parties holding together in spite of internal national differences. At worst the translation to a federal level of the squalid bickering between particular interests and the *immobilisme* associated with 'government by assembly' could discredit the whole undertaking in the eyes of the European people. It is, on the other hand, certainly the case that some Parliamentary systems (the British, for example) have so evolved in practice as to serve as instruments of aggregating interests and narrowing down conflict, so that Parliament now serves as a means of legitimizing authority rather than undermining it. However, this type of system depends not so much on the formal character of its institutions, as on the nature of the political culture and on the structure of its parties and groups. Simply to transpose such British Parliamentary institutions to a European level would be no guarantee that the features of political life which are associated with them would also reappear. Thus a major criticism of the 'Parliamentary' approach is that, while it does little to clarify what the nature of Parliamentary parties and groups in a federal system would be, the institutional arrangements it proposes would depend on these far more even than the institutions of the present Communities. Yet while doubts remain about the likely characteristics of European political parties, one must continue to be sceptical about the Parliamentary system as a means of injecting some kind of political dynamic into the unifying process.

Alternative proposals stress the need to take account of recent disillusionment with the conventional western systems of Parliamentary Government and to look for a different model. The alternative means of creating real political leadership at a European level could in principle be several and deserve to be critically examined at length as part of preparation for the time when a federal system can be established. We shall select here just one particular scheme which happens to favour a system of direct election of a European executive. According to this scheme the real decision-making body would be a Federal Council (of anything from nine to fifteen members) which would be elected every five years or so by universal adult suffrage according to a list system of voting. Competing fixed lists of candidates (which could not be modified by the voters) would be presented to the electorate in the member countries and would comprise a fixed distribution of candidates between the different nationalities. If no list obtained more than a certain percentage of the vote at the first ballot (say 40 per cent), then a second ballot could be held some time later at which alliances between lists would be permitted. At the same time as the election of the Council, voting would take place for a Federal Assembly which would be given power to amend and approve federal legislation introduced by the Council. However, in order to obviate the deadlock between executive and legislature which results in some federal systems, the Federal Council should have the power to hold referenda and the members of the Council should not be responsible to the Assembly at least for the first three years of their five-year term. The simultaneous election of Council and Assembly would be expected to avoid a situation in which any particular Council faced a hostile majority in the Assembly.

The main objectives of this scheme are to transpose to a European level the conflict between the two major political tendencies (radical against conservative), and to avoid the instability and consequent popular disaffection associated with multi-partism. By vesting the power of initiative and the responsibility of government in a multinational executive authority it aims to weaken the centrifugal tendencies of national or other particular interests and to combine the features of a directly elected executive as in the USA with those of a collegial executive as in Britain. The proposed Federal Council would be given responsibility, not just for economic affairs, but also for foreign policy and defence, and even educational and cultural affairs. It would be entrusted with an exclusive right to the use of force (a property which is often regarded as a defining characteristic of government). However, a number of doubts spring to mind about the scheme. For example, how is one to ensure that the multinational Federal Council does not behave as a purely representative, deliberating body, rather like the present Commission, its members dividing on the basis of their nationality? Is it entirely clear that national and other particular interests will not succeed in blocking progress by bridling the Council through obstruction in the Assembly?

We are not concerned here with analysing these proposals in detail, but rather with giving examples of recent thought on ways to inject political dynamic into the unifying process. Such schemes are themselves only at the stage of thought-provoking ideas. They have one positive feature in common—they realize that European unification cannot proceed without some firm political basis. They also share the same fundamental weakness, which is that none of them can hope to succeed without some concerted initiative on the part of some or all of the national governments in western Europe, and even now that de Gaulle has gone such action is most unlikely in the foreseeable future. Whether one seeks to develop the existing Communities into a political unit perhaps by taking advantage of the new merger Treaty or looks for some new initiative in some new field, whether one regards the Parliamentary system as a satisfactory basis for a federal Europe or favours some other arrangement, the practical obstacle is the same—the national governments have to be made to give up a key part of their sovereignty.

Perhaps, following the passing of the regime of General de Gaulle, an initiative towards this end can be taken within the framework of the existing Communities. Perhaps it would be more realistic to seek some initiative from outside the present Communities—say from the British government—but designed to gain the support of its existing members. These are questions which go beyond the terms of reference of our present study. But this study has served to show the basic principles upon which any such new initiative must be based, namely, the creation before anything else of a central, federal political leadership based on some means of direct legitimation in the member countries. We have already admitted that little is known about the processes by which such a leadership might come to be established. Moreover, in view of the atmosphere of social and political reconstruction which seems to be sweeping western Europe, it would probably be premature to set out with a rigid political structure in mind. However, we devote the last section of this chapter to a brief consideration of ways in which the organized activity of Europeans might be restructured and redirected in ways which would be of some immediate practical relevance.

EUROPEAN UNIFICATION IN THE 1970s

Research on European unification has for some time now concentrated almost exclusively on aspects of the existing European Communities. There have been good reasons for this, though one of the chief of these has been utilitarian in that the Communities (especially the Commission itself) have pursued a strikingly liberal attitude towards academic and other investigators—not only reacting favourably to their requests for information but even offering financial assistance towards their projects. (This attitude is significant: bodies which exercise real power—as the Commission needs to do—are far less anxious to reveal their secrets to outsiders. In many ways—although this is biting the hand that fed one—the Commission sometimes gives the impression of being just one big Department for Public Relations.) This open and often self-critical attitude is no doubt a hangover from the partisan phase of the Commission's organization and represents a sort of proselytizing zeal for the European cause. In the circumstances of today, as we have diagnosed them, it might distract research and inquiry from other pursuits which might prove more constructive than interpreting and understanding the working of the present Community institutions.

Like most other works on European unity in the last ten to fifteen years this book has also taken the existing Communities as its main subject matter and the role of the Commission as its central theme. Indeed, the research contained in this book, along with the synthesis we have provided of the work of other scholars in the field, was undertaken in the hope that some positive conclusion could be reached with regard to future action within the present Communities. If in the final analysis we have found ourselves in the position of having to bury Caesar, we are still convinced that many valuable (if cautionary) lessons can be drawn from the sort of analysis of his life which we have provided. Nevertheless, the main purpose of this book has been to point to the value of less narrowly-confined studies. Since the future of European unity must lie in finding some means of legitimizing effective leadership at a federal level, then much could be gained from the comparative study of politics, government and administration in western Europe. This already takes place, of course, in universities and other institutions, but it is not always conducted with the specific purpose of contributing to practical knowledge regarding the institutions of a future federal Europe. Much of this work might be highly speculative. Some of it will need to be painstakingly empirical. But there is a great deal of work to be done in this respect and, as we have suggested, it might bear more fruit in the long run than the more conventional study of international co-operation in Europe.

This is essentially something for the longer term. But even where immediate action is concerned committed Europeans might well set their sights on the future. One possible interpretation of our study could be that the attempt to construct Community institutions has been premature, in that there is as yet no adequate political base for European institutions. The case for achieving European unity as soon as possible is extremely convincing and, in terms of everyday life, Europe may in practice already be more united than its national leaders would like to admit. There is still much to be done, however, in building up political forces to support a federal political system in Europe. These forces have been sorely neglected up to now because of the bureaucratic nature of the present Communities.[1]

Generally speaking we have attempted in this book to divide approaches to this problem into two main types—the 'functionalist', or 'gradualist' approach, as represented by the founders of the present Communities, and a more 'radical' approach, which has criticized the Communities for lacking a firm political basis and for failing to sustain sufficient political impetus. To the 'gradualists', the first essential step to political union is seen as the creation of Community institutions with functions of a 'supranational' character. An impetus towards political unification is expected to follow as a reaction

[1] See A. Spinelli, *The Eurocrats: Conflict and Compromise in the European Community*, Baltimore, USA, Johns Hopkins Press, 1968, pp. 133–200.

320

to these institutions. At the same time, other steps towards building up a political impetus are not precluded. Indeed, the founders of the present Communities required that the European Parliament should eventually be directly elected and then obtain increasing powers of control over Community decisions (although not according to a fixed timetable). Nevertheless, in the 'gradualist' approach European political parties or European elections are not seen as prerequisites of successful integration. Indeed, as we have seen, there was no attempt to settle in advance the political issues which were expected to arise in the course of adopting common social and economic policies: European integration should be seen as being politically 'neutral'.

On the other hand, the 'radicals' place a much greater emphasis on the need for a political element at a Community level and have criticized the existing Communities for depending on the continuing support of the member governments, particularly where essential steps towards political union are concerned. Thus, for example, the 'radicals' would like direct elections to a European Parliament and financial autonomy for the Community Executive to be built into a pre-arranged timetable or, better still, perhaps, to follow a European referendum or some other act of appealing directly to the people.

Superficially it seems as if the nature of French European policy during the General's tenure of office must have weakened the 'gradualist' case, depending as this did upon the apparent willingness of the national governments to take further steps towards unity. In fact, the 'gradualists' have been able to argue that the Gaullist regime was a quite exceptional phenomenon which did not fit the general pattern of national support for European objectives. Thus, following the General's departure, the way forward would seem to be open again, since it is in the interests of all the national governments concerned to co-operate in gradual steps towards political union.

A certain amount of optimism is clearly consistent with the immediate reactions of the Six governments following de Gaulle's resignation.[1] Although there are still serious reservations and hesitancies on specific points, and although the measure of commitment of a new French President cannot be absolutely certain, it is obvious that an enormous obstacle has now been removed. It does now seem (in the summer of 1969) that discussions on British entry may open

[1] See J. Pinder and R. Pryce, *Europe after de Gaulle*, Penguin Books, 1969, pp. 184–6.

in the near future and that steps will be taken again within the Communities towards economic union. It is also highly likely that the Commission might once again find the opportunity to propose some extension of its own powers and those of the European Parliament at the expense of the powers of the Council of Ministers and the national governments.

Thus, it may appear to some observers that the 'functionalist' approach has been vindicated by the General's resignation and that 'defeatist' talk about the present Communities is no longer warranted. We do not wish in the context of this book to reach any final conclusion one way or the other regarding the 'gradualist' approach to European political unity. For one thing, it is not really meaningful to talk about the movement for political unification in Europe in terms of a conflict of clear-cut theories or doctrines. The attitudes, proposals and ideas we have labelled as 'gradualist' or 'radical' are essentially those of practical men, not philosophers. As members of the European movement they share essentially the same basic political objectives. However, the weight of the evidence presented in this book is against the arguments that have been put forward to justify the institutional arrangements of the present Communities and it supports the view of those Europeans who have criticized the present Communities for lacking any real political element of their own and for depending on the continuing support of national governments. The history of General de Gaulle's tenure of office as President of France does not really affect this conclusion. It is based, not on a finding that consensus among the member governments on long-term ends is impossible, but rather on a view that even short-term consensus is insufficient substitute for real political leadership. It is more or less conceded here that the trend in western Europe over the long term seems to point inexorably towards greater social and economic interpenetration across national boundaries. The ideological attitudes of particular governments can only slow this process down and probably cannot halt it; (although we would suggest that the effect of General de Gaulle's anti-European policy is evidence that the European movement was over-optimistic even on this score). What is maintained here, however, is that this process is not sufficient by itself to bring the benefits expected from integration. There must be separate provision for a legitimate, autonomous political authority at a federal level before integration can be regarded

322

as worthwhile. This authority will be ineffective if it is bureaucratic-ally organized like the present Commission. Instead it must be directly based on some kind of political support which is at the same time independent of the national governments. We suspect that this in turn must require some electoral process on party lines designed to bring to power a European government with a distinct programme of action at a federal level. Such a federal government is necessary because it is simply not practicable, however much the national governments concerned declare themselves to be committed to European unity in the long run, to entrust integration of social and economic policy in the short term to a set of institutions which rely for guidance and support on a number of different governments. Such a situation must, we suggest, turn the Executive part of the Community institutions into a bureaucracy. This is not only ineffi-cient as a means of making decisions, but also prevents the growth of political commitment and dynamism at a Community level.

The main question, of course, and one which this book is unable to answer satisfactorily, is by what immediate steps such a federal political authority could be established. Our conclusions do suggest, however, that a shift of emphasis is required. The detailed, slow and arduous work of integrating various sectors of social and economic administration should give way to a more direct kind of political action. The authority of the national governments at a Community level needs to be replaced by that of some new set of representatives with their own source of support. Clearly, before this can be achieved the national governments will have to be encouraged to abdicate their control of Community decisions, and active support for federalism will have to be mobilised in the countries concerned. It is without doubt of the most crucial importance for any general plan of action that, as we have tried to show, any federal political system must depend on mobilised public opinion and cannot be achieved unless the existing national governments have either been won over or undermined. This is not to say that direct action is sufficient, for the mobilisation of support for European unity might well require the existence of institutions to act as catalysts or as objects of support and will need to be fired by a vision of what a federal Europe would be like. What is clear, however, is that in this respect the existing institutions might prove wanting now that they risk losing their partisan, pioneering orientation and threaten to become nothing much more than bureaucratic agencies of the national governments. It will be said in reply to this that the Commission does, in fact, convert national officials to European objectives, both through employing them on secondment, and by co-opting them into the decision-making process of the Community. This cannot be of much value, however, if the Commission, and the Community decision-making process, are essentially bureaucratic undertakings. Furthermore, Europeans would be better advised not to tie their energies down in the tortuous process of reaching Community decisions, (which in any event do not seem to take them far in the direction of political unification), but to liberate these energies for reforming the present institutions or trying to build a new Community.

However, what if steps are taken now towards injecting the present Communities with some political element, say, by the introduction of direct elections to the European Parliament and a decision to give the Commission financial resources of its own? It is generally the wisest course in social and political action to seek change incrementally and to take advantage where possible of existing laws and institutions. Naturally, other things being equal, it would be best to work through the existing Communities, but it must be stressed that it is essential for successful integration to inject some political element into the Communities. Direct elections to the European Parliament would be pointless unless at the same time determined steps were taken to ensure that it was the Parliament and not the national governments whose approval was essential for making Community decisions. Even so it is far from clear what future arrangements are envisaged within the EEC for selecting future Community political leaders, or for approving legislation without the need to appeal to national governments, and so on. However desirable it may be to build on existing structures, the development of an independent political basis for unification is a more urgent need for the cause of European unity than the preservation of the existing Communities.

There is evidence that a new generation of Europeans combines their support for political unification of Europe with a desire for a fundamental restructuring and renewal of existing political forms. We have not taken much account of this view here, mainly because it points far beyond the scope of the present book, but partly also because such issues should probably not be treated in the context of dispassionate research. Indeed, one of the main limitations of this book is its tendency to refer to such concepts as 'political leadership', 'political authority', 'political element', without developing in any positive way what living forms these concepts should take. The main reason for this limitation is that we do not wish to prejudge the issue as to what form a future united Europe should take. It could be that the model for such a united Europe will not be existing political forms as we know them within the nation states. Thus our conclusions pass the initiative to all those who hold some view of the shape of a future political union of Europe. What such people have to say is extremely relevant, particularly in view of the urgent need for the modern European movement to find some rallying point for mobilising political support.

The thought that political union might involve political upheaval or other unpredictable events often seems to be unwelcome to the leaders of the European movement. On the other hand there probably is no ready-made, simple, 'one best way' to move from the present situation to a United States of Europe. No constitutional lawyer or political scientist, no experienced diplomat or committed federalist, can suggest straightforward steps which will produce political structures to meet such an objective. What matters is that, in spite of this, the political aspect of unification is crucial and any attempt by the European movement to ignore that fact would be fatal for their cause. Indeed, perhaps what the movement is trying to lose in seeking a federal Europe are the very institutional structures which exist in the present nation states. Perhaps the difficulties of unification which we have discussed in this book arise from the very inadequacies of conventional European political structures. We have argued that the European movement would benefit itself in future by paying more attention to fundamental questions such as these and by not giving so narrow and pragmatic an interpretation to political union.

CHAPTER 13

BUREAUCRACY AND POLITICS—
SOME QUESTIONS FOR FUTURE
RESEARCH

Our special study of the role of Commission of the European Communities has already enabled us to point to some general conclusions regarding the role of bureaucracy in relation to politics. Thus we found that the Commission came increasingly to exercise purely delegated, administrative functions and that this was related to its tendency to acquire a more and more bureaucratic organization.[1] Conversely the more it became suited to performing relatively mechanical, routine tasks (even where these needed the exercise of considerable discretion of an administrative kind), the Commission would be able to show less and less of the creativity and initiative demanded of a body capable of promoting political unity in Europe.[2] Similarly, the more it compromised its role as initiator and upholder of the common interest by co-opting national officials and Permanent Representatives into the decision-making process, the less it would be capable of laying down with any efficacy the norms of legitimate behaviour within the Community.[3] This seems to lead us to resuscitate the dichotomy between politics and administration, even though this has become rather disreputable among students of government.[4] However, in so far as there does seem to be a marked incompatibility between the Commission's 'political' role as promoter of the common interest and its 'bureaucratic' role as administrator and mediator, our work suggests that the dichotomy does still have some important operational value.[5]

[1] See pp. 290–3 above.
[2] See pp. 257–64 above.
[3] See pp. 284 90 above.
[4] See, for example, B. Chapman, *The Profession of Government*, London, George Allen & Unwin, 1959, pp. 273–95; C. J. Friedrich, *Constitutional Government and Democracy*, New York, Harpers, 1936, pp. 386–410.
[5] See pp. 234–40 above.

While in its early years the Commission might have seemed to be more like an autonomous, federal executive in embryo than like the administrative, implementative part of the Community's system of institutions, in the course of time the latter has grown to be more and more the true description. Our confidence in regarding the Commission as a bureaucracy was increased when we saw that the character of its internal organization and the behaviour of its members and personnel increasingly came to fit the criteria associated with bureaucracy just as much as did its external relations with other parts of the Community system. What is more, there seemed to be something almost inevitable about this development, for it seemed to be directly related to the delegated nature of the Commission's formal powers and to its need to adopt a mediative function in relation to the real political authorities of the Community (the national governments). The evolution of its organization into a 'mechanistic' type could be directly related to the external relationships of the Commission, in that bureaucratic methods of personnel administration, and a decision-making process that stressed hierarchy and formalism, were developed almost as a defence against infiltration from extraneous groups and influences and against opposition to its own development.[1]

This seems to give an almost tautological theme to our study: a body with essentially delegated functions (a 'bureaucracy') reveals an essentially mechanistic ('bureaucratic') organization.[2] However, although the Commission became more and more like the conventional type of bureaucracy, for a long time it seemed to function quite differently and it was certainly not intended to take such a form by the committed Europeans who founded the Communities. How then, can we classify it in terms of the normal institutions of a political system? It is evidently not the same sort of institution as the typical executive branch of government, whose members lead a political party or parties, or are directly elected into office; nor for that matter is it entirely the same as a purely administrative organ

---

[1] See pp. 242–64 above.

[2] This proposition is incomplete, of course, for it makes no reference to the 'vicious circle' of bureaucracy, whereby the bureaucratic features of the internal organization feed back on its external relationships and keep these at a delegative implementative level (see pp. 113–14 above). Bureaucrats resist the taking of initiatives and withdraw into routine, programmed activity where they feel more secure.

of the state organized and staffed according to classical bureaucratic principles. Indeed, if we attempt to list the main formal characteristics of the Commission in quite general terms, we get an interesting combination of 'political' and 'bureaucratic' qualities:

(1) Its members are appointed not elected to office, and the criteria of appointment do not include representation, (at least not formally and explicitly). Technical qualifications for membership are not formal and explicit, but are implied and understood, (even if only at the level of general technical competence). Appointment is at the discretion of legitimized political leaders (the national governments acting together).

(2) Membership of, or allegiance to, a particular political party is not usually a condition of membership, but the members are not expected to be anonymous or impersonal. Moreover, the members (and also to some extent the staff) of the Commission are expected to show a considerable degree of personal commitment to the aims of the organization, however vaguely these may be expressed and however long the term in which they are to be accomplished. Such commitment is probably a more important factor than salary or other material benefit in motivating participation in the organization at most levels.

(3) The members constitute the leaders of the organization and appoint their own staff, largely on the basis of open, competitive examination to test qualifications and merit. There is formal specialization and division of labour, but the members are constituted on a collegial basis and the organization is meant to be bound together by common leadership. Thus, the leaders are separated from the rest of the organization (by being separately appointed and bound by collegiality), and there is no formal way of passing from its lower ranks up to this leadership by promotion according to seniority or merit.

(4) The Commission's formal powers are delegated, being derived partly from the Treaty of Rome and partly from regulations passed by the Council of Ministers. (It does, however, also have power to make delegated legislation in consultation with other parties.)

(5) The Commission (in the person of its members) is solely responsible for interpreting and exercising its powers, subject only to judicial review, the threat of vote of censure by the European Parliament, and the need to take into account the views of this and

other consultative bodies. Such consultation may be used by the members, along with other forms of public exposure, as a means of mobilizing direct support for their aims.

It is clear merely from this listing of formal characteristics that the Commission is a most interesting hybrid kind of body. 'Political' characteristics such as a sense of shared commitment and purpose, relative independence of the national governments, the right to publicize its views and to canvass moral support, a collegial system of leadership which is not bound by the same rules as the rest of the organization, are found alongside bureaucratic traits such as the fact that the members are appointed not elected, that its powers are delegated not intrinsic and that it is not directly accountable to a Parliament or an electorate. However, this is a good point to recall that this juxtaposition of seemingly contradictory formal characteristics is not entirely accidental or irrational. In the circumstances of the Community, as seen particularly by people such as Jean Monnet and others more or less associated with the 'functionalist' approach to integration, the establishment of a supranational institution with these extraordinary features had a special appeal.

In the first place, the Commission was entrusted with protecting and furthering the European idea, to which it had to remain firmly committed, and with acting in strict independence of the governments of member States. It had to have means of mobilizing support for further integration. On the other hand, a directly representative kind of body was undesirable because it would have challenged the sovereignty of the member States. At the same time, some scholars have argued that such a body would have 'over-responded' to elements hostile to further integration. The European idea could be regarded in a sense as being too fragile for that kind of exposure.[1] Finally, the Commission's task was to be an extremely technical one, particularly in the first years, and the service of men, chosen to a large extent for their competence as much as for their conviction, was essential.

As we have seen, a body of this sort did for a time prove to be highly suitable for furthering integration under the circumstances prevailing in the early years of the Economic Community. While the member governments (the real sources of political authority both

---

[1] A. Etzioni, *Political Unification*, New York, Holt, Rinehart and Winstone, 1965, p. 75.

at a national and at a Community level) did not resist the long-term goal of political unity, then the Commission was able to carry short-term measures designed to lead to that goal (such as the removal of barriers to trade, the free movement of labour and services, and the adoption of a common policy on cartels and restrictive practices). The Commission achieved this by remaining firmly committed to the long-term goal of political unity, interpreting it in technical terms in the present, and thereby 'selling' its short-term implications to social and economic groups. However, in order to continue implementing measures of integration in the present, it had to compromise different national, social and economic differences, and the only way to sustain a short-term consensus was by mediating between these and even co-opting their representatives into the decision-making process. We have already traced in detail how this tended to detract from the Commission's political role.[1]

This was not the only cause of discomfort on the Commission's part. Eventually, it was bound to evolve common policies in vital sectors of economic and social activity, and here, too, it was faced with the need to reconcile different ideologies, which were already active at a national level. Thus there was not consensus about the proper role of public authorities in economic management and this made the evolution of common economic and industrial policies more difficult. Even when and if consensus can be found on this fundamental question, the Commission will be faced with the need to take over from member governments the responsibility for defining the public interest in social and economic affairs—a responsibility which strains all the resources of legitimacy and support which political authorities, even at a national level, can muster. In such conditions a body with only hybrid political form is inadequate.

A body like the Commission shares with the conventional type of administrative organization the essential quality of acting within defined fields of action on the basis of an established consensus of values. At the international level, as we have seen, such a basis must be the ideologies and interests of the leaders of nation states, who, in the absence of political leadership mobilized at a federal level, retain real power. A 'supranational' bureaucracy does not seem on the evidence we have collected to have resources enabling it to overcome opposition to its long-term aims from such national

[1] See in particular pp. 234–93 above.

330

political leaders. What is more, it is not even in a position to take their place in mobilizing support for measures in the long-term common interest.

We believe that it would be worth while to examine briefly here the possibility that these findings and the hypotheses based upon them might have wider relevance beyond study of political unification. Perhaps it is that the process of bureaucratization, to which the Commission of the European Communities seems bound to submit, affects all organizations of this type. However, what follows cannot be more than tentative with respect to bodies at a national level and we shall do no more than simply suggest questions for future research. The general circumstances under which the Commission has functioned do not at first sight seem to have much in common with the conditions under which the parts of a national government have to work. However, once various qualifications are made to allow for the transfer from an international to a national level, it is clear that the role of the Commission is analogous to a bureaucratic role recognized in the national context by a number of recent writers.

The kind of political role demanded of the Commission is very similar to the role which bureaucracies are increasingly being asked to perform in the making of social and economic policy. Particular sections of the French higher civil service have often been described as acting as if they were independent of the current political leaders of the state, and were presumably committed to certain long-term values. Moreover, they have also seemed to be in a position to champion these values, if not by actually taking power through the electoral process, then at least by identifying themselves publicly with certain policies.[1] What is more important is that the French postwar experiment with economic planning seems to have called forth a totally different type of official from the anonymous, impersonal, career bureaucrat, conventionally associated with the civil services of western Europe.[2] The process of planning itself seems to

[1] See Chapman, *op. cit.*, pp. 280–4; E. Strauss, *The Ruling Servants*, London, George Allen & Unwin, 1961, pp. 179–228; R. Gregoire, *The French Civil Service*, Brussels, International Institute of Administrative Sciences, 1965, *passim*.

[2] See A. Shonfield, *Modern Capitalism*, London, Oxford University Press, 1965, pp. 138–9; J. and A-M. Hackett, *Economic Planning in France*, London, George Allen & Unwin, 1963, pp. 37–48; E. F. Ridley, French Technocracy and Comparative Government in *Political Studies*, February 1966, Vol. XIV, No. 1, pp. 34–52.

require public administrators to commit themselves and the people to long-term ends at the expense of flexibility and responsiveness in the short term. The public interest is identified with the long-term goals of the planners, rather than with the results of shifting political compromise in the present. The planners have, therefore, to be at one remove from the immediate demands of groups and parties, and even, perhaps, from the nervous reactions of their ministers. They must take on an almost judicial role of protecting the long term interest against inroads in the short term. Their role is not, however, truly judicial, for the plan has to be 'sold' to a sceptical public, with the result that the planners are involved in direct confrontation with interest groups, members of parliament, and even the mass public, in an effort to rally support, (sometimes against the short-term policies of the government of the day).[1] At no time, however, do they become real political leaders. Their independence of politics is crucial, for they represent a consensus which has emerged in the course of drawing up the plan. Their only commitment is to the plan itself. Then again, their power is partly technical; the engineering of consensus involved in a *économie concertée* results not so much from an underlying social and political unity as from a skilled putting to gether of varying demands in a way which pays off to every important sector. Perhaps the key selling feature of the plan is that it must work, and for this reason the social and economic technician wields a special power.

Take, for example, the following remarks from a recent major work comparing the way economic policy is made in a number of modern capitalist countries:

'. . . the head of a national planning organization has the obligation to engage in a certain type of politics. His job as a public servant is to lead a lobby for long-term economic growth inside the government; this may conflict with the party politician's short-range imperatives. Like the governor of the central bank, he is ultimately subject to the orders of the government of the day, but it is expected of both governor and head planner that they will urge the policies which they judge to be right, in their fields of expertise, on the country at large as well as on the government, and do so with clarity. Plainly this does not give either of them a licence for unrestrained feuding. But it does make them politicians of a discreet

[1] Shonfield, *op. cit.*, pp. 221–36, 385–427.

variety.'[1] His study of the role of planners in the modern capitalist state led this author to identify a particularly prevalent type of public figure whom he calls the 'independent official'. This type is found more in France (where civil servants are accustomed to identify with some notion of the public interest which may well outlive the tenure of office of party politicians) than in Britain (where the civil servant is conventionally expected to be no more than the cypher of his minister).[2] The author goes on to imply that the adoption in Britain of a similar concept of public service will be essential if we are to succeed in achieving the same kind of coherence and efficacy in our economic policy-making as the French seemed to him to have achieved in theirs. What is most interesting from our point of view is that his ideal example of what he means, indeed, the 'apotheosis of independent officialdom', is the Commission of the EEC, on the merits of whose combined independence, expertise and commitment he expounds at length. If anything he tends to underestimate the extent to which the members of the Commission themselves are politicians rather than bureaucrats, ministers rather than civil servants, but the conclusions he draws add an interesting rider to our findings here:

'What is striking is that probably the most radical and complicated set of reforms of our time, those undertaken by the European Economic Community, have been achieved substantially by a group of appointed officials at one remove from the conventional democratic process. The moral of this is not that the representative process is dead, but that it may well assume additional and more subtle forms than the conventional parliamentary encounter. Effective democracy has always depended on a limited suspension of judgement by the electors, on a willingness to clothe people with power and then give them a period of time for action, before reporting back to those from whom they derived their mandate. The principle has been further extended in postwar national planning; the plans formally recognize that decisions once made cannot be quickly unravelled. In the short or medium term they are irrevocable. The work of the European Commission offers another kind of example of the contemporary political method at work.'[3]

1 Shonfield, *op. cit.*, p. 410.
2 *ibid.*, p. 234.
3 *ibid.*, p. 405.

We have isolated here, it seems, a phenomenon of some general interest, recognized by one highly respected social scientist as 'the contemporary political method at work'. It would be most interesting to trace its other applications in modern government. To do this here would take us far beyond the scope of the present work, but we cannot resist pointing to ways in which the questions raised here in connection with the Commission of the European Communities might be followed up in other (national) contexts. We do this in the hope that other studies will take up where we left off.

It would be valuable in the first instance to follow up the comparison between the role of the Commission and that of government planners in western capitalist countries to see how far the role of the planners does fit our own general description of this hybrid type of bureaucracy. It would also be useful to know whether other sectors of government and public administration could be found performing the same or a similar role. Our suspicion is that the phenomenon of bureaucracy, so designed to perform a political role, might be quite widespread in highly developed capitalist politics, and that responsibilities parallel to the Initiative and Normative functions of the Commission of the European Communities are quite widely assigned to the higher Civil Service, particularly in the economic sector. The book from which we have already quoted is, in fact, only one of several published in the United Kingdom in recent years implying that sound economic management in modern conditions of government necessitates an expanded role for public officials, if not a general 'politization' of the relevant parts of the state bureaucracy.[1]

Our own study of one particular, and in some ways unusual, case has implied that there may be serious limitations to the effectiveness of such a 'politized bureaucracy'. The 'vicious circle' of bureaucracy seems to affect this type just as much as it affects the more conventional administrative organization. At least, it seems that its effectiveness depends overwhelmingly on the general political circumstances of the time, on the disposition of the major political parties and groups (or of the national governments in an international

[1] In addition to Shonfield *op. cit.*, see B. Chapman, *British Government Observed*, London, George Allen & Unwin, 1963; S. Brittan, *The Treasury Under the Tories*, London, Penguin Books; 1969; Evidence from The Labour Party and The Liberal Party, The Fulton Committee on the Civil Service 1966–68, The Civil Service, Vol. 5(2), London, HMSO, 1968, pp. 652–78.

context), and on the degree to which electorates and key political activists are positive or neutral with regard to the aims the bureaucracy is intended to serve. We would assume that the growth of bureaucracy with hybrid political features is associated with an expanded role of the state in economic and social affairs, the application of modern techniques of national planning, and mistrust of conventional forms of democratic politics, such as Parliamentary accountability, ministerial responsibility, and so on. We would also expect such a form of government to appeal mainly to those who regard the conventional socialist/free enterprise cleavage as an outdated or irrelevant basis for political dissent. It would probably be championed by those who see the real problems of modern government as being fundamentally those of sound economic management, or, in other words, of applying modern techniques of planning and administration in response to the competing demands of organized interest groups. In so far as the more conventional parts of the political system, such as parties, elections, and parliament, had not been 'modernized' to take account of such needs, the same people would reasonably seek to entrust the public interest to technicians at one remove from conventional politics but possessing a highly developed professional sense of the 'public interest'. Thus, in the case of the European Communities, the interests of the citizens of member countries were seen as being tied up with further integration of the economies, (and later of the politics), of member States. The national governments, however, had in the past tended to champion their peoples' interests largely by inter-governmental conflict and by economic and political nationalism. Thus the peoples' interests could best be served by some common, supranational body, responsible for asserting general, European values over selfish, national ones.

On the other hand, we would expect a 'politized bureaucracy' to be extremely unpopular with those still adhering to a socialist/free enterprise cleavage, or indeed with anyone who rejected the so-called 'consensus politics' of modern western democracies. In fact, the Commission's role as a kind of political leadership became less and less effective as the apparent consensus regarding long-term European political unity began to collapse in the face of the hostile policies of General de Gaulle. Is it the case, whenever 'consensus politics' does collapse and cleavages (whether of nationalism or of economic and

335

social principle) reassert themselves, that the bureaucracy must be bound to adopt a purely mediative and administrative orientation? Under such circumstances, certainly, the long-term conception of the public good cannot safely be entrusted to an independent, delegative body.[1] But, as we have seen, the promotive role of the bureaucracy could break down even when there is relative consensus on long-term ends. How much consensus would be needed to support it indefinitely?

This reduces the particular bureaucratic phenomenon we have been studying to a consequential feature of 'consensus politics', depending for its effectiveness on the widespread acceptance of a ruling ideology. Such a body can be of value only if one regards politics as an essentially technical, functional business of reconciling different social and economic demands. We put forward this conclusion with some confidence in the context of the establishment and development of the Commission of the European Communities, but we have not collected evidence regarding national political systems. However, we believe that extension of this kind of inquiry at the national level would be worthwhile.[2]

---

[1] Note, for example, the mounting criticism within France of the power of 'technicians' and others within the higher ranks of the civil service. Such criticisms go beyond a call for administrative reforms and imply that the civil service has become in some way too closely identified with the 'ruling ideology' of consensus politics, drawing attention to such features of the higher administrative echelons as their narrow social base, their servility to the regime, and their natural conservatism. See, in particular, J. Mandrin, *L'Enarchie: ou les mandarins de la société Bourgeoise*, Paris, Club Jean Moulin 1967—an extraordinary diatribe on the products of *L'Ecole Nationale d'Administration*; but also, in more restrained language, Club Jean Moulin, *L'Etat et le Citoyen*, Paris, Editions du Seuil, 1961, p. 140. Such comments form part of the general debate in France on the merits and dangers of 'technocracy': see, J. Meynaud, *La Technocratie: Mythe ou Réalité*, Paris, Payot. 1964; J. Billy, *Les Techniciens et le Pouvoir*, Paris, Plon, 1963. F. F. Ridley, *op. cit.*

[2] Most recent work on the political role of the bureaucracy has been confined to the context of developing countries, see, for example, J. La Palombara *Bureaucracy and Political Development*, Princeton, New Jersey, Princeton University Press, 1963; and J. P. Nettl, *Political Mobilisation*, London, Faber and Faber, 1967. See also Fred Rigg's work on the specific case of Thailand: Rigg's conclusions in the developmental context are strikingly similar to our own in the context of the 'developed' European Communities: Fred W. Riggs, *Thailand: The Modernisation of a Bureaucratic Polity*, Honolulu, East-West Center Press, 1966 and *Administration in Developing Countries: The Theory of Prismatic Society*, Boston, Houghton Mifflin, 1964.

INDEX

341

Martino, E., 270
Maud'huy, Comte de, 222
Mediative function, *see* functions
Meeting of Heads of Cabinets, 154, 155, 265
Meeting of Presidents, 152 ff., 159
Messina Conference (1955), 23
MLF, 187, 197
Monde, Le, 268
monetary policy, 47, 62, 243, 295, 302, 304, 305, 314, 315
Monnet, Jean, 19 ff., 23, 31, 52, 295, 299, 300, 329
Morocco, 67
Movimento Federalista Europeo, 17, 96

Netherlands, 21, 70, 123, 125, 126, 128, 129, 132
See also Benelux
neutrality, 68
Nigeria, 67
Noël, Emile, 249, 250
Nordic Union, 33, 192
Normative function, *see* functions
North Atlantic Alliance, 21, 30
North Atlantic Treaty Organization (NATO), 197
Norway, 68, 314

organization:
bureaucratic, 102, 104–15, 209, 233, 234, 249 ff., 266, 272 ff., 326 ff.
'common culture', 113, 117, 209, 215, 260 ff. *passim*, 273, 309; partisan, 209, 213 ff., 230, 259, 266, 309 ff.
porous, 228 ff., 257 ff., 266, 291, 309 ff.
technocratic, 213, 214, 230
See also bureaucracy; civil service; Commission
Organization of European Economic Co-operation ((OEEC), 17, 236

overseas dependencies, former, 66, 67

Paliano, C. di, 252n
parties, political, 45, 50, 98, 104, 115, 295, 316
patent law, 65
Petrilli, G., 252n
Pinder, John, 304
Powell, Sir Richard, 197
prices, agricultural, *see* agriculture

Rasquin, M., 252n
regional development policies, 63 ff., 166, 167, 217–33, 258, 304
Règlement Intérieure, *see* Rules of Procedure
restrictive trade practices, *see* competition, regulation of
Rey, Jean, 179, 183, 192, 194, 195, 198, 208, 252n, 265
Riker, W. H., 37, 38
Rochereau, H., 252n
roulement, 149, 164. *See also* Commission: secondment
Rules of Procedure (*Règlement Intérieure*), 247 ff., 255, 265

Scandinavia, 175
Schaus, L., 252n
Schuman, R., 18
Schuman Plan, 19
science and technology, 63, 65, 295, 306, 307, 314, 315
Maréschal Committee for, 281
Servan-Schreiber, J.-J., 305, 306
Selznick, Philip, 95, 110, 111, 113, 241
Six, the, *see* Belgium; Benelux; France; Germany; Italy; Luxembourg; Netherlands
SOCOREC, 222, 224
Spain, 68
specialization, 88, 95, 102, 106 ff. *passim*, 126, 131, 141, 143 ff. 150, 162, 201, 203 ff., 213, 243 ff., 263

343